Second Edition 1988

Bicycling
the Backroads
OF SOUTHWEST WASHINGTON

By Erin and Bill Woods

Maps by Helen Sherman

Cartoons by Dale Martin

The Mountaineers, Seattle

The Mountaineers: Organized 1906
"...to explore, study, preserve and enjoy
the natural beauty of the Northwest."

Published by The Mountaineers
306 2nd Avenue West, Seattle, Washington 98119
First edition, March 1980
Second edition, March 1988

Manufactured simultaneously in Canada by Douglas & McIntyre, Ltd.
1615 Venables Street, Vancouver, British Columbia, V5L 2H1

Designed by Marge Mueller
Edited by Karen Boush
Cover Photo: Lake Tapps from Pierce County's
    Lake Tapps Park (Tour 100)

Manufactured in the United States of America

Library of Congress Cataloging-in-Publication Data

Woods, Erin.
  Bicycling the backroads of southwest Washington / by Erin and Bill
Woods ; maps by Helen Sherman ; cartoons by Dale Martin. —2nd ed.
    p.   cm.
  Includes indexes.
  ISBN 0-89886-150-0 : $9.95
    1. Cycling—Washington (State)—Guide-books. 2. Cycling paths—
Washington (State)—Guide-books. 3. Washington (State)—
Description and travel—1981—Guide-books.   I. Woods, Bill,
1925-   II. Title.
GV1045.5.W2W67 1988   87-35917
917.9704'43—dc 19   CIP

NOTE ABOUT RIDE NUMBERING

Do not look for missing pages. The tours in this book start at number 94 to follow in sequence those in *Bicycling the Backroads Around Puget Sound* and *Bicycling the Backroads of Northwest Washington* (The Mountaineers, Seattle, Washington). This numbering system was adopted to facilitate cross-referencing and compilation using tours from all three books. Tours numbered 1 to 54, when cited, refer to the first title, and tours 55 to 93, when cited, refer to the second title.

CONTENTS

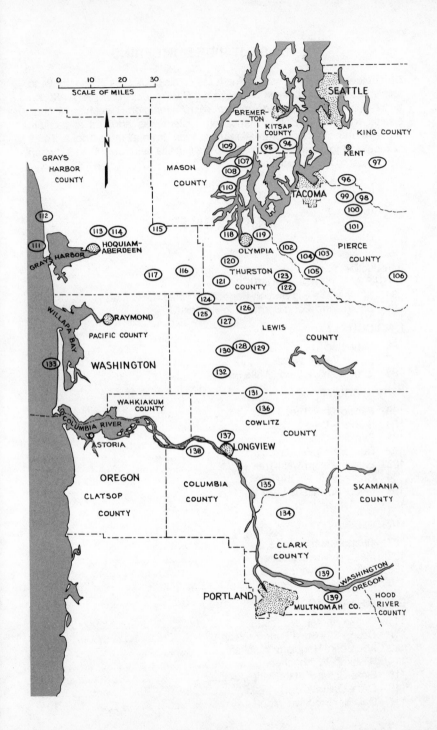

SCALE OF MILES
0   10   20   30

N

GRAYS
HARBOR
COUNTY

SEATTLE

BREMER-
TON

KITSAP
COUNTY

KING COUNTY

KENT

⑨⑤ ⑨④

⑨⑦

MASON

COUNTY

⑩⑨

⑩⑦

⑩⑧

⑨⑥

TACOMA

⑨⑨ ⑨⑧

⑩⓪

⑪②

⑪③ ⑪④

HOQUIAM-
ABERDEEN

⑪⓪

⑩①

GRAYS HARBOR

⑪①

⑪⑧ ⑪⑨

OLYMPIA

⑪⑤

⑩②

PIERCE

⑪⑦ ⑪⑥

⑫⓪

THURSTON

⑩④ ⑩③

COUNTY

⑫①

COUNTY

⑫③

⑩⑤

⑩⑥

WILLAPA BAY

RAYMOND

⑫②

⑫④

PACIFIC COUNTY

⑫⑤

⑫⑥

⑫⑦

WASHINGTON

LEWIS

COUNTY

⑬⓪ ②⑧ ⑫⑨

⑬③

⑬②

WAHKIAKUM
COUNTY

⑬①

⑬⑥

COLUMBIA RIVER

ASTORIA

COWLITZ

COUNTY

⑬⑦

LONGVIEW

⑬⑧

OREGON

COLUMBIA

COUNTY

⑬⑤

SKAMANIA

COUNTY

CLATSOP

COUNTY

⑬④

CLARK

COUNTY

WASHINGTON

OREGON

⑬⑨

PORTLAND

⑬⑨

MULTNOMAH CO.

HOOD
RIVER
COUNTY

4

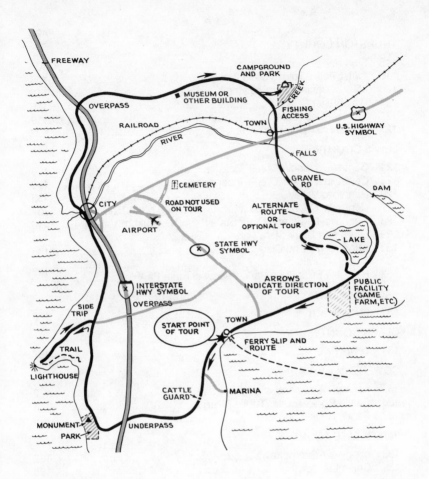

FREEWAY

CAMPGROUND
AND PARK

MUSEUM OR
OTHER BUILDING

CREEK

OVERPASS

FISHING
ACCESS

RAILROAD

TOWN

U.S. HIGHWAY
SYMBOL

RIVER

FALLS

GRAVEL
RD

CEMETERY

DAM

CITY

ROAD NOT USED
ON TOUR

ALTERNATE
ROUTE
OR
OPTIONAL TOUR

AIRPORT

LAKE

STATE HWY
SYMBOL

ARROWS
INDICATE DIRECTION
OF TOUR

INTERSTATE
HWY SYMBOL

PUBLIC
FACILITY
(GAME
FARM, ETC.)

OVERPASS

START POINT
OF TOUR

TOWN

SIDE
TRIP

FERRY SLIP AND
ROUTE

TRAIL

LIGHTHOUSE

CATTLE
GUARD

MARINA

MONUMENT
PARK

UNDERPASS

6

INTRODUCTION

The resurgence in the 1970s of the bicycle as a recreational and transportation vehicle has encouraged the start of what is hoped will be a network of bicycle routes and trails in western Washington. The Burke-Gilman Trail, from Gas Works Park in Seattle to Log Boom Park in Kenmore, although vigorously opposed in its planning stages by adjoining landowners, is now a coveted and highly popular recreational facility, as well as a commuter route for University of Washington students. The Sammamish River Trail, from Redmond to Bothell, is rapidly becoming popular, and eventually will be linked up with Burke-Gilman. The Interurban Park Trail, from Tukwila to Pacific on the Pierce County line, also attracts many cyclists, even though it is punctuated with several detours and only partially improved.

Urban trail systems, however, are often heavily occupied and as a result present an element of danger. The accident rate per mile can be significantly higher than the rate on adjacent roadways, and cyclists must be constantly on the alert to avoid colliding with other trail users, including beginning cyclists, joggers, roller skaters, dogs, equestrians, and parents pushing baby strollers.

Once having acquired a degree of cycling proficiency, most bicyclists prefer to tour on quiet backroads. Although in Washington State such roads have a high degree of connectivity, there are several areas where only busy highways offer a reasonable means of passage. Progress is being made

"THIS SAYS TO TURN LEFT."

here, too, with the opening to bicyclists of interstate highway shoulders throughout the state, with only urban areas excluded. On secondary highways, upgrading of design to federal standards provides paved shoulders for cyclists to ride comfortably out of the automotive traffic pattern.

The Washington State Department of Wildlife, which has jurisdiction over the state's fishing and hunting access areas, has marked many of these convenient stopping areas as conservation parks, requiring users to have a current fishing, hunting, or conservation license. In particular, Tour #105 in this book begins at one of these marked areas. Other routes that may require a license for use of rest areas are Tours 98, 121, 122, 123, 135, and 138. Before starting on any one of the above tours, purchase of a conservation or equivalent game license is recommended.

For many years, two primary alternatives for overnighting bicycle tourists have been low-cost campgrounds and higher-cost motels. Campgrounds often are dominated by noisy recreational vehicle occupants, and shower facilities may leave something to be desired. Motels are sterile, impersonal institutions and may be rather expensive for the solo cyclist. Now there is another alternative represented by the increasing number of bed-and-breakfast (B & B) opportunities in Washington State. Finding out about them, however, may not be easy. Some are listed in local telephone directories, some advertise in tourist magazines or are registered with listing agencies, and many depend on word-of-mouth promotion. To assist bicyclists in taking advantage of this new opportunity, a listing is provided of B & B telephone numbers and locations in the index of this book. Some have been checked out by the authors, many have not.

Aside from this, you are on your own. Ride safely and enjoy your touring.

Erin and Bill Woods

SAFETY CONSIDERATIONS

Safety is an important concern in all outdoor activities. No guidebook can alert you to every hazard or anticipate the limitations of every reader, so the descriptions in this book are not representations that a particular trip is safe for your party. When you take a trip, you assume responsibility for your own safety. Some of the trips described in this book may require you to do no more than look both ways before crossing the street; on others, more attention to safety may be required due to terrain, traffic, weather, the capabilities of your party, or other factors. Keeping informed on current conditions and exercising common sense are the keys to a safe, enjoyable outing.

The Mountaineers

BICYCLING THE BACKROADS
OF SOUTHWEST WASHINGTON

94 SOUTHWORTH–GIG HARBOR–KOPACHUCK STATE PARK

STARTING POINT: Southworth ferry terminal. From I-5 in Seattle take exit 163 or 163A (Spokane Street and West Seattle). Cross Duwamish Waterway to West Seattle, climb hill, and at traffic signal continue through on Fauntleroy Avenue (follow Vashon ferry signs). Park in Lincoln Park (south parking lot) 2 blocks north of Fauntleroy ferry terminal. Take bicycles on ferry to Southworth. From I-5 in Tacoma, take exit 132 (State Route 16) and follow across Narrows Bridge to Kitsap Peninsula. Turn right on Sedgwick Road 14 miles north of bridge and follow to Southworth ferry terminal parking lot.

DISTANCE: 35 to 51 miles.
TERRAIN: Strenuous hills.
TOTAL CUMULATIVE ELEVATION GAIN: 2300 to 3100 feet.
RECOMMENDED TIME OF YEAR: Any season.
RECOMMENDED STARTING TIME: 8 to 10 A.M. from Southworth ferry terminal.
ALLOW: 6 to 8 hours; 1 day or overnight.

POINTS OF INTEREST
Gig Harbor shops
Kopachuck State Park

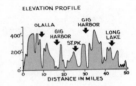

The Southworth–Port Orchard route (Tour #44) has long been a favorite of cycle-touring Seattle residents for its close-in starting point, beautiful scenery, easy hills, and moderate traffic. The tour described here shares all but one of these virtues, the difference being the hills. The eastern edge of southern Kitsap Peninsula presents a high bluff cut by several stream channels, making many ups and downs in the roads. This should not deter a determined cyclist, however, as the tour may be shortened at will, to almost any length or degree of effort, by taking advantage of short crossroads that cut the course at frequent intervals.

The scenery, although offering few seascapes, is nonetheless delightful for viewing cool, green forest, upland lakes and valleys, and occasional deep coves and bays. White pine and madrona vary the usual sights of fir, hemlock, and alder of second-growth forests, with evergreen huckleberry, sword fern, and oceanspray filling in the understory. The upland lakes have shallow slopes supporting dense growths of water lilies. In the estuarial coves, great blue herons vie with ducks, grebes, and gulls for their share of aquatic tidbits.

Gig Harbor has developed a handicraft orientation, and its stores are favored by shoppers looking for unusual arts and crafts. Several restaurants and cafes offer a variety of fare.

By using Kopachuck State Park as an overnight stop, the touring cyclist can test his bicycle camping gear close to home before setting out on longer trips. Hot showers, secluded campsites, and waterside picnic shelters make this one of Washington State's better-appointed parks. A group camp area is available by reservation with the park manager. A boat anchorage with nearby restroom and showers caters to marine visitors.

MILEAGE LOG

0.0 Southworth ferry terminal. Head uphill on **State Route 160.**

0.3 Left turn on **Sedgwick Road** and head uphill.

2.8 Turn left on **Banner Road** as Sedgwick tops a summit. Dip down, cross Fragaria Creek, and climb out again at mile 5.9. Views of Colvos Passage and Point Defiance at mile 8.1. Descend steep, curving hill to Olalla on the shores of Puget Sound.

9.2 Left turn on **Crescent Valley Road** by Olalla store as Olalla Valley Road goes right. Wind up out of the valley. Road changes name to **Crescent Valley Drive N.W.** as it enters Pierce County at mile 11.6.

15.7 Turn right on **96th Street N.W.** toward Gig Harbor and Tacoma. City park on right at bottom of hill at mile 15.9; picnic lunch stop.

16.1 Left turn on **Harborview Drive** in Gig Harbor as Vernhardson Road continues up a steep hill. *Note: Short tour turns sharp right on Peacock Hill Avenue at 16.5 and picks up mileage log at 32.2.* Continue left with Harborview around harbor. Cafe at 17.6.

17.8 Turn right on **Pioneer Way** at blinking red light as Harborview angles left. Crank up steep hill. Cross State Route 16 on overpass at mile 18.5. Road changes name to **Wollochet Drive N.W.** and winds down to tip of Wollochet Bay.

20.8 Right turn on **Artondale Drive N.W.** as Wollochet bends left along bay. Road is renamed **78th Avenue N.E.** and **Whitmore Drive N.W.**

23.9 Turn left at stop sign as Ray Nash Drive N.W. joins from the right.

25.0 Continue straight toward Kopachuck State Park on **Artondale Drive N.W.** Arletta store is 1.0 mile to the left. 56 Street N.W. goes left into Kopachuck State Park at mile 26.0 as Artondale Drive changes name to **Kopachuck Drive N.W.** *Note: State park is a possible overnight stop; see text for facilities.*

27.6 Cross a small inlet and continue on **Ray Nash Drive** as it enters from the right. Small grocery here.

28.3 Turn right toward State Route 16 on **Rosedale Street N.W.** and climb a long hill. Enter Gig Harbor at mile 30.8. Observe 25-mph speed limit as road dives down a steep hill.

31.3 Left turn at stop sign on **Stinson Avenue.**

31.5 Go straight on **Harborview Drive** as Stinson ends and follow Harborview to the right around the harbor.

32.2 Turn left on **Peacock Hill Avenue.** Enter Kitsap County at mile 36.7.

37.7 Right turn on **S.E. Nelson Road** as Peacock ends.

38.0 Turn left on **Fagerud Road S.E.,** which executes two bends and descends hill.

39.1 Right turn on **S.E. Olalla-Burley Road** as Fagerud ends.

39.5 Turn left on **Wallace Road S.E.** then bear left on **Olalla Valley Road** by Olalla Food Center.

42.2 Left turn on **S.E. Mullenix Road** toward Port Orchard, Bremerton, and Tacoma.

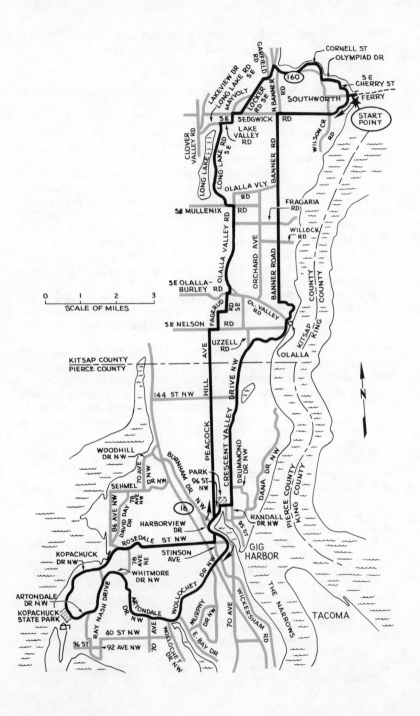

42.4 Turn right on **Long Lake Road S.E.** as Mullenix starts down a long hill. Cycle past Long Lake.

44.9 Right turn at wye on **Lake Valley Road S.E.** as Long Lake Road turns left. Road bends left again shortly.

45.6 Turn right on **S.E. Sedgwick Road** as Mayvolt Road S.E. goes on.

45.8 Turn left on **Locker Road S.E.** Start down long hill at 46.1.

47.5 Right turn on **State Route 160** as Locker ends at bottom of hill.

48.5 Turn left on **Cornell Street**, marked Dead End. Continue along water.

49.1 Go around vehicle barrier in Harper and continue on **State Route 160**.

49.5 Turn left on **Olympiad Road** as shoreline swings left. Follow **Olympiad Drive** left at 49.9 as Nokomis Road goes right.

50.4 Left turn on **S.E. Cherry Street** as Olympiad is marked Dead End.

50.8 Turn left on **State Route 160** toward ferry landing in Southworth.

51.1 Southworth ferry terminal; end of tour.

95 SOUTHWORTH–LONGBRANCH– GIG HARBOR

STARTING POINT: Southworth ferry terminal. From I-5 in Seattle take exit 163 or 163A (Spokane Street and West Seattle). Cross Duwamish Waterway to West Seattle, climb hill, and at traffic signal continue through on Fauntleroy Avenue (follow Vashon ferry signs). Park on side streets uphill from Fauntleroy ferry terminal. Take bicycles on ferry to Southworth. From I-5 in Tacoma, take exit 132 (State Route 16) and follow across Narrows Bridge to Kitsap Peninsula. Turn right on Sedgwick Road 14 miles north of bridge and follow to Southworth ferry terminal parking lot.

DISTANCE: Total, 107 miles: first day, 42 miles; second day, 37 miles; third day, 28 miles.
TERRAIN: Hilly.
TOTAL CUMULATIVE ELEVATION GAIN: 6800 feet: first day, 2200 feet; second day, 2700 feet; third day, 1900 feet.
RECOMMENDED TIME OF YEAR: Any season.

RECOMMENDED STARTING TIME: 9 A.M. from Southworth ferry terminal.
ALLOW: 3 days.
POINTS OF INTEREST
Seascapes between Southworth and Port Orchard
Manchester State Park
Penrose Point State Park
Minter Creek Salmon Hatchery
Kopachuck State Park
Gig Harbor shops

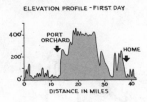

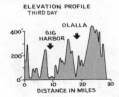

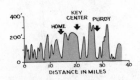

Seattleites have often asked for an overnight or multi-day tour that travels over low-traffic roads, has reasonably short mileages, and starts from the Seattle area. Specifications such as these sound nearly impossible to meet, yet this tour does come close. In its short span of 100 miles or so, it offers a wide variety of scenery: the salty seascapes along Puget Sound, frequented by migrating waterfowl of many varieties (ducks, geese, grebes, loons, scoters, and murres, to name a few); inlets from the Sound punctuating the forest scenery, pointing long fingers up creek estuaries; forests of alder, maple, fir, hemlock, and cedar, as well as stands of white and lodgepole pine; and the plateau area, with upland lakes, creek valleys, and dairy farms.

There is variety in the towns, too. Harper, Manchester, Point Fosdick, and Longbranch all offered ferry service to the mainland at one time or another but now are sleepy little communities tucked away in out-of-the-way places, their old piers gradually crumbling with decay. Port Orchard still has passenger ferry service to Bremerton and the naval shipyards and has grown to be a thriving city. Gig Harbor, on the other hand, caters to boaters and tourists with its handsome marina and many small arts and crafts shops.

Camping accommodations at Penrose and Kopachuck state parks include the usual automobile-oriented campsites secluded among trees and shrubbery around a campground loop road and restrooms with coin-operated hot showers for a welcome clean-up opportunity. Picnic shelters shed the rain in inclement weather. For group outings, both parks have group camp areas, available by reservation with the park manager.

Although much of the tour is through rural country, food is available at convenient points in the itinerary. On the first day, the restaurants and fast-food shops in Port Orchard offer a wide choice of fare. The restaurant in Home is an option for dinner, or perhaps the chowder house in Longbranch. For the second day, the Home restaurant is open for breakfast, and Purdy is convenient for lunch. Two small grocery stores not far from Kopachuck State Park may be visited for dinner materials. On the third day, Gig Harbor is close enough for breakfast, and if a morning of sightseeing and shopping is desired, then lunch there is in order as well. A pleasant city park along Crescent Lake Creek in Gig Harbor may be enjoyed with a picnic lunch. From here the end of the tour is only a few hours away, and cycle tourists may board a ferry for home without a care for the long lines of weekend or holiday automotive traffic. Even with the many hills on this ride, it is a good multi-day tour from Seattle's metropolitan area.

MILEAGE LOG

FIRST DAY

0.0 Southworth ferry terminal. Head east and uphill on **State Route 160**.

0.3 Turn right on **Cherry Street** by gas station just up the hill from ferry terminal.

0.7 Right turn on **Olympiad Drive**, keeping right as Nokomis intersects at mile 1.2.

1.5 Turn right at stop sign on **State Route 160**.

2.0 Go around barrier and continue along waterfront on **Cornell Street** in Harper as S.R. 160 turns left and starts uphill.

2.5 Right turn on **State Route 160** for 1.0 mile of traffic.

3.5 Turn right on **Yukon Harbor Drive** and descend to waterfront again.

4.4 Bear right on **Colchester Drive** into Manchester.

5.9 Left turn at stop sign on **Main Street** in Manchester. Crank up steep hill one block, then turn right on **Beach Drive**. Side road to Manchester State Park at mile 8.5.

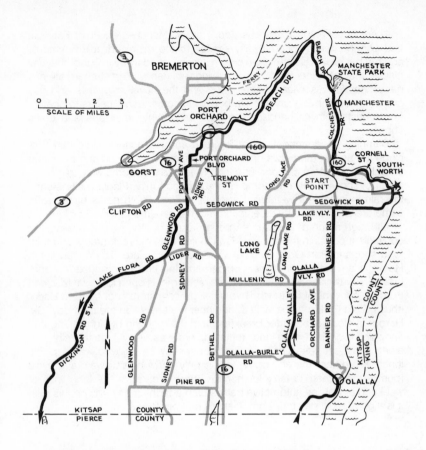

13.5 Bear right on **Bay Street** in Port Orchard as **State Route 160** joins from the left. Cafes, fast-food shops in Port Orchard along Bay Street. Cross Sydney Avenue at traffic light at mile 14.0.

14.3 Left turn on **Port Orchard Boulevard** and start uphill.

15.3 Turn right at stop sign at top of hill on **Tremont Street** as Port Orchard Boulevard ends.

15.5 Left turn on **Pottery Avenue**. Go under State Route 16 at mile 16.3. Road name changes to **Sidney Road**.

17.1 Turn right on **Glenwood Road** and cycle into forest.

19.1 Continue straight on **Lake Flora Road** toward Clavinwood and Wye Lake as Glenwood Road goes left to Camp Niwana. Road name changes to **Dickinson Road S.W.** at mile 21.9, and to **Carney Road S.W.** at mile 25.3.

29.1 Turn right toward Belfair on **State Route 302**. Busy traffic, narrow shoulder.

29.7 Turn left on **Bliss Cochrane Road KPN** by health-care facility.

31.5 Left turn on **Bay View Road KPN.**

31.9 Turn right on **Van Slyke Road KPN**, then left on **Hall Road KPN** as Van Slyke ends.

32.5 Right turn on **South Vaughn Road KPN** by Key Peninsula Civic Center in Vaughn. Cross inlet at end of Vaughn Bay.

32.9 Bear left and uphill on **Lackey Road KPN** as South Vaughn Road goes right.

36.1 Bear right on **Key Peninsula Highway KPN**. Restaurant on left at mile 37.9, grocery at mile 38.1.

38.3 Turn left on **Hoff Road KPS** just after crossing bridge over tip of Van Geldern Cove. Road is renamed **Lorenz Road KPS**.

40.2 Continue on **Delano Road KPS** as it enters from the right by Lake Bay Marina and grocery.

41.0 Turn left on **158th Avenue KPS** toward Penrose Point State Park, turning left toward camping area as road forks.

41.7 Campground area, Penrose Point State Park.

SECOND DAY

0.0 Campground area of Penrose Point State Park. Head out entrance road, which becomes **158th Avenue KPS** as it leaves the park.

0.6 Left turn on **Delano Road KPS**, which bends right after 0.4 mile and is renamed **142nd Avenue KPS**, and finally **Meridian Road KPS**.

3.3 Turn left on **158th Avenue KPS** as Meridian ends at stop sign. Road name changes to **Reeves Road KPS** and finally **40th Street KPS**.

4.6 Left turn on **Key Peninsula Highway KPS** as 40th Street ends. Longbranch Mercantile, marina, and chowder house at mile 5.4.

7.0 Right turn on **76th Street KPS** as Key Peninsula Highway is marked Dead End. Road name changes to **Whiteman Road KPS** at 9.8. 40th Street KPS goes left to Whitman Cove at mile 10.6.

13.4 Bear left at stop sign on **Key Peninsula Highway KPS**. Pass restaurant at mile 14.9.

20.1 Turn right on **92nd Street KPN** at flashing amber light in Key Center by cafe and grocery. Road bends left immediately and is renamed **Cramer Road KPN**. YMCA Camp Seymour on right at mile 21.1, just after road crosses tip of Glen Cove.

22.8 Right turn on **Creviston Drive KPN.** as S.R. 302 appears ahead. Minter Creek Salmon Hatchery on left at mile 23.6.

25.6 Bear right toward Gig Harbor on **State Route 302** and endure traffic for 0.8 mile.

26.4 Continue straight on **Goldman Drive N.W.** as S.R. 302 bends right.

27.1 Left turn again on **State Route 302** and cross tip of Carr Inlet on causeway with wide, paved shoulder.

28.0 Bear right through business area in Purdy at junction of S.R. 302 with Purdy Drive. Cross Purdy Drive at 28.2 and continue on **Goodnough Drive N.W.** Cross Purdy Drive with Goodnough again at mile 29.0.

29.9 Turn right on **Woodhill Drive N.W.**, which turns a corner after 0.7 mile and is renamed **70th Avenue N.W.**

31.6 Right turn on **Sehmel Drive N.W.** as 70th Avenue ends.

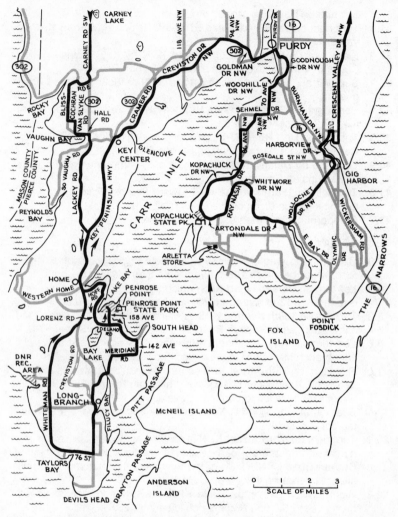

32.1 Bear left on **78th Avenue N.W.** at top of hill. As it bottoms out and bends right the road is renamed **Chapman Drive N.W.**, and then **96th Street N.W.**

33.0 Left turn on **86th Avenue N.W.** as 96th Street is marked Dead End. Gas-grocery store on left at mile 33.9. Road bends left at mile 34.0 and is renamed **Rosedale Street N.W.**

34.3 Turn right on **Ray Nash Drive N.W.**

35.0 Continue straight on **Kopachuck Drive N.W.** toward Kopachuck State Park as Ray Nash Drive bends left by small grocery.

36.6 Right turn on **56th Street N.W.** into Kopachuck State Park. Camping area on the right 0.1 mile down the hill.

THIRD DAY

0.0 Entrance to campground area of Kopachuck State Park. Head uphill out of park on **56th Street N.W.**

0.1 Right turn on **Artondale Drive N.W.**

1.0 Continue on **Ray Nash Drive N.W.** as it enters from the right at a wye.

2.2 Right turn on **Whitmore Drive N.W.**, which bends after 1.2 miles and is renamed **78th Avenue N.W.** and finally **Artondale Drive N.W.**

5.2 Bear left on **Wollochet Drive N.W.** at T junction. Cross State Route 16 on overpass at mile 7.3. As it enters Gig Harbor, road dives down steep hill and is renamed **Pioneer Way**. Watch for 25-mph speed limit.

8.1 Left turn at flashing red light at bottom of hill on **Harborview Drive**. Follow Harborview along waterfront; cafe.

9.7 Turn right on **96th Street N.W.** City park on left at 10.0.

10.2 Turn left on **Crescent Valley Drive N.W.** Enter Kitsap County at mile 15.2.

17.4 Bear left on **Olalla Valley Road** by Olalla grocery and post office.

23.3 Turn left on **Banner Road** as Olalla Valley Road ends.

25.2 Right turn on **Sedgwick Road** as Banner ends.

27.7 Turn right on **State Route 160** as Sedgwick ends.

27.8 Southworth ferry terminal; end of ride.

96 KENT–PACIFIC

STARTING POINT: City of Kent's Russell Road Park. Take exit 149 (State Route 516) from I-5 and follow State Route 516 down the hill toward Kent. Turn left on Meeker Street at traffic light at bottom of hill, cross bridge over Green River, and take next left on Russell Road.

DISTANCE: 26 miles.
TERRAIN: Flat with a few hills.
TOTAL CUMULATIVE ELEVATION GAIN: 300 feet.
RECOMMENDED TIME OF YEAR: Any season.
RECOMMENDED STARTING TIME: Anytime.
ALLOW: 4 hours.
POINTS OF INTEREST
Kent and Auburn bicycle routes
Interurban Trail

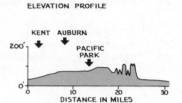

ELEVATION PROFILE

A handsome document published by King County in 1978 outlines the master plan for the Interurban Park Trail. Although much of the trail has been paved, few of the planned facilities have been constructed and several detours remain. When completed, this trail will provide recreational opportunities for bicyclists, joggers, hikers, and horseback riders over a distance of approximately 14.5 miles through the Green River and Stuck River valleys between Fort Dent Park in Tukwila and a trailhead in Pacific, the southern terminus. Puget Sound Power and Light Company, in a generous bid for good public relations, granted an easement over the old electric-railroad bed on which the trail is and will be built. The original electric railway between Seattle and Tacoma, dating back to the turn of the century, was a financial success for about 20 years, but as hard-surfaced, parallel roads were constructed and the era of the automobile began, decreased patronage on the electric railway eventually pulled the switch. The cities of Tukwila, Renton, Kent, Auburn, Algona, and Pacific, along with King County, are responsible for constructing and maintaining trail sections under their jurisdictions.

This Kent-Pacific tour follows the signed Kent bicycle route along both sides of the Green River and through downtown Kent. The Interurban Trail bypasses downtown Auburn to Algona and Pacific, where low-traffic roads continue back through Auburn. Restrooms and picnic facilities are found in Pacific's city park, where views along the dikes of the Stuck River change with the seasons. Red-breasted merganser and goldeneye ducks make their way up the rivers during winter, while mallards and coots paddle around all year. Wintertime fishermen build small, smoky fires among the blackberry brambles along the riverbanks. Great blue herons fly regular sorties over the valley and peruse the few marshy wetlands that still remain. Many residents take advantage of King County "pea patch" gardens along the Green River Road north of Auburn to grow lush vegetables in the fertile valley soil. Only a short score of years ago farming was the principal activity in the Green River Valley, but today few farmers remain. Along Frager Road, strawberries still thrive in farms where they are harvested by hundreds of U-pickers, and corn covers other sections of cultivated acreage.

Combining this ride with Tour #3 from *Bicycling the Backroads Around Puget Sound* provides a scenic 40-mile backroad loop through the Green River Valley from Tukwila to Pacific.

MILEAGE LOG

0.0 City of Kent's Russell Road Park. Head north past the barricade through the parking lot toward park exit.

0.3 Right turn on **S. 240 Street**. Cross State Route 181 (68 Avenue S., Washington Avenue) at mile 0.9 as road is renamed **James Street**. State Route 167 passes overhead at mile 1.1.

1.4 Right turn on **4th Avenue** and continue through downtown Kent.

1.8 Left turn on **Gowe Street** with Interurban Trail sign, then right on **3 Avenue S**. As it leaves Kent, the road is renamed **78 Avenue S**.

2.8 Cross the Green River and turn right on **S. 262 Street**, which bends left and parallels State Route 167. Cross S. 277th Street at mile 4.2 and continue on frontage road, marked Dead End. Road bends left at mile 4.8 and is named **S. 285 Street**.

5.0 Turn right past bollards on **Interurban Trail**. Cross thoroughfares at 5.4, 7.8, and 8.6. Benches under State Route 18 overpass at 8.1; grocery and cafe in Algona at 9.9.

11.0 Left turn on **3 Avenue S.W.** in Pacific as Interurban Trail ends. Pass Pacific City Hall and Union Station cafe.

12.1 Right turn into Pacific Park. Playground equipment, picnic areas, restrooms, river frontage along the Stuck River. Continue on 3 Avenue S.W. after leaving the park. Road bends left at mile 12.5 and is renamed **Skinner Road**.

12.9 Turn right on **Ellingson Road**, go under railroad trestle, and turn left on **A Street S.E.** Heavy traffic, but sidewalk is available.

13.2 Right turn on **37 Street S.E.**

14.0 Left turn on **M Street S.E.** Cross State Route 164 (Auburn Way S.) and continue on M Street S.E. at mile 15.2.

16.0 Right turn on **3rd Street S.E.**

16.2 Left turn on **R Street S.E.** Cross Main Street at mile 16.6.

17.1 Right turn on **8 Street N.E.** and cross Green River. Ramped bridge sidewalk available.

17.2 Turn left from left turn lane on **104 Avenue S.E.** toward golf course.

18.2 Left turn toward golf course on **Green River Road**. Golf course on the right at 19.0; cafe.

22.1 Cross Central Avenue in Kent and continue on **S. 259 Street**.

22.7 Bear left on gravel path as road bends right, and follow trail under State Route 167 bridge. Continue on blacktop road at other end of trail.

23.3 Left turn on **State Route 181 (S. Washington Street)**, cross the Green River, and turn right on **Frager Road S.**

24.7 Turn right on footbridge suspended beneath the S.R. 516 bridge over the Green River. Follow path west along the dike on other side, past the Kent Golf Course.

25.5 Continue on path under Meeker Street Bridge and turn right on old roadway up to sidewalk (marked bike route) along north margin of Meeker Street.

25.9 Turn left on **Russell Road** and return to Russell Road Park at mile 26.2.

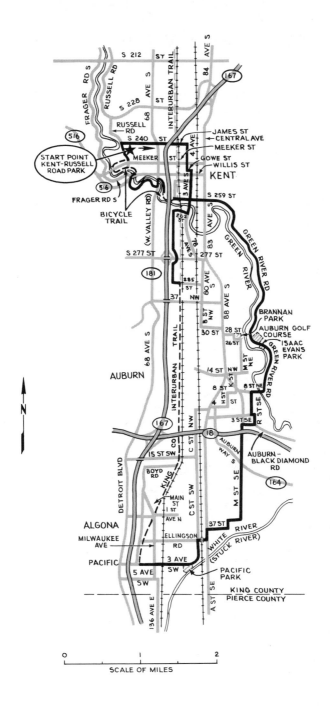

97 MAPLE VALLEY–VEAZIE

STARTING POINT: Lake Wilderness King County Park. From I-405 in Renton take exit 4A, Renton – Maple Valley Road S.E. (State Route 169). Drive 16 miles to Maple Valley. Turn right on Witte Road for 0.8 mile, then left into Lake Wilderness Park.

DISTANCE: 33 miles.
TERRAIN: Flat to moderate plus one steep hill.
TOTAL CUMULATIVE ELEVATION GAIN: 1500 feet.
RECOMMENDED TIME OF YEAR: All seasons.
RECOMMENDED STARTING TIME: 8 to 9 A.M.
ALLOW: 4 to 5 hours.
POINTS OF INTEREST
Maple Valley Grange
Black Diamond Bakery
Green River Gorge
Nolte State Park

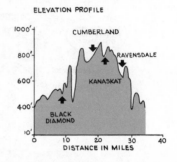

ELEVATION PROFILE

In Maple Valley, near the starting point of this ride at Lake Wilderness Park, the Maple Valley Grange offers a pancake breakfast on the third Sunday of each month from 8 A.M. to 1 P.M., a great send-off for this tour. At Lake Wilderness Park a full range of facilities is offered among tall trees and green lawns. Several varieties of ducks frequent the lake, including the usual hungry, panhandling mallards. Near the park the route crosses a bridge over an abandoned railroad grade that until recently was used for transporting coal from the mines in and around Black Diamond.

Nolte State Park on Deep Lake is the logical picnic lunch stop for this ride. Deep Lake, the recipient of the waters of Deep Creek, has no surface outlet, but year-round springs on the edge of nearby Green River Gorge provide the obvious answer to the question of where the water goes. In inclement weather or if prepared food is desired, the Cumberland Cafe offers a good menu. On opening day of fishing season, in April, the Cumberland fire hall holds a ham, eggs, and pancake breakfast.

Two other parklike facilities lie adjacent to the route: the Lake Wilderness Arboretum is at present undeveloped but has nature trails and a few picnic tables; the Green River Gorge Camp and Picnic Area, managed by the Washington State Department of Natural Resources (DNR), is primitive but creates an opportunity to incorporate this trip in an overnight tour.

Scenery on this ride is rural, with minor samples of fringe suburbia and a few short exposures to the traffic on State Route 169. Tall trees, dense forest, and bucolic cow pastures are the order of the day, with automobile traffic at a minimum. Take this tour for a different facet of versatile King County.

MILEAGE LOG

0.0 Parking lot of Lake Wilderness County Park. Leave park and head out entrance to Witte Road.

0.7 Turn left on **Witte Road S.E.** Cross Kent-Kangley Road (State Route 516) at 2.3. Witte Road eventually bends right and becomes **S.E. 276 Street**.

3.0 Turn left on **216 Avenue S.E.** as Witte Road ends. Cross railroad tracks at mile 3.4, dip down to creek valley, and climb out again. Food services available at Lake Sawyer at mile 3.9. Road bends right at mile 4.5 and is renamed **224 Avenue S.E.** Optional side trip left on S.E. 296 Street to Lake Sawyer public boat ramp with small parking area and restrooms. At 5.7 the road changes name again to **Lake Sawyer Road S.E.**

6.6 Turn left on **S.E. Auburn–Black Diamond Road** as Lake Sawyer Road ends.

6.9 Right turn on unmarked road by small restaurant. Mailboxes indicate this is **Morgan Street**. As it enters Black Diamond, the road is renamed **Railroad Avenue**. High-calorie treats at Black Diamond Bakery at mile 7.8; doughnuts generally gone by 10:30 A.M. Continue out of town on Railroad Avenue.

8.1 Turn right on **Third Avenue (State Route 169)** and continue through dip past Jones Lake.

8.5 Right turn on a narrow, dirt road (looks like a driveway) as S.R. 169 heads uphill. Follow dirt road around a bend and uphill through forest planting, where it is named **257 Avenue S.E.** Patchy, oiled surface begins at 9.3.

9.5 Left turn on **S.E. Green Valley Road**. *Note: For connections with other tours, turn right to Flaming Geyser Park, Green River Valley, and Auburn.*

10.0 Turn right toward Enumclaw on **Enumclaw–Black Diamond Road (State Route 169)** and continue on paved 18-inch shoulder. Plunge downhill and cross Green River Gorge at 10.9. Bridge has sidewalk, allowing bicycles to stop and get off roadway for sightseeing. An eight-foot-wide paved shoulder begins on the other side of the bridge, heading uphill. Pass entrance to Green River Gorge Camp and Picnic Area (DNR) at 11.5.

12.4 Turn left on **S.E. 385 Street** as S.E. 383 Street goes right, then turn left on **Enumclaw-Franklin Road S.E.**

12.6 Right turn on **S.E. 384 Street**. After climbing a short but very steep hill, the road turns right and is renamed **276 Avenue S.E.**

13.7 Turn left on **S.E. 392 Street** as 276 Avenue ends. Continue over low ridge and descend into Enumclaw valley.

14.7 Left turn on **Veazie-Cumberland Road S.E.** toward Kanaskat and Cumberland. This open pasture area was once the community of Veazie. Cross Coal Creek at 15.0. Nolte State Park Recreation Area, suggested lunch stop, on the left at 16.2; day use only. Pass Cumberland Cafe and grocery at mile 17.5 and continue on **Cumberland-Kanaskat Road S.E.** Pass Palmer-Kanaskat State Park entrance at mile 20.4, cross the Green River, and continue through Kanaskat.

21.9 Cross the main-line Burlington Northern Railroad tracks on a high bridge and turn left toward Kent on **S.E. Retreat-Kanaskat Road**.

The BPA Raver power substation and high-tension switchyard is on the left as power lines pass overhead. Lake Retreat Baptist Camp is on the right.

25.3 Left turn on **Kent-Kangley Road S.E.** as Retreat Road ends.

26.4 Turn right on **Landsburg Road S.E.** toward Issaquah and North Bend by the Ravensdale Market. Crank over a hill.

27.8 Left turn on **S.E. Summit-Landsburg Road** from a downhill run.

28.6 Bear right on **S.E. 252 Street**, which shortly bends and becomes **S.E. 248 Street**. Road plays leapfrog with the Seattle Cedar River water pipeline, changing name to **240 Avenue S.E.** and eventually merging with the gravel-surfaced pipeline road for 0.1 mile.

30.4 Left turn on oiled surface of **S.E. 244 Street** by locked gate.

30.9 Turn right on **Maple Valley–Black Diamond Road S.E. (State Route 169)** and proceed along marginally navigable gravel shoulder.

31.7 Turn left on **Witte Road**.

32.5 Left turn toward Lake Wilderness County Park.

33.2 Back at starting point.

"WE ALWAYS GET A GOOD TURNOUT FOR A FOOD RIDE."

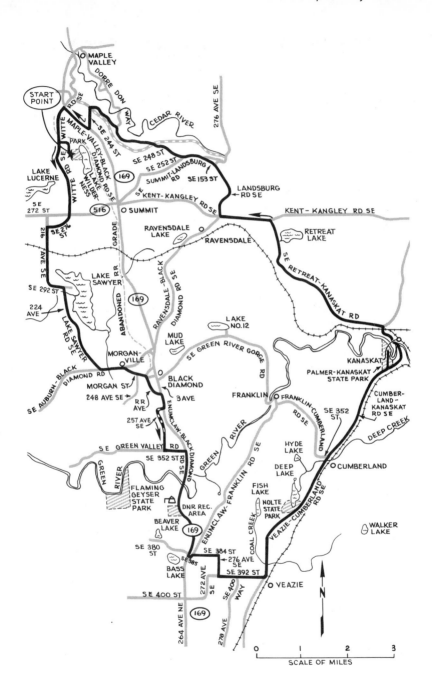

98   ENUMCLAW–AUBURN (White River)

STARTING POINT: King County Park in Enumclaw. From the north take exit 4A (State Route 169) from I-405 to Enumclaw and State Route 410 to the park. From the south take exit 135 (State Route 410) from I-5 to the park.

ALTERNATIVE STARTING POINT: Public fishing access on Green River, 2 miles east of Auburn. Take Green Valley–Black Diamond exit from State Route 18 east of Auburn, turn east on Auburn–Black Diamond Road, then right on Green Valley Road 0.1 mile to fishing access. *Note: Conservation license required.*

DISTANCE: 43 miles.
TERRAIN: Moderate with one steep hill.
TOTAL CUMULATIVE ELEVATION GAIN: 1000 feet.
RECOMMENDED TIME OF YEAR: Any season.
RECOMMENDED STARTING TIME: 9 A.M.
ALLOW: 5 hours.
POINTS OF INTEREST
Lake Tapps Power Flume
Lake Tapps Pierce County Park

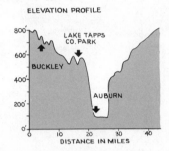

The White River, as it descends from the Mud Mountain Dam near Enumclaw to the flood plain at Auburn, cuts a narrow gorge through a broad, 600- to 700-foot plateau, with Enumclaw on one side and Lake Tapps on the other. Pierce County claims the Lake Tapps plateau on the south side of the White River, while King County is the governmental entity to the north.

This tour traverses the plateau on both sides of the river, dropping briefly to the Auburn plain to recross the White River and climb out of the Green River Valley to the plateau again. These uplands as a rule remain in a semi-rural state with many acres devoted to pastureland for the numerous dairy farms. Horses canter along the fences in corrals and pastures by large homes scattered across the plateau. White-faced Hereford cattle graze many acres while a carefully manicured sod farm sits near the edge of the plateau high above the White River.

The Lake Tapps power flume is filled by water diverted from the White River a short distance upstream from the highway bridge near Buckley. As the tour leaves Buckley, the flume courses alongside through a series of lakes and canals. It is a wood-lined structure with cross braces as it passes under the Sumner–Buckley Highway at the Lake Tapps Highway junction.

The tour route through Auburn circumvents the heavy traffic of Auburn Way, using sidewalks and an underpass. The exposure to secondary thoroughfares, limited to a portion of Auburn's signed bicycle route, is minimal and quickly left behind. The pleasant scenery and easy terrain (with the exception of one hill) make this an enjoyable ride in southern King County.

MILEAGE LOG

0.0 Parking area of Enumclaw King County Park. Leave park and head west on **State Route 410 (Roosevelt Avenue E.)**. Keep on left-hand shoulder.

0.1 Turn left on **284 Avenue S.E.** by Farman's Pickle Factory.

2.7 Turn right on **S.E. Mud Mountain Road**. White River rolls by in canyon on the left; dairy farms on the right.

5.8 Turn left on **State Route 410**. Cross the White River and enter Pierce County. Cross Lake Tapps power flume, climb hill, and enter Buckley. Cafes, groceries. Road shoulder oiled but rough; traffic busy.

6.7 Turn right on **Park Avenue** in Buckley. Road bends left and is named **Naches Street N.** at 7.1.

7.3 Turn right on **Mason Avenue**. Turn right at stop sign and cross power flume at 8.8 as road is renamed **Sumner Buckley Highway**.

11.1 Turn right on **Buckley Tapps Highway E.** just before highway re-crosses power flume. Continue along cliff above White River. Terrain changes from flat to rolling; traffic almost nonexistent. Pass several dairy farms. Lake Tapps comes into view at mile 15.7.

17.4 Turn left on **198 Avenue E.** toward Lake Tapps Pierce County Park.

17.8 Proceed through park gate and bear right toward peninsula park area. Restrooms, food concession, marina, and picnic area; fair-weather lunch stop. After lunch continue north past barricade and along lakeshore dike.

18.7 Bear left on dirt path as road is barricaded ahead, then turn right on **9 Street E.**

18.8 Turn left and head downhill on **Coby Road**. Enter King County at mile 19.3. Road changes name to **Randall Avenue S.E.** and **53rd Street S.E.** as it swings left and continues downhill.

20.3 Bear right on **Kersey Way** and continue downhill. Cross the White River and continue into the city of Auburn on **R Street S.E.** State Route 164 (Auburn Way) arches overhead at mile 22.7.

22.8 Road bends left and becomes **17 Street S.E.** To avoid heavy traffic at next corner, bicycles should get up on sidewalk. Bear right alongside **Auburn Way**.

23.1 Bear right with **M Street**, leave sidewalk, and pick up Auburn bicycle route signs. Cross railroad tracks just after State Route 18 roars overhead at mile 23.7.

23.8 Turn right with bike route sign on **3rd Street S.E.**

24.1 Right turn on **R Street S.E.** As the street turns left and rounds a corner it is renamed **Auburn–Black Diamond Road**. Execute another crossing of railroad tracks. State Route 18 crosses overhead at mile 25.5.

25.6 Turn right on **S.E. Green Valley Road**. Alternative starting point at Green River fishing access is on the left at 25.7. Strawberry fields offer U-pick opportunities during June and July.

26.6 Right turn on **Academy Drive S.E.** by a dairy farm with Holstein-Friesian cows. Climb a forested, winding road to the Enumclaw plateau. Seventh-Day Adventist Auburn Academy spreads over the terrain at the top of the hill at mile 27.5. Keep left with Academy Drive as it bends and twists through an attractive residential community.

27.7 Left turn on **32nd Street S.E.** at stop sign as Academy Drive ends.

28.0 Turn left on **37th Street S.E.** as busy highway appears ahead.

28.1 Continue on **Lemon Tree Lane** as 37th Street turns right.

28.5 Right turn on **Orchard Street S.E.** as Lemon Tree Lane is marked Dead End. Road surface becomes unpaved for 0.3 mile as road is renamed **148 Avenue S.E.**

29.0 Turn left on **S.E. 368 Place** as 148 Avenue ends. Road turns left and is renamed **S.E. 372 Street**, then bends right and becomes **156 Avenue S.E.** As road bends left again, it is renamed **S.E. 376 Street**. Pass large homes on multiacre lots.

30.1 Right turn on **160 Place S.E.** Continue as S.E. 380 Place comes in from the right at stop sign at mile 30.3.

30.7 Road turns left and is renamed **S.E. 384 Street**. Mt. Rainier appears on the horizon.

31.6 Right turn on **180 Avenue S.E.** by Newaukum Grange Hall. S.E. 408 Street, an old concrete highway, joins from the right at mile 33.1.

33.6 Bear left at wye with old highway as it is renamed **S.E. 416 Street**.

34.4 Bear right with old highway on **192 Place S.E.**

34.8 Bear right on old highway as it becomes **196 Avenue S.E.** Cross State Route 164 at mile 35.6. Road turns left at 36.8 and is renamed **S.E. 456 Street**. A sod farm presents acres of beautiful green lawn. *Note: If ride started from Auburn or Buckley, turn right on 220 Avenue S.E. by old schoolhouse at mile 38.4 to shorten tour by 7 miles; otherwise, stay on S.E. 456 Way.*

39.1 Turn right on **S.E. 452 Street** just after 456 Street bends left (north) and is renamed **228 Avenue S.E.**

40.1 Jog left on **244 Avenue S.E.** at stop sign, then immediately turn right on **S.E. 456 Street**. Cross State Route 410 at mile 40.9. As it traverses a section of Enumclaw the road is locally renamed **Warner Avenue**.

42.6 Left turn on **284 Avenue S.E.** as S.E. 456 Street ends.

43.1 Right turn on **Roosevelt Avenue E. (State Route 410)**.

43.2 Back to starting point at Enumclaw King County Park.

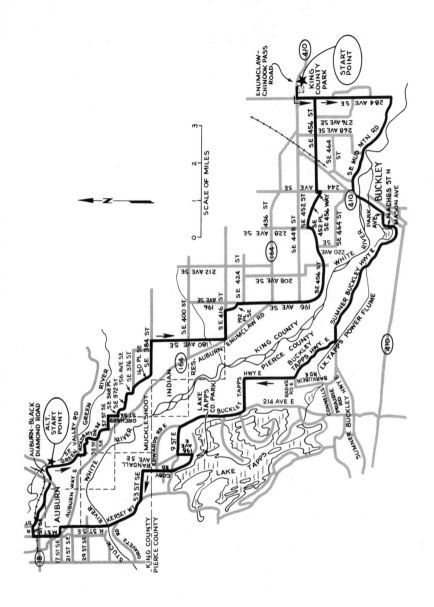

31

99 PACIFIC–LAKE TAPPS

STARTING POINT: Pacific Park, city of Pacific. From the north take exit 2A from I-405 and follow State Route 167 south to Pacific. The park is on 3rd Avenue S.E. along the Stuck River. From the south take exit 127 (State Route 512) from I-5. Pick up State Route 167 near Sumner and proceed north to Pacific.

DISTANCE: 30 miles.
TERRAIN: Hilly.
TOTAL CUMULATIVE ELEVATION GAIN: 900 feet.
RECOMMENDED TIME OF YEAR: All seasons.
RECOMMENDED STARTING TIME: 9 A.M.
ALLOW: 4 to 5 hours.
POINTS OF INTEREST
Lake Tapps Pierce County Park
Bulb farms along Puyallup River

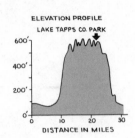

ELEVATION PROFILE
LAKE TAPPS CO. PARK
DISTANCE IN MILES

Before the turn of the century the White River flowed north through what is now south Auburn to empty into the Green River. In one of its major rampaging floods, it overflowed the valley floor and washed a deep channel around the bluff into Stuck Creek and thence to the Puyallup River. Once settled into its new channel, it never returned to the Green. As it winds around the bluff and flows south to the Puyallup, the river is now alternatively called the White River or the Stuck River.

In about the year 1900, the power company of Stone and Webster built a small diversion dam on the White River near the town of Buckley. A channel and flume system directed the water into a lake we know today as Lake Tapps. To make the large lake, the forest around several small lakes was logged off and gaps in the ridges diked; the stumps were left and still are visible at low water.

At the northwest corner of the lake the water follows an exit channel and plunges through penstocks to generators at the White River Power Plant, 500 feet below in the valley at Dieringer. In the early 1900s, Puget Sound Power and Light Company acquired this rather unusual system to help power its electric railways in and around Tacoma. It is still an important element in Washington State's network of electric-power-producing facilities.

The White River originates at the terminus of the Emmons Glacier on the north slope of Mt. Rainier. After the slowly moving glacier grinds and pulverizes the rocks and soil, the silt emerges with the water at the river's source. When diverted from the river into the series of small lakes forming the channel to Lake Tapps, the silt settles out, forming fine, gray mud. A large dredge periodically maintains the settling basin by scooping out the mud and building up the adjoining banks.

About the year 1957, Puget Power sold land adjoining the lake to developers, retaining title of the lakefront up to the high-water, 545-foot elevation level. In the intervening years Lake Tapps has seen the growth of an extensive residential community along its many miles of shoreline.

In winter months, when river flow declines and power demand increases, Puget Power draws the lake down to feed the power turbines, slowly shrinking the reservoir and exposing huge stumps along the muddy edges. When the spring runoff begins, usually around the first of April, the company increases the diversion of water from the White River to a maximum allotment of 2000 cubic feet per second. By the middle of May, Lake Tapps is filled and ready for the many summer recreational activities that occur on and around the lake: powerboating, waterskiing, swimming, and bicycle touring.

Two parks offer picnicking on a warm, sunny day: Bonney Lake Park on the southwest corner of Lake Tapps, and the Pierce County park at the northeast corner. The food concession at the county park is not open before Memorial Day, but there are picnic tables on the peninsula's lawn. A rapid, plunging return to the valley floor completes an exhilarating tour.

MILEAGE LOG

0.0 Pacific city park. Leave park and turn left (west) on **3rd Avenue S.E.**
0.4 Left turn on **Butte Avenue S.** Cross County Line Road and enter Pierce County at 0.9. Road changes name to **139th Avenue E.**
1.4 Right turn on **8th Street E.** as 139th Avenue ends.
1.6 Cross railroad tracks and turn left on **136th Avenue E.** Pass homes with small gardens, old orchard trees, and green fields.

"*TAIL*" *GUNNER*

2.6 Left turn on **24th Street E.** as 136th Avenue ends. Cross railroad tracks at 2.7. Road bends right by sod farm and is renamed **142nd Avenue E.** Rhubarb and strawberry fields along the road.

4.6 Cross Stuck River, enter Sumner, and immediately turn left on **Puyallup Street.**

5.0 Right turn on **Williams Avenue** as Puyallup ends.

5.2 Cross angled railroad tracks and turn right on **Wood Avenue.** Follow Wood through Sumner, crossing Main Street with traffic light in the city center at mile 5.7.

6.4 Left turn on **Gary Street** as Wood Avenue is marked Dead End.

6.5 Right turn on **Valley Avenue** as Gary ends.

6.8 Cross State Route 410 on overpass and almost immediately turn left on **74th Street E.** toward Riverside Drive E. Road makes a couple of bends and becomes **Riverside Drive E.** as bulb fields come into view on the left. Pierce County Riverside Park on the right at mile 7.8.

8.9 Turn left on **McCutchen Road E.** as Riverside Drive goes on to cross the Puyallup River. Start uphill as the road winds around a bend.

9.9 Turn left on **Rhodes Lake Road E.** as McCutchen crests a summit. Continue climbing through forest. Houses appear as the road levels out again.

11.2 Left turn on **Angeline Road E.** An attractive dairy farm with white-painted wooden fences adds interest to a lush, green valley. State Route 410 roars overhead at mile 12.8.

13.2 Bear left on **Old Buckley Highway** as Angeline ends.

13.5 Turn hard right on **Church Lake Road** just before the highway tops a summit by a small grocery.

14.5 Left turn on **West Tapps Highway E.** Bonney Lake Park is on the right at mile 15.2; restrooms, picnic tables, and swimming beach in summer.

15.7 Bear right on unmarked fork as main thoroughfare goes left. Missing name signs should say **West Lake Tapps Highway.** At the next intersection turn left on **195 Avenue N.E.**

16.1 Right turn at the next side road on **195 Place E.**

16.4 Right turn on **56 Street E.** as 195 Place ends. 56 Street soon bends left and is renamed **West Tapps Highway.** Overlake Island Drive goes right at 16.5. Jenks Park at mile 16.9 posts prominent Members Only signs as road is renamed **West Tapps Drive E.**

17.3 Right turn on **Lakeridge Drive.** Glimpses of Lake Tapps between the houses.

18.9 Right turn on **West Tapps Drive E.** High-tension power transmission lines sizzle overhead.

19.6 Right turn with **West Tapps Highway** as Sumner-Tapps Highway goes left. Cross power canal to penstock head gates at mile 20.5 and climb a short hill.

21.6 Right turn on **9 Street E.** as 182nd Avenue E. continues toward Auburn.

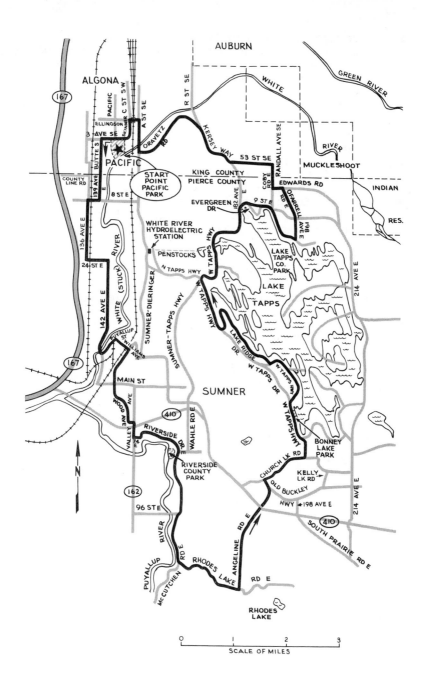

22.4 Right turn on overgrown, narrow roadway behind barricade across road from grocery and cafe. The road goes along the top of a dike holding back the waters of the lake. At mile 23.1 a chain link fence and gate form another barrier on the dike road at the boundary of Lake Tapps Pierce County Park, but bicycles and pedestrians can circumvent the obstacle. The park offers picnic tables, restrooms, and views of the lake and Mt. Rainier. A section of the park farther south along the lake offers more picnic tables, a shelter, and a badminton court.

23.3 Exit the park and turn left toward park exit gate. Road becomes **198 Avenue E.** as it leaves the park.

23.7 Cross 9 Street E. and continue on **OFarrell Road E.**

24.2 Turn left on **Edwards Road E.** as OFarrell ends.

24.5 Right turn on **Coby Road E.** as Edwards ends. Auburn city-limit sign at mile 24.7 marks the King County line. Road changes name to **Randall Avenue S.E.**

25.0 Road bends left and becomes **53rd Street S.E.**

25.7 Right turn on **Kersey Way** as 53 Street ends. Plunge downhill as traffic picks up.

26.8 Turn left on **Oravetz Road** near bottom of hill as bridge over Stuck River comes into view.

28.2 As Oravetz ends, turn right on unmarked highway (later marked **A Street S.E.**). Almost immediately cross Stuck River on narrow, two-lane bridge with busy traffic and no sidewalks.

28.7 Left turn on **41st Street S.E.** at traffic light. Road is almost immediately renamed **Ellingson Road**. Go under railroad trestle.

28.8 Turn left on **C Street S.W.** Next street sign names it **Skinner Road**. Road turns a corner at 29.2 and becomes **3rd Avenue S.E.** as Stuck River rolls out from under railroad bridge on the left.

29.5 End of tour at Pacific Park.

100 SUMNER–LAKE TAPPS

STARTING POINT: Pierce County Riverside Park in Sumner. Take the Valley Avenue exit from State Route 410 in Sumner and turn south on Valley Avenue. Turn left almost immediately on 74 Street E. toward Riverside Drive. Follow Riverside Drive 1 mile to park. Access routes to State Route 410 include: from the south, exit 127 from I-5 (State Route 512); from the north, exit 2A from I-405 (State Route 167).

DISTANCE: 23 miles.
TERRAIN: Rolling terrain with one major hill.
TOTAL CUMULATIVE ELEVATION GAIN: 850 feet.
RECOMMENDED TIME OF YEAR: All seasons.
RECOMMENDED STARTING TIME: 8 A.M. to noon.
ALLOW: 3 to 4 hours.
POINTS OF INTEREST
Connells Prairie Battle Monument
Lake Tapps Pierce County Park

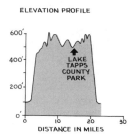

ELEVATION PROFILE

Water and power: these two ingredients go together in many ways, and touring around the Lake Tapps power reservoir can bring them into focus (see Tour #99). Pierce County Riverside Park occasionally feels their full effect when the Puyallup River reaches flood stage and deposits fine glacial silt all over the grounds of the park. Sometimes the flood waters rise high enough to cover McCutchen Road with a thin, silty layer. Debris of twigs, pieces of wood, and vegetation lodge against the fences and among the trees and bushes, and several houses show a brown high-water mark. But nature is not always destructive; she can also be beautiful, as in the tumbling, misty, roaring spectacle of nearby Victor Falls.

Muscle power comes into play as the bicyclist negotiates steep hills up to the Lake Tapps plateau, and a plentiful supply of water is needed for the body to accomplish this feat on a hot summer day. The dense, forested hillsides and lush, green pastures project a lovely scene typical of our northwest area, the result of its surfeit of water in the form of rain.

Over much of its route this tour takes the bicyclist through forest, farmland, and inland residential areas. Occasional glimpses of Lake Tapps appear as its many arms seek avenues of escape. Mt. Rainier soars skyward from its pedestal on the southeastern end of the lake. For the adventuresome, several side roads to islands in the lake offer additional waterscape and miles of interesting exploration.

MILEAGE LOG

0.0 Parking area, Pierce County Riverside Park. Leave park and turn right (south) on **Riverside Drive E.**

1.2 Turn left on **McCutchen Road E.** as Riverside Drive bends right and approaches a bridge over the Puyallup River. Start up steep hill at mile 1.9.

2.2 Turn left on **Rhodes Lake Road** at summit of hill and continue climbing for another 0.8 mile.

3.5 Turn left on **Angeline Road E.** State Route 410 roars overhead at mile 5.1.

5.5 Turn left on **Old Buckley Highway E.** and go uphill on old concrete pavement.

5.8 Turn sharp right on **Church Lake Road** as Old Buckley Highway approaches a summit by a grocery store.

7.3 Bear left on **Kelly Lake Road E.** at a small wye.

7.8 Left turn on **214 Ave E.** as Kelly Lake Road ends.

8.1 Turn right on **Connells Prairie Road E.**

9.1 Bear left on **Barkubein Road E.** by Connells Prairie Battle Monument. Cross bridge over Lake Tapps power flume at 9.2. As it bends right at mile 9.9, the road is renamed **Radke Road East**.

10.2 Turn left on **Buckley Tapps Highway E.**

15.1 Left turn and uphill on **198 Avenue E.** toward Lake Tapps Pierce County Park.

15.4 Proceed through park gate and bear right toward peninsula park area. Restrooms, concessions, and picnic area; fair-weather lunch stop. After lunch continue north past barricade and along lakeshore dike.

16.5 Bear left on dirt path as road is barricaded ahead, then turn left on **9 Street E.**

17.0 Turn left on **182nd Avenue E.** The road winds up and down and crosses the power canal to the White River Power Plant penstocks at 18.2.

19.1 Go straight on **Sumner-Tapps Highway E.** as West Tapps Highway goes left. Climb a short rise and enjoy a long, straight descent on wide, paved shoulder.

21.4 Pass under State Route 410 and continue on **166 Avenue E. (Wahle Road E.).**

22.3 Turn right on **Wood McCumber Road E.** as Wahle ends.

22.5 Left turn on **Riverside Drive E.**, then right into entrance of Riverside Park.

22.6 End of ride.

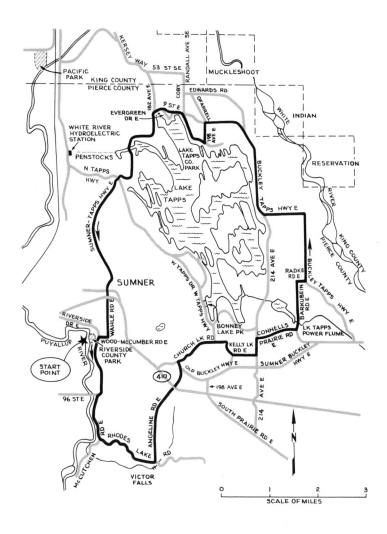

101 BUCKLEY–ORTING

STARTING POINT: White River High School Annex in Buckley. From the south, take exit 127 (State Route 512) from I-5 to the State Route 410 interchange and take State Route 410 east to Buckley. From the north, take exit 2A from I-405 and follow State Route 167 and State Route 410 to Buckley. Turn east on A street as Park Avenue goes west at the northeast edge of town and park along A Street by high school annex.

ALTERNATIVE STARTING POINT: Lions Club Park in Orting. Take Valley Avenue exit from State Route 410 in Sumner and follow State Route 162 south to Orting.

DISTANCE: 32 miles.
TERRAIN: Hilly with some flat.
TOTAL CUMULATIVE ELEVATION GAIN: 800 feet.
RECOMMENDED TIME OF YEAR: All seasons.
RECOMMENDED STARTING TIME: 9 A.M.
ALLOW: 5 hours.
POINTS OF INTEREST
Victor Falls
Puyallup Salmon Hatchery

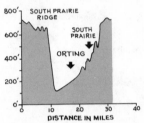

ELEVATION PROFILE

Located in northeastern Pierce County, Buckley and Orting trace their origins back to the 1870s and 1880s, when the first settlers arrived to farm and log the land, work for the Northern Pacific Railroad, or dig coal in the nearby mining towns of Wilkeson, Carbonado, and Burnett.

Today, a century later, logging continues to be an important industry in the nearby Cascade foothills, but the mining operations stopped many years ago. The Northern Pacific moved its main line north to Kanaskat in King County, merging in 1970 with the Chicago, Burlington and Quincy to form the Burlington Northern Railroad. Farming, also, is no longer important to the economy of Buckley, and only a few dairy farms persist near Orting. Pierce County is slowly but surely losing its agricultural lands, yet it still maintains a rural atmosphere.

As this bicycle tour leaves Buckley, it passes small, private woodlots and homes with orchards, gardens, horses, cows, sheep, and chickens. Hinkleman Road, narrow and patchy, is not conducive to fast-moving traffic. Pleasant country scenery continues along 112 Street E. (formerly called Pipeline Road), which follows the Tacoma water pipeline originating high up the Green River Gorge. The view from the ridge overlooking the sparsely settled South Prairie Creek Valley 300 feet below is most impressive. Winter tourists may catch a glimpse of ducks on little Rhodes Lake as they round a corner and begin the exhilarating plunge downhill to the Puyallup River Valley. Several small streams tumble off the hillside and rush noisily to the silt-laden Puyallup. At McMillin, traffic picks up along State Route 162, but a frontage road beside a former bulb farm, now platted for residential development, lessens the ordeal of this section of highway. Massive Mt.

Rainier appears in all its glory at the end of the valley, brightening the spirits of all.

State Route 162 has three-foot-wide paved shoulders as it leaves Orting and heads up the valley of South Prairie Creek, which joins the Carbon, another silt-laden river, near the traffic-free backroad of Pioneer Way. Horses occupy the small pastures near the homes along the Lower Burnett Road. Old masonry structures, possibly once powder magazines for the coal mines, crumble among the trees. The route continues along this narrow, winding road as it negotiates the steep, enchanting canyon of South Prairie Creek and emerges on top of the plateau at the old mining town of Burnett, where rows of look-alike "company" houses line the street. Traffic continues to be minimal and scenery rural as the route returns to Buckley.

MILEAGE LOG

0.0 White River High School Annex in Buckley. Head west on **North A Street**, cross Highway 410, and continue on **Park Avenue**. Road bends left at mile 0.6 and is renamed **Naches Street N.**

0.8 Right turn on **Mason Avenue** at stop sign.

1.0 Bear left, then right on **Hinkleman Road E.** at unmarked wye and proceed along narrow, oiled roadway.

1.9 Turn left on **Mundy Loss Road E.** at stop sign as Hinkleman ends. Cross State Route 410 at mile 2.0.

2.3 Right turn on **112th Street E.** A small airstrip appears on the left at mile 4.0.

5.9 Turn sharp left on **South Prairie Road E.**

6.3 Right turn on **Prairie Ridge Road E.**

6.5 Right turn on **120th Street E.** as Prairie Ridge Drive continues into the mobile-home community of Prairie Ridge. *Note: For an unusual view of South Prairie Creek Valley, the side trip into Prairie Ridge and along the trail at the edge of the bluff leads to 214th Avenue and back to the route. See map, page 43.*

8.1 Turn right on **198th Avenue E.** as 120th Street ends. The marshy shores of Rhodes Lake show dimly through the trees on the left. The road bends left at 8.4 and is renamed **Rhodes Lake Road E.** A tall surge pipe for the Tacoma water line stands on the left. At mile 9.4, near the bottom of a downhill run, the water department facilities of Bonney Lake appear on the left. Just beyond the end of the fence and guardrail, a faint trail leads 30 yards or so to the precipice of Victor Falls. Caution is urged in exploring here; there are no guardrails, and a slip may result in a vertical fall of 70 feet. Victor Falls are the property of Bonney Lake, and authorized tours may be arranged by calling city hall at 863-6318.

10.9 Bear left at wye on **McCutchen Road E.** View of Puyallup River below.

12.2 Bear right on **128th Street E.** and cross the Puyallup River as road ahead is marked Dead End. The Tacoma Water Department pipeline crosses its own bridge on the left.

12.9 Left turn on **State Route 162** by McMillin Grocery.

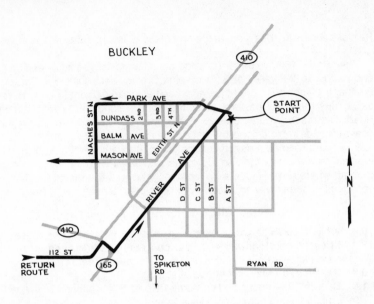

14.4 Turn right on **Old Pioneer Way E.** and continue parallel to highway.

15.9 Continue right on **State Route 162** as Old Pioneer Way ends. Orting Lions Club Park on the right in Orting at 16.7; picnic lunch stop. A drive-in before the park and a cafe beyond offer indoor lunches. Follow S.R. 162 through Orting as it bends right and left.

18.1 Bear left with S.R. 162 as Orville Road E. goes right to Electron. Puyallup Salmon Hatchery on the left at 19.2.

20.4 Turn right on **South Pioneer Way** and continue parallel to the highway.

24.8 Left turn in South Prairie on **Emery Street** as Pioneer Way ends, then turn right on **State Route 162** and pass a grocery store on the left. Climb hill out of town.

25.9 Turn right and down a short hill on **Lower Burnett Road**. Road meanders along South Prairie Creek with Mt. Rainier in the distance. Cross bridge over creek at 27.2 and start uphill.

27.6 Turn left on **State Route 165** in old mining town of Burnett. Cross high bridge over South Prairie Creek.

28.4 Bear left at wye on **State Route 162** toward South Prairie and Orting.

28.6 Cross bridge over abandoned railroad cut and turn right on **Mundy Loss Road E.** toward White River Middle School.

29.6 Right turn on **112th Street E.**

30.8 Turn right at wye on **State Route 165**, then immediately left on **River Avenue**. Roadside park with picnic tables on the left. Continue on River Avenue through Buckley.

31.5 Turn right on **A Street** at stop sign and return to starting point.

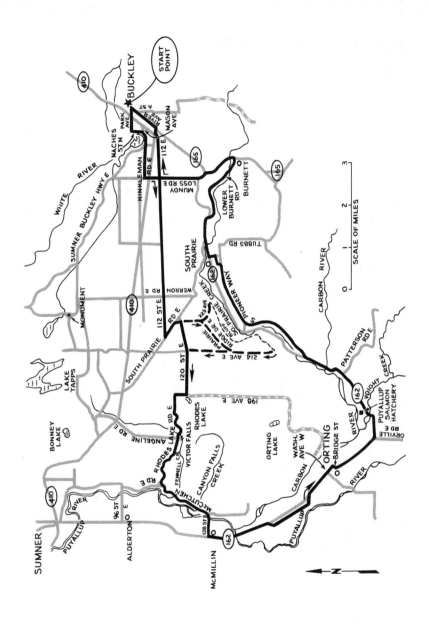

102 DU PONT–MCKENNA

STARTING POINT: Parking spaces along main street in Du Pont. Take exit 119, turn west on Steilacoom Road, and then immediately left on Barksdale Street in Du Pont.

DISTANCE: 35 miles.
TERRAIN: Moderate to flat.
TOTAL CUMULATIVE ELEVATION GAIN: 500 feet.
RECOMMENDED TIME OF YEAR: Any season.
RECOMMENDED STARTING TIME: 9 A.M.
ALLOW: 4 to 5 hours.
POINTS OF INTEREST
Medicine Creek Treaty monument in Old Nisqually
Centralia City Light Hydroelectric Plant
Fort Lewis training facilities

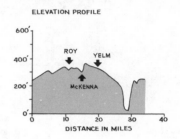

ELEVATION PROFILE

    Much of the area covered in this tour is rich in historical background. Among the earliest white settlers in the northwest were the farmers of the Hudson's Bay Trading Post, who established Fort Nisqually amid their farmlands atop the bluff west of what is now the town of Du Pont. The Fort Nisqually area was acquired by the E. I. Du Pont Nemours Company in 1900 for the manufacture of dynamite, a product that has contributed greatly to the clearing of farmlands, mining of coal, and construction of our nation's roads and highways. The little town of Du Pont, established as the company's town, is now without a namesake, as the Du Pont property was acquired by the Weyerhaeuser Company in 1976. About the only reminder of the original fort settlement accessible to the public is a plaque on a boulder west of the fenced plant commemorating an observatory site used to establish the geographic location by star sightings. Rough, unimproved roads lead around the fence to the memorial.

    The Medicine Creek Treaty, negotiated by Governor Stevens in 1854 as a covenant between the United States of America and the Indian tribes of Nisqually, Puyallup, and Squaxin, is commemorated by a monument in Old Nisqually. This small plaque on a boulder hardly seems fitting for a document that has caused such uproar over Indian fishing rights.

    History of another sort is represented by the Centralia City Light Hydroelectric Plant, near Yelm. Although dwarfed by the hydroelectric facilities on the Columbia River, the three turbines of this power plant have supplied a major portion of Centralia's electricity since the plant's construction in 1928. A diversion dam several miles up the Nisqually River (see Tour #123) supplies water to the power canal feeding the penstocks. The plant's entrance road crosses an emergency spillway built to divert the canal's flow if an unplanned shutdown of the turbines occurs. Tours of the hydroelectric facility and the upstream diversion dam may be arranged by contacting the plant supervisor at least two days in advance. Write to Centralia Light Department Superintendent, 1102 N. Tower, Centralia, WA 98531, or call 736-7611.

McKenna owes its existence to a lumber mill established in 1906. Although the mill is gone, the town continues a sleepy existence. The big, old bunk-house that once housed mill workers is today an attractive home for old folks. Large trees shade the lawns around the home, while the Nisqually River ripples by on its way to Puget Sound.

Roy, platted in 1884 with the name of Muck, also has many memories. The general store, built in 1889, still does a thriving business. Much of the town is decorated in Western style, and the major crowd-drawing event is the Roy Rodeo. A delightful little park along Muck Creek invites passersby for a picnic lunch.

Apart from these smaller bits of history, and dominating the major portion of this tour, is the Fort Lewis Military Reservation. The fort was established as a training area at American Lake by the U.S. War Department in 1906. In 1917 the citizens of Pierce County donated real estate for the establishment of Camp Lewis. Enlarged over the years, the camp has become Fort Lewis, and has served as a base and training area for five wars. After many years of operation as an open fort, Fort Lewis was closed to the public in early 1987. Visitors must now acquire passes at the visitor center by the main gate.

MILEAGE LOG

0.0 Starting from automotive service station on **Barksdale Street** in Du Pont, head out to freeway interchange, cross I-5 on overpass, and immediately turn left on freeway entrance northbound. Continue on wide shoulder of **I-5**.

2.2 Bear right on **Exit 120** and continue right through Fort Lewis main gate to Visitors Information Center. Pick up day pass and continue on shoulder of **41st Division Drive**.

2.6 Turn left at traffic light on **Colorado Avenue**. Cross Pendleton Avenue at mile 3.6 and continue on **4th Division Drive**.

6.1 Turn left on **East Gate Road** as 4th Division Drive ends, and continue through east gate checkpoint.

8.7 Cross cattle guard and railroad tracks, and immediately turn right on side road and cross another cattle guard. Cross cattle guard at mile 10.7, and railroad tracks at 10.8. Enter Roy on **Warren Street**. *Note: To visit Roy city park on Muck Creek, turn right on Cedar Street at mile 11.1.*

11.2 Turn left on **Water Street** in Roy, cross railroad tracks, and turn right on **McNaught Street (State Route 507)**. Cafe and grocery in Roy. Go through McKenna (grocery, deli) at mile 16.0, cross the Nisqually River, and enter Thurston County.

17.0 Cross bridge over railroad tracks and immediately turn right on **Old McKenna Road S.E.** As it executes a bend, the road is renamed **Bridge Road S.E.**

18.6 Left turn on **Railway Street S.E.** Road is renamed **First Street** as it enters Yelm.

20.1 Turn right across railroad tracks on **State Route 510 (Yelm Avenue)** as S.R. 507 continues on in Yelm city center. Grocery, cafes, city park.

22.6 A dirt road leads right, by a sign announcing the Centralia City Light Hydro Plant. This is an interesting 0.9-mile side trip to penstock head gates and view of valley power plant. For a view, follow dirt path to the right just past diversion gates. Do not continue down to hydro plant unless appointment has been made for visit (see text). Return to S.R. 510 and continue north.

26.6 Bear right on **Reservation Road S.E.**

29.4 Right turn on **Old 99 Highway S.E.** as Reservation Road ends. Old Nisqually Store and Medicine Creek Treaty monument at mile 30.1. Cross Nisqually River and enter Pierce County at mile 30.8. Climb long hill.

33.0 Turn right at freeway entrance on **I-5** northbound toward Tacoma and Seattle. Continue on shoulder, keeping right around weighing station.

35.1 Bear right on **Exit 119** toward Du Pont.

35.3 Left turn across overpass and continue through traffic light on **Steilacoom Road**.

35.4 Turn left toward Du Pont on **Barksdale Street** just after crossing railroad tracks, and return to start point.

"Sorry, Sir. You must have a gate pass."

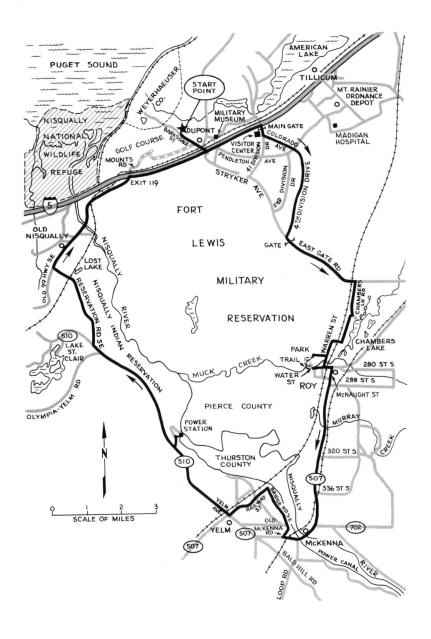

103 GRAHAM–NORTHWEST TREK

STARTING POINT: Parking lot of Graham Grange Hall in Graham. From the north take exit 2A from I-405 and follow State Route 167, State Route 512, and State Route 161 (south) to Graham. From the south take exit 127 (State Route 512) from I-5 and State Route 161 south to Graham. Park near the grange hall across from the Graham Post Office on 224th Street E.

DISTANCE: 40 miles.
TERRAIN: Moderate to hilly.
TOTAL CUMULATIVE ELEVATION GAIN: 1200 feet.
RECOMMENDED TIME OF YEAR: Any season.
RECOMMENDED STARTING TIME: 9 A.M.
ALLOW: 5 to 9 hours.
POINTS OF INTEREST
Northwest Trek, Tacoma's Zoological Park.
Spring flowers

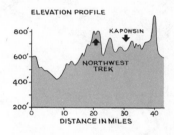

ELEVATION PROFILE

Northwest Trek, a wildlife preserve created from a 600-acre cattle ranch, perches atop a plateau overlooking Ohop Lake near Eatonville. Originally just a dream of two private citizens, it shows what can be accomplished when diligent efforts are made to obtain the cooperation of local governmental agencies and the financial help of the general public.

Dr. and Mrs. David Hellyer had the vision of a park devoted to the exhibition and preservation of northwest animals and birds in their native habitat. They wanted the animals free to roam about their ranch, each species occupying its own ecological niche on the land. The Hellyers also wanted the public to be able to observe the animals. In 1971 they approached the Tacoma Metropolitan Park Board with an offer: they would donate the land for the natural zoo in return for the privilege of remaining in their home on the shore of Horseshoe Lake for as long as they desired. The park board approved the idea and put a bond issue before the citizens of Tacoma to fund the park. It took two tries, but in 1973 the people of Tacoma voted for the bond issue and Northwest Trek became a reality, opening its door to visitors in July 1975. A major portion of the park is enclosed by a secure fence to exclude predators and to allow animals to roam freely. In propane-powered trams, visitors travel 5.5 miles of paved road to view the wildlife within the enclosure. Herds of bison and elk graze the green meadows while white- and black-tailed deer browse the forest. A few moose seek out the wetlands. Wild turkey gobblers make their cacophonic proclamations and strut for the benefit of their hens. Canada geese stake out nesting areas by several small marshy lakes; one such lake boasts a beaver lodge. Ubiquitous mallards and coots prefer the big lake and are occasionally joined by rarer species such as the gadwall. Tundra swans add their beauty to the scene. Great blue herons fly in and out of the ponds and lakes. Changing with the seasons, the wild bird population attracts the avid bird watcher.

Outside the main herbivore area, predatory timber wolves share their four-acre enclosure with a black bear, with whom they have reached a mutual nonaggression understanding. The public is invited to walk through a display area that has been cleverly designed so that small animals such as otter, beaver, raccoon, fisher, skunk, marten, and wolverine appear in a natural outdoor setting among man-made dens, lodge, stream, and ponds.

A five-mile-long nature trail traverses the hillside overlooking Ohop Lake and offers the hiker interesting botanical explorations. Picnic tables, food service, gift shop, and restrooms also complement this unique wildlife preserve.

While bird and wild animal lovers will enjoy Northwest Trek, those who relish the sight of wildflowers growing in their natural state will find several interesting species along the roadsides of this tour; flowers of the open prairie, dense forest, and lush greensward weave a colorful tapestry.

MILEAGE LOG

0.0   Leave grange hall parking lot, turn right on **224 Street E.**, and proceed gently downhill. Cross railroad tracks at mile 0.8. Fenced pastures with cattle.

1.9   Left turn on **70 Avenue E.** Pass a small group of homes and enter forest. Mahonia and kinnikinnick grow in the stony soil.

4.1   Right turn on **260th Street E.** Horse ranches with occasional large oak trees in the pastures alternate with forests of Douglas fir.

5.6   Jog left on **State Route 7** as 260th Street appears to end, then turn right and continue on 260th Street. In the springtime blue camas lilies and blue campanulas (bluebells) bloom along the roadside and underneath the trees in the open forest. Cross cattle guard and enter open range at mile 7.1; Fort Lewis Military Reservation on the right. Large fir trees have the shape of trees in an open forest.

7.5   Bear left with 260th Street E. as Rice Kandle Road E. continues on. Meadowlarks sing from trees and wires.

8.1   Left turn on **8th Avenue E.** and cross another cattle guard as 260th Street E. ends. Military Reservation is on the right. Cross two small creeks. Stop and cross 304th Avenue E. at mile 10.8. Road bends left at 12.3 and becomes **Kinsman Road E.** as forest closes in.

14.0   Left turn on **State Route 702** as Kinsman is marked Dead End. Proceed through Weyerhaeuser Tree Farm, harvested and replanted in 1963.

16.2   Junction State Route 7 as S.R. 702 ends. Cross S.R. 7 and continue on **Eatonville Cutoff Road**, which shortly bends right.

18.4   Left turn on **Jensen Road E.** as Eatonville Cutoff proceeds downhill. Road is narrow and winds through forest. Pastures open up around a small lake. Road bends left and up a very steep hill at mile 19.6.

20.4   Turn left on **State Route 161** as Jensen Christian Road ends.

20.5   Right turn on **Trek Drive E.** toward Northwest Trek.

21.5   Northwest Trek, a Pacific Northwest wildlife preserve. Open daily 10 A.M. until one hour before sundown, April through October. Open Wednesday through Sunday from November through March.

Children are half price; group rates for 12 or more are available on request. After visiting the park retrace route back on park entrance road.

22.5 Right turn on **State Route 161**.

24.8 Bear left on side road toward Camp Arnold at milepost 11. Road eventually is marked **Webster Road E.**

27.2 Right turn on **Kapowsin Highway (304th Street E.)** at stop sign.

31.2 Continue with **Orville Road E.** as it joins from the right at blinking red light. Grocery at this corner.

31.6 Cross bridge over railroad tracks and immediately bear left on **Griggs Road E.** Lake Kapowsin appears below on the right.

31.7 Left turn uphill on **Browne E.** and zigzag through Kapowsin, eventually heading north (left) on **158th Avenue E.** Pedal over several short hills.

33.9 Left turn on **264th Street E.** as 158th Avenue ends. Morgan Lake appears in a pasture on the left at 34.3. Cross Orting-Kapowsin Highway E. at 35.1. Magnificent view of Mt. Rainier to the east.

36.9 Right turn on **110th Avenue E.** and climb a hill past dairy farm. On a clear day in spring Mt. Rainier appears white all the way to the bottom of its 14,000-foot massif. Top the hill at 38.1 and plunge down the other side. Road zigzags left and right as it is renamed **240th Street E.** and **108th Avenue E.**

39.5 Left turn on **224th Street E.** as 108th Avenue ends. Cross State Route 161 at mile 39.9.

40.0 End of tour at Graham Grange Hall in downtown Graham.

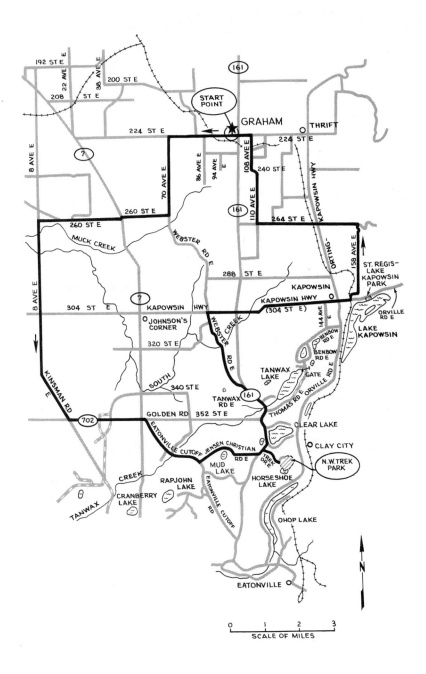

104 GRAHAM–ROY–KAPOWSIN

STARTING POINT: Parking lot of Graham Grange Hall in Graham. From the north take exit 2A from I-405 and follow State Route 167, State Route 512, and State Route 161 (south) to Graham. From the south take exit 127 (State Route 512) from I-5 and State Route 161 south to Graham. Park near the grange hall across from the Graham Post Office on 224th Street E.

DISTANCE: 40 miles.
TERRAIN: Flat to moderate.
TOTAL CUMULATIVE ELEVATION GAIN: 1000 feet.
RECOMMENDED TIME OF YEAR: Any season.
RECOMMENDED STARTING TIME: 9 to 10 A.M.
ALLOW: 5 to 6 hours.
POINTS OF INTEREST
None outstanding

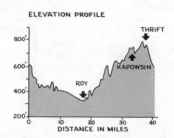

ELEVATION PROFILE

Cows graze unconcernedly in broad open prairies; a few turn their heads to watch bicycles as they wheel by. Deciduous trees, bare of leaves in winter, support a crop of lichens reminiscent of biblical tales of manna. Occasional swampy patches grow crops of cattails and steeplebush. Blue camas lilies along the roadside in spring are followed in summer by the bluebell campanula and tall orange tiger lily.

At almost the halfway point, Roy offers a cafe, grocery, and park picnicking facilities. An old railroad water tank, rehabilitated, serves as a standpipe for the town's water supply. Next door to the rodeo grounds, a colorful sign reminiscent of the early Wild West advertises an old tavern. These are the highlights of this tour; details may be filled in by the rider.

MILEAGE LOG

0.0 Leave grange hall parking lot and turn right on **224th Street E.**

1.3 Turn right on **82nd Avenue E.** Road bends left at mile 2.0 and is renamed **Eustis-Hunt Road E.**

2.8 Left turn on **204th Street E.** as Eustis-Hunt Road ends. Road executes bends to left and right and is renamed **Knoble Road E.**, **200th Street E.**, and **38th Avenue E.**

6.6 Turn left on **192nd Avenue E.** just after crossing railroad tracks.

8.6 Turn left on **8 Avenue E.** Cross State Route 7 at mile 9.2. Gas station and cafe.

9.6 Turn right on **208th Street E.**

10.6 Left turn on **State Route 507** and proceed along paved shoulder. Enter Roy city limits at mile 17.0. As it enters main part of town, road bends right, then left on **McNaught Street**. *Note: To visit city park, go straight on Water Street as highway bends left. Park is at foot of Water Street, accessible by footbridge over Muck Creek.*

17.2 Roy city center. Grocery and cafe; lunch stop. After lunch, head back (north) along **State Route 507**.

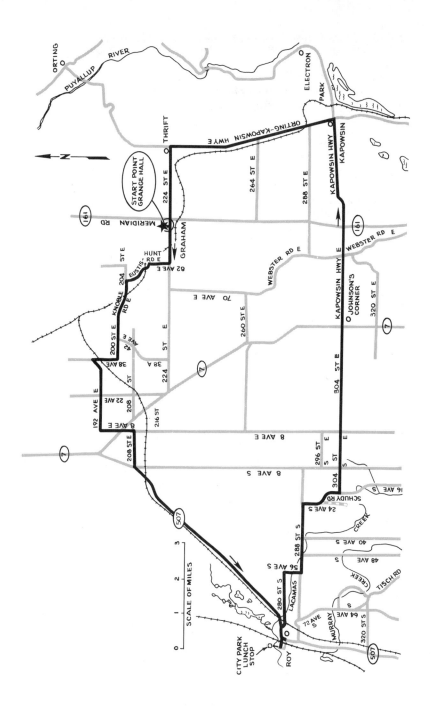

17.3 Bear right on **280th Street S.** as S.R. 507 swings left. Cross railroad tracks at mile 17.6. Road turns corner at mile 18.8 and is renamed **56th Avenue S.**

19.3 Left turn on **288th Street S.** as 56th Avenue is marked Dead End.

21.3 Turn right on **24th Avenue S.** by Lacamas Valley Ranch.

21.8 Bear left on **Schudy Road** as 24th Avenue goes on unpaved.

22.7 Left turn on **304th Street S.** Cross State Route 7 at mile 27.2 and continue as 304th Street is renamed **Kapowsin Highway E.** Grocery. Cross State Route 161 at mile 30.0.

33.1 Left turn on **Orting-Kapowsin Highway E.** at flashing light in Kapowsin. Grocery, tavern.

37.6 Turn left on **224th Street E.** at blinking amber light. This is Thrift. Cross State Route 161 in Graham at 39.6 and return to starting point at Graham Grange Hall.

"HE IS REALLY SOLD ON THE ADVANTAGES OF SEW-UPS."

105 OHOP–ROY–HARTS LAKE

STARTING POINT: Public fishing access on Lake Ohop. From the Seattle area take exit 2A from I-405, and follow State Route 167, State Route 512, and State Route 161 (south) to Orville Road E. Turn left and proceed 0.5 mile to fishing access. From the south take exit 127 (State Route 512) from I-5 and State Route 161 south 20 miles to Orville Road E. Turn left and proceed 0.5 mile to fishing access. *Note: Parking privileges now require conservation license, available for a nominal fee at sporting goods stores.*

DISTANCE: 53 miles.
TERRAIN: Moderate to hilly; 5 miles of unpaved roads.
TOTAL CUMULATIVE ELEVATION GAIN: 2000 feet.
RECOMMENDED TIME OF YEAR: Avoid spring thaw (March through mid-May) and opening week of hunting season (mid-October); otherwise any season.
RECOMMENDED STARTING TIME: 9 A.M.
ALLOW: 7 to 8 hours, 1 day, or overnight.

POINTS OF INTEREST
Views of Mt. Rainier

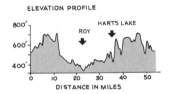

ELEVATION PROFILE

Houses crowd the shoreline along Lake Ohop, allowing glimpses of the lake and recreational boaters. A spring, gushing through a pipe to a concrete basin along the road, is a popular stop for motorists and bicyclists alike. Faint smoke plumes rise from the brick kilns at Clay City near the head of Ohop Lake as the valley continues to the end of Lake Kapowsin. The tall silhouette of Mt. Rainier stands on the horizon, overlooking the upland plateaus and valleys of southern Pierce County. Poorly suited to grain or vegetable crops, the land supports a suburban fringe of houses, grass for dairy and beef cattle and riding horses, and trees from which more houses will be built.

Open prairies, some natural and some with an assist from Homo sapiens, green up in spring with a lush crop of grass. Prairie flowers such as the blue camas lily brighten the roadsides. Signs proclaim the border between the Fort Lewis Military Reservation, and open cattle range. (Watch out for the cattle guards!) Ant mounds, some as large as three feet tall, digest a continually refreshed crop of grasses and needles.

The trees at first seem merely decorative: open-grown firs and lichen-covered oaks. Occasional stands of fir are overcrowded, badly in need of thinning. But these are private lands, neglected by Paul Bunyan for many years. When the commercial forest (primarily Weyerhaeuser's) appears, the hillsides bear evidence of the giant's fabled scythe. But all is not desolation, as young trees, hand-planted and cared for, are turning the hills green again for another crop of timber several decades hence.

From the hilltops the route descends to the glacial valley of the Ohop, with its dairy farms. A bicycling hazard occasionally encountered here is wind-blown spray from a "honey sprinkler" so take care. Eventually the creek winds back to its source at Ohop Lake and the starting point for this tour.

As a one-day tour this ride may be a bit long and strenuous for some. An alternative is to plan an overnight stay at Gil's Resort on Harts Lake. A small grassy tenting area is reserved away from the crowded automotive camp. Water, picnic shelter, and pit toilets are the primary facilities. A snack bar and store with limited food selections provide relief from carrying extra food supplies. For more information write to Route 1, Box 75, Roy, WA, or telephone Yelm, 458-7093.

MILEAGE LOG

0.0 Public fishing access on Ohop Lake. Leave parking area and turn right on **Orville Road E.**

8.1 Stop at blinking red light and continue on **Orting-Kapowsin Highway E.**

8.7 Left turn on **288th Street E.** Cross State Route 161 at mile 11.5.

13.0 Turn right on **Webster Road E.** as 288th Street ends. Gain summit, descend steep hill. Road changes name to **70th Avenue E.**

14.9 Left turn on **260th Street E.**

16.3 Turn left on **State Route 7**, then immediately right again on **260th Street E.** Cross cattle guard and enter open range area at mile 17.8.

18.1 Bear left with 260th Street E. as Rice Kandle Road E. continues on.

18.8 Turn left on **8th Avenue E.** as 260th Street E. ends and cross another cattle guard. Leave range area. Cross Muck Creek and South Creek.

20.5 Right turn on **288th Street E.** just before 8th Avenue E. starts up steep hill. Large ant hills appear near mile 21.7. Cross Lacamas Creek at mile 24.0.

24.5 Turn right on **56th Avenue S.** Cross Lacamas Creek. Road bends left at mile 25.0 and is renamed **280th Street S.**

26.5 Cross railroad tracks and bear left on **State Route 507** into Roy.

26.6 Continue on **Water Street** toward city park as State Route 507 turns left to business district on McNaught Street (cafe, grocery). Cross railroad tracks, jog right on Warren Street, and continue on Water Street to end, where a footbridge leads right across Muck Creek to park at mile 26.8; lunch stop. After lunch, recross footbridge and head south on **Rounge Street.**

27.0 Left turn on **Huggins-Grieg Road** by rodeo grounds.

27.2 Turn right on **McNaught Street (State Route 507)** and ride out of town.

27.6 Left turn on **288th Street S.**

28.3 Bear right on **Lyons Road S.** as 288th Street bends left. Road is renamed **74th Avenue S., 70th Avenue S.**, and **72nd Avenue S.** in succession.

30.4 Turn left on **Tisch Road**. High-tension power lines hum overhead 1 mile later. Road changes name to **56 Avenue S.**

33.0 Right turn on **State Route 702**, then left on **58th Avenue S.** 0.5 mile later road bends right and becomes **360 Street S.**

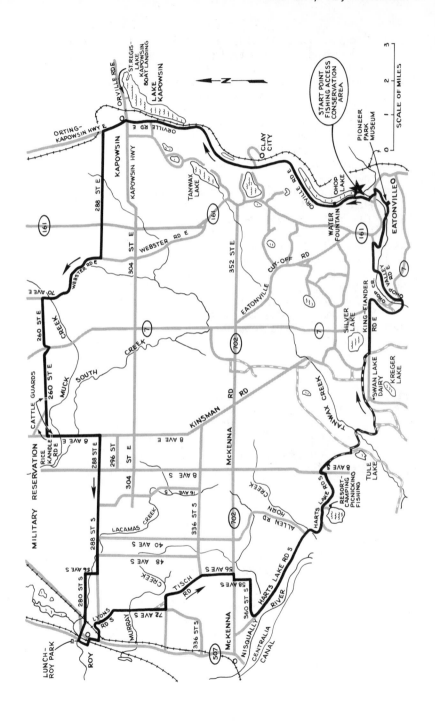

34.7 Turn sharp left on **Harts Lake Road S.** At mile 38.7 is Harts Lake public fishing access with toilets; a private resort with camping area is on right; groceries and snack bar.

40.0 Bend left with thoroughfare on **8th Avenue S.** and turn right almost immediately on narrow, oiled, one-lane road. Pavement ends at mile 40.6. Descend hill.

41.2 Left turn at major intersection by gravel pit, then immediately right 0.1 mile later. Cross Tanwax Creek at mile 41.9.

42.9 Bear left on unmarked fork at top of hill as thoroughfare continues right. Continue with another thoroughfare as it joins from the right 0.2 mile farther.

44.9 Turn right at intersection, then immediately left on paved **King-Fiander Road E.** as Dean Kreger Road continues on.

46.7 Turn right on **State Route 7** by Ohop Grange. Wide, paved shoulder. Descend into Ohop Valley, begin climb on other side.

48.3 Left turn on **Ohop Valley Road E.** and bear right with oiled surface toward Pioneer Farm Museum. Cross Ohop Creek at mile 49.5.

50.3 Bear right at T junction at stop sign. Cross valley again.

52.2 Turn sharp left on **State Route 161 (Eatonville Highway).**

52.3 Go by Ski Park Road and bear right on next road, marked Dead End. Go around barricades and cross bridge.

52.7 Right turn on **Orville Road E.** and cycle along Ohop Lake.

53.2 Turn right into fishing access on Ohop Lake; end of tour.

"IS THIS THE SKYLINE TRAIL?"

106 MT. RAINIER

STARTING POINT: King County Fairgrounds, Enumclaw. From the south take exit 127 (State Route 512) from I-5 to Puyallup and State Route 410 to Enumclaw. From the north take exit 142A (State Route 18) from I-5 to Auburn and State Route 164 to Enumclaw, or from I-405 take exit 4A (State Route 169) to Enumclaw. Turn right from S.R. 410 by Farman's Pickle Factory on 248 Avenue S.E. as highway leaves Enumclaw, and proceed south 0.5 mile to King County Fairgrounds. Park inside gates. (Make arrangements with fairground manager.)

DISTANCE: Total, 162 miles: first day, 63 miles; second day, 43 miles; third day, 56 miles.
TERRAIN: Mountainous.
TOTAL CUMULATIVE ELEVATION GAIN: 10,100 feet: first day, 2800 feet; second day, 4200 feet; third day, 3100 feet.
RECOMMENDED TIME OF YEAR: Weekend after Labor Day to first weekend in October.
RECOMMENDED STARTING TIME: 8 to 9 A.M.
ALLOW: 3 days.
POINTS OF INTEREST
Mt. Rainier National Park
Views of Mt. Rainier

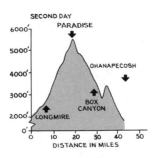

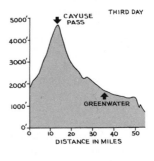

ELEVATION PROFILES

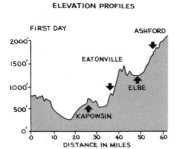

Until a few decades ago Paradise Park on the slopes of Mt. Rainier was at the terminus of a dead-end road. With the completion of the Stevens Canyon Road in 1957, it became a short side trip on a popular weekend drive. Addition of a wide, well-graded access road, attractive visitor center, and extensive hard-surfaced walking trails now make Paradise a popular tourist center whose parking lot is congested with automobiles, tour buses, and recreational vehicles. The popularity of the area for automotive traffic during the summer, and closure of roads by snow at other times of the year, limit to a few short weeks in autumn the optimum interval for enjoying this tour by bicycle. Even then, sudden changes of mountain weather require precautionary planning and provisions.

In order to limit the mileage to what can be accomplished comfortably in a three-day tour, and to protect automobiles parked at the starting point during the tour, it is recommended that arrangements be made with the King County Fairground manager (telephone 825-7777) to park inside the locked gates of the fairground complex. A fee is charged for this service.

Dairy farms dominate the scene as bicyclists leave the fairgrounds and ride along the White River. The rough shoulders and busy traffic of State Route 410 are endured for a brief river crossing. Traffic is minimal through the Pierce County towns of Buckley and South Prairie as open, rural vistas greet the eye along South Prairie Creek. The route turns south along the Puyallup River, where a small lumber mill processes logs beside Orville Road. The high canyon crossing of the Puyallup River affords a view of the milky-gray waters, full of silt from the Tahoma and Puyallup glaciers on Mt. Rainier. Summer cabins and an increasing number of year-round residences line the delightful winding road along Ohop Lake. The State Department of Wildlife maintains a public fishing access at the south end of the lake.

Occasional striking views of Mt. Rainier along the Alder Cutoff Road near Eatonville give the camera buff reasons for stopping. An operating passenger steam train beckons in Elbe for a no-effort side trip to Mineral to view the mountain from a different vantage point. Foothills block the view as the Nisqually entrance to Mt. Rainier National Park is approached, but the mountain soon appears in all its glory. Blazing patches of red and yellow splash across the hillsides and stand out against the gray rock and evergreen trees. Icy-white glaciers sparkling against a bright blue sky complete the colorful autumn spectacle.

Several points along the way, such as the Kautz Mudflow, entice the cyclist to stop and enjoy the inspiring vistas or walk the short scenic trails. In 1947 torrential rains caused the snout of the Kautz glacier to collapse, damming the canyon and forming a lake. Eventually the lake broke through and surged down the creek canyon, carrying tons of rock and mud along with it into the forest below and wiping out everything before it. In keeping with National Park Service land management policy, natural forces were left to heal the scars of this devastating flood. Today a new forest is growing in the soil brought down with the avalanche.

Spectacular Christine and Narada falls provide welcome excuses for stopping on the way up to Paradise, as do metal plaques explaining the views from Rieksecker Point and Canyon Rim. The gray (Canada) jay and Clark's nutcracker enjoy sharing a bit of your lunch at these viewpoints, and also are popular attractions at the Paradise Visitor Center. Dressed in their mid-season brown-and-white attire, white-tailed ptarmigans occasionally stop traffic as they cross the road near the Paradise summit. In winter their all-white plumage makes them practically invisible against the snow.

In season, flowers of all colors and shapes cover the gentle slopes above the Paradise Visitor Center. Hard-surfaced trails lead travelers to a fantastic alpine garden. Strict adherence to trail travel is encouraged to protect the fragile vegetation and to keep erosion of the fine pumice soil to a minimum.

At an elevation of 5420 feet, the weather at Paradise can be capricious during early fall, so bicyclists must be prepared for colder temperatures.

Warm clothes should be available for the downhill trip to Ohanapecosh. As the road begins its descent of the Paradise Valley, brown furry marmots sun themselves on large boulders. Framed by red-and-gold-leafed huckleberry bushes, Reflection Lakes double the grandeur by duplicating the image of the magnificent mountain. The road then executes a sharp hairpin turn as it plunges down the canyon. Shrubby Sitka alder and vine maple cling to the steep ridge on the north side, while several waterfalls cascade down the slopes to the south. The second of two tunnels signals the approach to the box canyon of the Muddy Fork of the Cowlitz River, where restrooms and a scenic overlook provide a welcome stopping place. Golden-mantled ground squirrels and chipmunks frequent the area, accepting handouts and surreptitiously rummaging through handlebar bags or panniers for other tasty morsels. The viewpoint by Backbone Ridge offers one last look before the road traverses the Cowlitz Divide and dives down into the narrow Ohanapecosh Valley. Just before the road crosses the Ohanapecosh River, a sign proclaims an interesting side trip to the Grove of the Patriarchs. A one-mile trail leads past many huge old cedars and Douglas fir trees growing on an island in the river. Ohanapecosh, once a popular spa with cabins and baths that used water piped from hot springs, is now just another park campground. The cabins and baths have been removed and the hot springs restored to their original state. A spacious visitor center provides extensive displays of geology, natural history, and wildlife.

There are few views of Mt. Rainier on the road to Cayuse Pass, but the dense evergreen forest, laced with deciduous shrubs and trees, presents a beautiful scene, and in early fall the coming of winter can be presaged by snow. Again, plenty of warm clothes must be available for the descent from Cayuse Pass. Once the descent is begun, the exhilarating pace discourages bicyclists from frequent stops. One mountain viewpoint requires crossing the highway, as do views of the White River channel. The roadside waterfalls of Crystal Springs are interesting but unheralded by signs or information plaques. At the base of the hill, soon after leaving National Forest land, the shoulder widens out, lessening competition with the fast automotive traffic. Without the scenic attractions of the mountain and its waterfalls, prevailing tailwinds encourage bicyclists to complete this tour rapidly.

MILEAGE LOG

FIRST DAY

0.0 King County Fairgrounds, Enumclaw. Leave fairgrounds and turn left (south) on **284 Avenue S.E.**

2.3 Right turn on **Mud Mountain Road**. White River rolls by on the left.

5.5 Left turn on **Enumclaw-Buckley Road (State Route 410)**. Cross the White River, climb a hill, and enter Buckley.

6.3 Left turn by drive-in on **Park Avenue**, then right on **River Avenue**.

7.1 Continue on **State Route 165** as it joins from the right.

8.6 Right turn on **State Route 162** toward South Prairie at road junction. Pass through South Prairie at mile 11.1. Cross the Carbon River at mile 15.3. Puyallup Salmon Hatchery at mile 17.0.

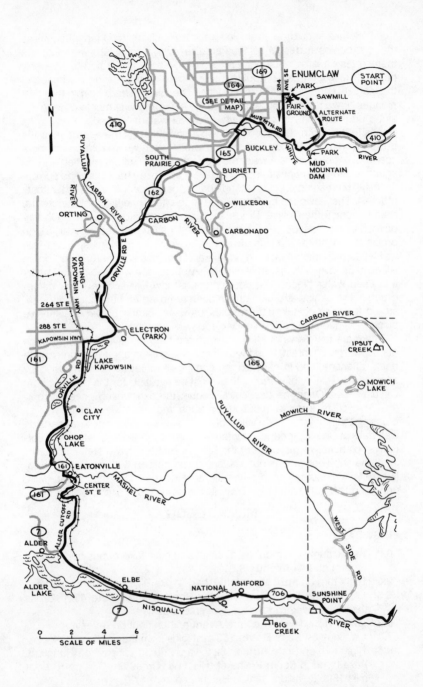

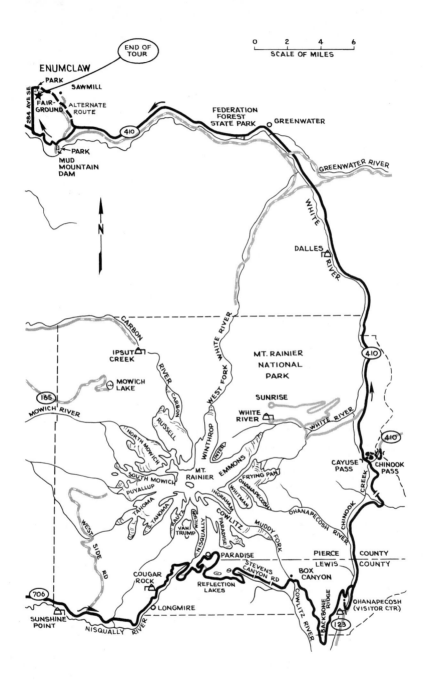

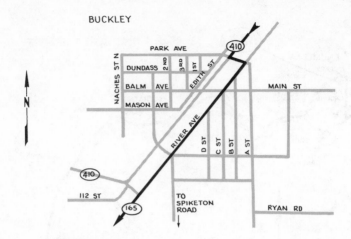

17.5 Left turn on **Orville Road E.** as S.R. 162 continues right into Orting. Cross Puyallup River at 21.0. Road to Electron (park, view) goes left at mile 24.5.

26.7 Left turn with Orville Road E. at Kapowsin Junction (blinking red light, grocery). Route continues south along Lake Kapowsin and Ohop Lake toward Eatonville.

35.4 Pass public fishing access and at 35.7 turn left on faint trail to a partially barricaded bridge across Ohop Creek. Cross bridge and continue on roadway on other side.

36.0 Bear left and uphill on **State Route 161**.

36.7 Right turn on business route in Eatonville by Eatonville sign. Grocery and cafes.

37.1 Left turn on **Center Street E.** by U.S. Post Office. As the road leaves town it is marked **Alder Cutoff**. A climb to two summits precedes a short descent to Alder Lake.

44.5 Left turn on **State Route 7** toward Mt. Rainier National Park. Tacoma City Light Alder Lake Recreation Area on the right at mile 47.8. Enter Elbe at mile 49.2. Cafe, grocery, steam train rides. Watch for acute-angled railroad tracks.

49.4 Continue on **State Route 706** in Elbe as S.R. 7 goes right toward Morton. Pass through Ashford at 56.9; last grocery for two days. Sign points right on Kernahan Road two miles to Big Creek National Forest Camp and Skate Creek Road at mile 59.7; overnight camping. Pass Copper Creek Inn at mile 60.8 and Alexander's Manor at 62.0.

63.4 Nisqually entrance to Mt. Rainier National Park; motel, several lodges, and bed-and-breakfast accommodations nearby. Sunshine Point Campground is another 0.3 mile past the entrance.

SECOND DAY

0.0 From the Nisqually entrance, where a nominal entrance fee is levied on bicyclists, continue into Mt. Rainier National Park. Pass Sunshine

Point Campground at mile 0.3; Kautz Mudflow at 3.3.

6.4 Park headquarters at Longmire, elevation 2761 feet; nature trail, cafeteria and snack bar; Cougar Rock Campground entrance at 8.6.

10.6 Christine Falls, elevation 3676 feet; scenic footpath to view falls from under bridge.

11.8 Cross Nisqually River; elevation 3900 feet.

12.8 Bear right to Rieksecker Point Overlook; elevation 4212 feet.

13.9 Rejoin main road. View of Mt. Rainier from Canyon Rim Overlook at mile 14.5; elevation 4462 feet.

15.6 Narada Falls on the right; restrooms and footpath to view of falls.

16.4 Bear left toward Paradise at road junction. Begin a steep, two-mile climb ending at Paradise Visitor Center at mile 18.4; elevation 5420 feet. Cafeteria and snack bar open through first weekend in October. After exploring the many interesting exhibits, trails, and vistas, continue uphill past Paradise Inn and start downhill on one-way road.

21.0 Join main road and turn left toward Ohanapecosh. Pass Reflection Lakes at mile 22.5. Brake around a horseshoe turn at mile 24.6 and continue down **Stevens Canyon Road**. Proceed through two tunnels and emerge at Box Canyon of the Muddy Fork of the Cowlitz River at mile 29.5; restrooms and scenic overlook. Road continues downhill for two more miles before climbing again to a summit at mile 34.3, then dropping to a crossing of the Ohanapecosh River (elevation 2176 feet) at mile 40.0.

40.1 Right turn on **State Route 123** toward Ohanapecosh.

41.9 Turn right into Ohanapecosh Campground. Visitor Center at 42.2. No food concessions. Campground area begins 0.2 mile farther.

THIRD DAY

0.0 Leave Ohanapecosh Campground and turn left on **State Route 123**. Pass Stevens Canyon entrance to Mt. Rainier National Park at mile 2.3 and continue toward Cayuse Pass. Cross Panther Creek at mile 4.6 and begin inexorable climb. Pass massive rock outcroppings at mile 7.0; views into canyon below. Owyhigh Lakes Trail goes right at 8.3. Tunnel at mile 10.6.

13.3 Continue on **State Route 410** at summit of Cayuse Pass (elevation 4694 feet) as S.R. 123 ends. *Note: Chinook Pass is uphill to the right at an elevation of 5440 feet, a worthwhile 7.2-mile round trip.* If weather is cool, put on all available clothing and plunge downhill for 10 miles. Side road goes left to Sunrise at mile 17.0; to Crystal Mountain right at 21.7. Pass Dalles Campground at 28.9. Pass through Greenwater at mile 36.6; grocery and cafe. Federation Forest State Park Interpretive Center is at 38.3.

49.8 Left turn on **Mud Mountain Road** toward Mud Mountain Dam. Turn sharp right at mile 51.7 as main thoroughfare goes left into Mud Mountain Dam Park. Road bends right at mile 53.9 and is renamed **284 Avenue S.E.**

56.3 Right turn into fairgrounds; end of tour around Mt. Rainier.

107 TWANOH–MASON LAKE

STARTING POINT: Twanoh State Park. From Seattle take Bremerton ferry: follow signs to Belfair and Twanoh State Park on State Routes 3 and 106. Park in picnic area parking lot. From the south take exit 104 from I-5 in Olympia and follow U.S. 101 and State Route 106 to Twanoh State Park.

DISTANCE: 37 to 44 miles.
TERRAIN: Hilly.
TOTAL CUMULATIVE ELEVATION GAIN: 1450 feet.
RECOMMENDED TIME OF YEAR: Avoid major summer holidays and clam tides, otherwise, any season.
RECOMMENDED STARTING TIME: 8 to 9 A.M.
ALLOW: 5 hours.
POINTS OF INTEREST
Old water wheel near Union
Signboard in Union commemorating
    Hood Canal discovery

ELEVATION PROFILE

Fog softens the silhouettes of houses nudging the southern shoreline of Hood Canal. Views of the snow-covered Olympic Mountains are not possible on this morning. The campgrounds and beaches of Twanoh State Park appear deserted. Only the sounds of screaming gulls and cawing crows fill the air as they argue over scavenging claims on the carcasses of salmon along the little stream that bisects the park.

From another creek a broken flume leads to a deteriorating log building. An old water wheel with cast-iron rim, spokes, hub, and sheet-steel buckets turns no more. The wooden flume has rotted out. Once an interesting roadside attraction for visitors to Hood Canal, it receives hardly a passing glance today.

Many black-and-white ducks (bufflehead and goldeneye) dive for food deep under the water, while large flocks of American widgeon paddle near the shoreline, frequently upending and thrusting their beaks into the shallow muddy water for a tasty morsel. Surf scoters join grebes and loons along the many bays and coves of Hood Canal. A kingfisher's rattle shatters the quiet stillness as he lands atop a flagpole. An owl surveys the scene from a tall post. On second glance, the owl is identified as a cleverly carved wooden replica. Live cormorants sit upright on old pilings that march sporadically along the shoreline. Seals invade the cool waters, seeking their share of the fish population.

As the road climbs the hillside high above the canal the fog clears. Hundreds of acres of Christmas tree plantings march over the hills and valleys. Patches of snow lie beneath evergreen huckleberry and manzanita, which flourish in the stony, sandy soil. Frosted, red-berried kinnikinnick cascades down the banks of roadway cuts. Suddenly, a red-tailed hawk swoops low across the road into the brush, comes out with empty talons, and flies up into a nearby tree.

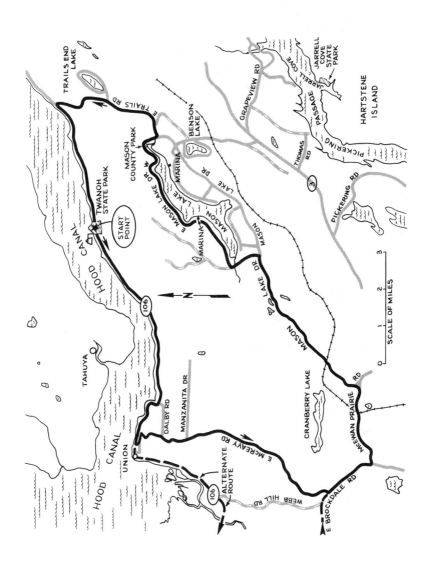

Faded signs advertising real-estate developments of Lake Limerick face the road along McEwan Prairie. Trees and brush surround a little frozen puddle of a lake. Along the southwestern shore of Mason Lake a Simpson Timber Company recreation area offers relaxation for employees. Behind locked gates and nestled among virgin Douglas fir and hemlock, the park wears the chilly, neglected cloak of winter. A mile up the lake the boating clientele of Calm Cove Marina will find service unavailable during the month of January. Mason County Park and fishing access near the northeast corner of the lake is attractive for a lunch stop, but posts a notice of closure from November through February.

Forest closes in as the hill between Mason Lake and Hood Canal first warms bicyclists as they climb, then cools them as they plunge toward the canal. On a winter day the last four miles of riding along Hood Canal are a bracing experience. Spring, summer, and fall will bring different sights and sounds, warmer weather, and the ebb and flow of automotive traffic.

MILEAGE LOG

0.0   Picnic area parking lot, Twanoh State Park. Leave the park and turn right (west) on **State Route 106**. Several restaurants and cafes line the highway. Old cast-iron water wheel at mile 5.5.

7.3   Turn left and uphill on **McReavy Road**. A few yards farther on State Route 106 is a scenic attraction—a highway department signboard commemorating Captain George Vancouver's discovery of Hood Canal. *Note: Those with an aversion to steep hills and a tolerance of traffic may choose to continue on S.R. 106 for 3.4 miles, left on Purdy Cutoff Road 2.8 miles, left on U.S. 101 1.9 miles, then left on Brockdale. This adds 3.0 miles to total distance.* Roadway is steep at first, but soon moderates and provides a view of the canal.

14.0   Turn left on **E. Brockdale Road** at stop sign as E. McReavy Road ends.

15.6   Left turn on **McEwan Prairie Road**. *Note: For a cafe lunch in Shelton, continue on Brockdale for 2.2 miles; turn left from left turn lane shortly after Alpine Way goes left. Shelton is at bottom of hill 1.1 miles farther. Return to McEwan Prairie turnoff after lunch.*

18.0   Turn left on **Mason Lake Drive** toward Mason Lake and Lake Limerick as McEwan ends. Grocery at 18.8. Lake Limerick roads go left just before and after crossing a creek under a railroad trestle at mile 19.3.

22.8   Turn left on **E. Mason Lake Drive West** toward Lake Trask. A small marina and grocery on the right at mile 25.8. At mile 28.9 Mason County Mason Lake Park offers picnic sites, modern restroom and boat-launching facilities.

29.5   Left turn on **E. Trails Road** as Mason Lake Drive ends. Road undulates slightly, then dives down an unusually steep hill.

32.8   Turn left at bottom of hill on **State Route 106** and proceed along Hood Canal waterfront.

37.0   End of ride at Twanoh State Park.

108 MASON LAKE–GRAPEVIEW

STARTING POINT: Visitor's parking lot of North Mason High School, near Belfair at toe of Hood Canal. From the north take ferry from Seattle to Bremerton, follow signs to Belfair. Continue on State Route 3 uphill from Hood Canal, under concrete railroad trestle to high school at top of hill. From the south take State Route 16 through Tacoma to Gorst and State Route 3 south to high school.

DISTANCE: 37 miles.
TERRAIN: Hilly.
TOTAL CUMULATIVE ELEVATION GAIN: 1500 feet.
RECOMMENDED TIME OF YEAR: Weekends, holidays, or when school is not in session.
RECOMMENDED STARTING TIME: 9 A.M.
ALLOW: 5 hours.
POINTS OF INTEREST
Waterscapes
Tree farms

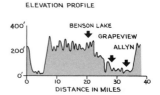

ELEVATION PROFILE

Mason County, among the least populated of the counties in southwestern Washington, offers many low-traffic backroads. Although well removed from the direct effects of suburbia, signs of population pressure are evident in summer homes springing up around the many forest-ringed lakes. Mason Lake, one of the largest in the county, features permanent residences in addition to two marinas and a county park with modern facilities.

Much of Mason County is devoted to tree farms. Good forest management practices are evident in the vigorous stands of Douglas fir, while the conical shapes of smaller, sheared trees attest to the energetic pursuit of the Christmas tree trade. Tree farms allow native shrubbery typical of the Hood Canal region to flourish. Evergreen huckleberry edges many of the roads and extends back into the forest. The glossy, green branches sought after by the florist trade command a high premium, as implied by the No Brush Picking signs posted at regular intervals. Other handsome evergreen bushes that thrive in the soil conditions of the lower Puget Sound country include the sticky laurel and the red-barked manzanita. The madrona tree, a larger relative, attains great size and grows abundantly along Hood Canal.

Wine and juice grapes were once an important crop cultivated on the hillsides above the inlets of lower Puget Sound, but today most of the vineyards lie abandoned and overgrown with weeds and trees. On Stretch Island, a few vineyards survive for the grape harvest and offer a short side trip for the curious. The nearby community of Allyn boasts a cafe for a late lunch, or just a snack to fuel cyclists up the long hill to the tour's end.

MILEAGE LOG

0.0 Parking lot of North Mason High School. Go out north entrance drive, turn right on **State Route 3**, and freewheel downhill on three-foot-

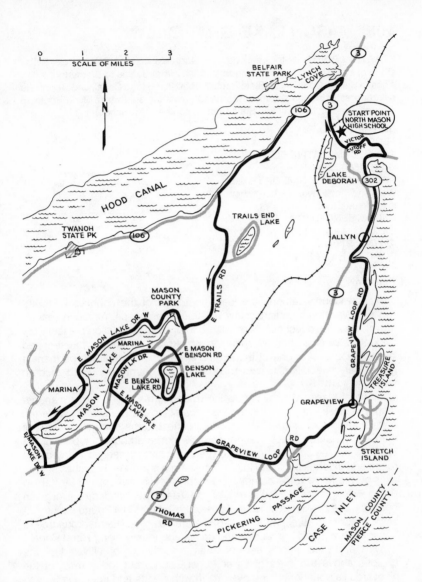

wide paved shoulder.

1.6   Turn left at a wye on **State Route 106** at bottom of hill. Wide, paved shoulder narrows to 18 inches or less. Grocery on right at mile 4.5. Occasional glimpses of Hood Canal through trees between homes.

5.6   Turn left and uphill on E. **Trails Road** toward Mason Lake County Park and Trails End Lake. Keep right at 7.2 as side road bears left to Trails End Lake.

9.0   Turn right on **E. Mason Lake Drive West**. Mason Lake County Park on left at mile 9.6; picnic sites, swimming, restrooms with hot showers. Calm Cove Marina at mile 12.8, grocery.

15.8   Left turn at stop sign on **E. Mason Lake Drive** as Mason Lake Drive West ends.

17.8   Turn left and downhill on **E. Mason Lake Drive E.** Mason Lake Marina on left at mile 19.8 (grocery) as road turns right, heads uphill, and is renamed **E. Mason Benson Road**.

20.7   Turn right on **E. Benson Lake Road** and follow around lake. Fishing access with toilets at mile 22.3.

22.4   Turn right on main road as Benson Lake Road ends.

24.3   Left turn on **State Route 3** as Mason Benson Road ends. A four-foot-wide paved shoulder eases traffic concerns.

24.8   Turn right on **Grapeview Loop Road** toward Grapeview, Stretch Island, and Treasure Island.

29.2   Turn left by Grapeview Store, fire station, and post office. Public boat launch at 29.9. *Note: For a visit to Stretch Island, go straight across bridge by fire hall.*

32.7   Right turn on **State Route 3** as Grapeview Loop Road ends. Cross Sherwood Creek and continue on wide, paved shoulder. Grocery and cafe in Allyn at mile 33.4. Public park and pier on right by church.

33.6   Continue straight at wye on **State Route 302** as S.R. 3 veers left and uphill.

35.5   Left turn on **Victor Cutoff Road** just before S.R. 302 crosses Coulter Creek. Crank uphill through forest.

36.8   Turn right into entrance of North Mason High School athletic field parking lot. Go through lot, around gate, and bear right on asphalt path around back of gymnasium.

37.2   Visitors parking lot of North Mason High School; end of tour.

109 BELFAIR–TAHUYA

STARTING POINT: Picnic area parking lot of Belfair State Park. From the Seattle area, take ferry to Bremerton and follow signs to Belfair via State Route 3. Turn right, then left (west) on State Route 300 at Belfair and continue to park entrance. From the Tacoma area, cross the Narrows Bridge on State Route 16 to Port Orchard and Gorst, then follow State Routes 3 and 300 to the park.

DISTANCE: 26 to 34 miles.
TERRAIN: Half flat, half hilly.
TOTAL CUMULATIVE ELEVATION GAIN: 1250 feet.
RECOMMENDED TIME OF YEAR: Avoid hunting seasons; otherwise, any time of year. Rhododendrons bloom from late May to early June.
RECOMMENDED STARTING TIME: 8:30 to 9:00 A.M.
ALLOW: 4 to 5 hours.
POINTS OF INTEREST
Views of Hood Canal

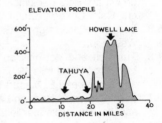

ELEVATION PROFILE

HOWELL LAKE

TAHUYA

DISTANCE IN MILES

Shaped like a long, crooked finger, the narrow extension of Puget Sound known as Hood Canal gouges a swath through Mason County, with the tip of the nail just touching Belfair. Nature has created many miles of glorious salt-water shoreline to explore and enjoy. The State of Washington claims several parcels along the canal and has developed them into parks. Belfair is the most advantageous home base for exploring the north shore of these sheltered waters in the shadow of the Olympic Mountains. Captain George Vancouver discovered the canal when he sailed into Puget Sound in 1792 and named it after fellow countryman Samuel Hood. The name stuck, though the possessive "s" in Hood's has been dropped.

A steep hillside rises above the north shore road, and summer homes vie with permanent residences in their competition to fill the available space along the narrow shoreline. Fifteen miles from the park the hillside recedes, allowing more breathing room for the houses as the canal executes its great bend and heads north. Tacoma's Lake Cushman Power Plant stands out as a prominent landmark across the canal.

The calm waters of Hood Canal provide a winter home for many varieties of ducks: goldeneye, bufflehead, and surf scoter, to name a few. Gulls and shorebirds explore the shallow mud flats near estuaries of small creeks. Eventually the road along the canal's east shore loses its hard surface and becomes very narrow as it skirts a high bluff. Much of this forested bluff land belongs to the state and is managed by the Department of Natural Resources (DNR). Sustained-yield logging practices give the people of Washington a continued source of state monies for the school fund. DNR also provides recreation areas by maintaining roads and building primitive camping and picnicking sites. Land that has been clearcut is quickly cleaned of debris and replanted to Douglas fir. Stands of young noble fir for the Christmas tree trade add diversity to the ridge-top landscape. Lodgepole pine and white

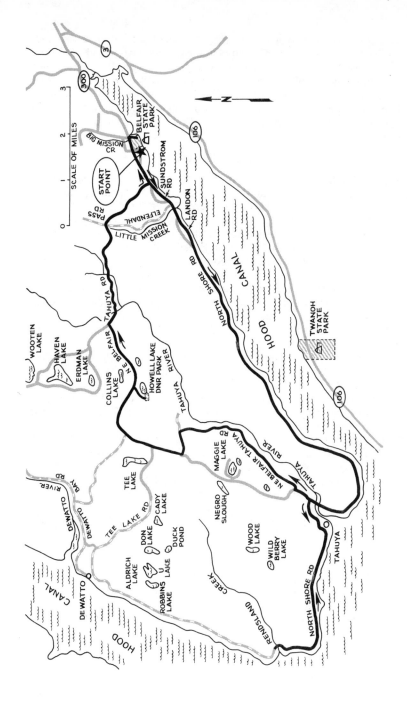

pine compete for toe holds with the evergreen madrona tree. The wild roadside rhododendron, flowering gem of the evergreen plant world, puts on a
dazzling display of rose-pink blooms during late spring. Bright, sunny days
open up vistas westward across the canal to the 6000-foot snow-covered
peaks at the southern end of the Olympic Mountain range. The scenery
changes with the seasons, making this an interesting tour at any time of
year. Diversity is the key word for an excursion that travels from sea level to
ridge crest and back again in the short span of only 34 miles.

MILEAGE LOG

0.0 Belfair State Park picnic area parking lot. Leave park and turn left
(west) on **State Route 300**. The state route designation ends after
0.4 mile and the road is named **North Shore Road**.

1.1 Bear left on **Sundstrom Road** for 0.3 mile diversion along the water,
then continue on **North Shore Road**.

2.4 Bend left on **Landon Road** for another waterfront diversion, this time
for 0.8 mile. **North Shore Road** crosses the estuary of Tahuya River
at mile 11.1. *Note: The tour eventually goes up Belfair Tahuya Road
to the right 0.1 mile beyond the bridge, but for more views of Hood
Canal, continue on North Shore Road.* Tahuya offers the services of
two grocery stores at mile 11.7.

15.5 Stop at bridge over Rendsland Creek, observe scenery, and turn
back along North Shore Road. *Note: North of this point the road de-
teriorates to a single-track gravel road with excessively steep grades,
and is recommended only for the hardy cyclist.* Return to Tahuya at
mile 19.4.

19.9 Turn left on **N.E. Belfair Tahuya Road** toward Haven Lake, Dewatto,
Tahuya Valley, and Maggie Lake shortly before North Shore Road
crosses the Tahuya River.

20.4 Bear right with Belfair Tahuya Road as Maggie Lake Road forks left
and heads steeply uphill toward Maggie Lake and Dewatto. Views of
Tahuya Valley.

24.6 Turn right at stop sign with Belfair Tahuya Road. Continue with main
thoroughfare as Tee Lake Road goes left to Tee Lake at mile 25.3.
Rhododendrons decorate roadsides at edge of forest.

27.2 Turn right into Howell Lake Recreation Area (DNR). Picnic tables and
pit toilets.

27.9 Turn right on main road again upon leaving Howell Lake Recreation
Area.

29.6 Right turn toward Belfair at T junction. Cross Tahuya River 0.3 mile
beyond and continue uphill along the valley of a tributary creek.
Cross Elfendahl Pass Road at mile 32.1.

33.9 Descend steep hill and turn left on **North Shore Road** as Belfair
Tahuya Road ends.

34.3 Turn right into Belfair State Park entrance. Those who have not had
enough exercise bicycling may go swimming in Hood Canal. Hot
showers are available at the camping area restrooms.

110 PICKERING PASSAGE

STARTING POINT: Parking area across road from Spencer Lake Tavern near Shelton in Mason County. From the north take the ferry from Seattle to Bremerton and follow signs through Belfair toward Shelton via State Route 3. Ten miles southwest of Allyn turn left on Pickering Road toward Hartstene Island, Spencer Lake, and Phillips Lake. Continue one mile to tavern and parking area. From the south take exit 104 (U.S. 101) from I-5 to Shelton, then State Route 3 eight miles to Pickering Road turnoff.

DISTANCE: 34 miles.
TERRAIN: Hilly.
TOTAL CUMULATIVE ELEVATION GAIN: 1900 feet.
RECOMMENDED TIME OF YEAR: Avoid opening week of fishing season; otherwise, any season.
RECOMMENDED STARTING TIME: 9 to 10 A.M.
ALLOW: 4 to 5 hours.
POINTS OF INTEREST
Jarrell Cove State Park
Views of Hammersley Inlet

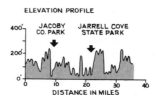

ELEVATION PROFILE

Perhaps to us wheel-happy landlubbers the name Pickering Passage does not ring a bell; even the name Hartstene means only an island somewhere in Puget Sound, probably not one of the San Juan group. To the boater and sailor, Pickering Passage is a narrow but important stretch of water in southern Puget Sound, between the Mason County mainland and Hartstene Island. Jarrell Cove extends from the passage into northern Hartstene Island, furnishing an ideal site for one of Washington's several marine state parks. Boaters tie up to the piers and several buoys anchored in the cove. A picnic area, restrooms with hot showers, and a few camping sites make Jarrell Cove State Park attractive. As a marine park, however, it is not designed for the motorist; its terra firma gateway stands at the end of a narrow, bumpy, gravel road.

Until the 1950s Hartstene Island (the natives spell it *Harstine*) was accessible only by boat or by a small ferry that crossed Pickering Passage to the western side of the island. Now Pickering Road carries traffic to a new bridge, which has opened the island to more intensive development. In spite of the bridge the island is still rather sparsely settled and provides several miles of traffic-free, although hilly, bicycling.

Blackberry vines climb over a large bull rail at the edge of an old log-rafting area in a finger of Jarrell Cove. Cables hold together a ramp of small logs, providing a slide for the released logs to skid down on their way to the shallow cove below, to splash or plop, depending on the tide. Deer roam freely across Hartstene Island and understand fully the principle that the shortest distance between two points is a straight line, even if it means almost colliding with a touring bicyclist.

The route of this bicycle tour follows roads along the shoreline of inlets and bays in southern Puget Sound. Dense forests cover much of the landscape, allowing only fleeting glimpses of the scenery across the waters. One viewpoint at Mason County Jacoby Park encompasses the timber-industry-dominated waterfront at Shelton, Mason County seat. Across Hammersley Inlet, private residences crowd the shoreline, sending their long, steep driveways up to the access road on the hillside above. Tugboats towing barges set no speed records as they chug along at a steady five to eight knots. On the southwestern horizon Mt. Rainier is often visible.

The Pickering Passage bridge provides an excellent vantage point for marine bird-watching. Scoters, loons, grebes, and murrelets are a few of the many species that dive and find nourishment in the sheltered, productive inlets and passages of Puget Sound. Ducks preferring fresh water fly in and out of Spencer Lake, where anglers enjoy seclusion among the water lilies.

MILEAGE LOG

0.0 Parking area across road from Spencer Lake Tavern. Turn right (west) and continue on **E. Pickering Road**.

0.9 Left turn on **E. Spencer Lake Road**. Fishing access on Spencer Lake at mile 2.0.

3.7 Left turn on **E. Shelton-Agate Road** as Spencer Lake Road ends by Pioneer School.

6.0 Turn right on **E. Agate Loop** and follow it as it bends left at mile 6.5. Cross Campbell Creek, view Chapman Cove, and crank up steep hill.

7.7 Right turn on **E. Crestview Drive**. Road bends left at mile 9.7 and is renamed **E. Shorecrest Drive**. Views of Oakland Bay and Hammersley Inlet.

10.1 Turn right on **E. Shorecrest Parkway**, then right again into Mason County's Jacoby (Shorecrest) Park. View the inlet and Shelton's industrial waterfront, and crank up out of the park again.

10.3 Turn left on **E. Shorecrest Parkway**, pass E. Shorecrest Drive, and turn right on **Kingston Way**.

10.6 Turn right at stop sign as Kingston ends. This is **E. Hillcrest Drive**.

10.7 Left turn on **E. Leeds Drive**. Views of Hammersley Inlet and Mt. Rainier.

12.0 Left turn on **E. Grunert Road** as Leeds ends.

12.1 Turn right on **E. Crestview Drive**. If this intersection looks familiar, you are right. Agate Grocery on the left at mile 12.9, where road name changes to **E. Agate Road**.

15.8 Bear left on **Pickering Road** as Agate Road ends.

18.7 Turn right at wye on **E. Harstene** (sic) **Bridge Road** to Hartstene Island. After crossing bridge, turn left on **North Island Drive** toward state park.

23.0 Descend a hill and turn left on **Wingert Road** toward state park. Wingert is a narrow, winding, gravel driveway, and is easy to miss.

23.8 Jarrell Cove State Park; lunch stop. If weather is inclement, a foot trail leads to a shelter on point at southwest end of park. After lunch, go back out entrance road and turn right on **North Island Drive**.

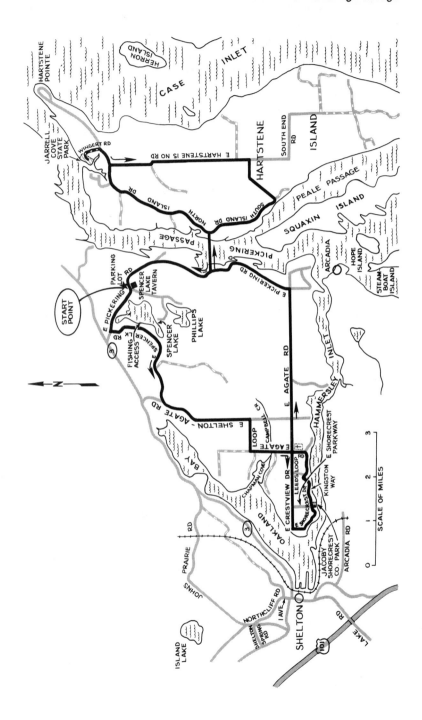

25.0 Turn left on **E. Hartstene Is. No. Rd.** by Community Hall.

28.4 Right turn on **South Island Drive** and freewheel down to near water level. View of Squaxin Island across passage.

31.6 Turn left and cross bridge over Pickering Passage back to mainland.

32.2 Right turn on **E. Pickering Road**. End of tour by Spencer Lake Tavern at 34.2.

GRAYS HARBOR COUNTY

111 OCEAN SHORES

STARTING POINT: Ocean City State Park. From the north take exit 104 (U.S. 101) from I-5, continue on State Route 8 and U.S. 12 to Aberdeen, and U.S. 101 to Hoquiam. Continue west on State Route 109 and turn south on State Route 115 to Ocean City State Park. From the south take exit 88B (U.S. 12) from I-5, pick up U.S. 101 in Aberdeen and State Route 109 at Hoquiam. Turn left on State Route 115 to the park. Park in picnic area parking lot near registration cupola.

DISTANCE: 20 to 25 miles.
TERRAIN: Flat.
TOTAL CUMULATIVE ELEVATION GAIN: 50 feet.
RECOMMENDED TIME OF YEAR: Any season.
RECOMMENDED STARTING TIME: Anytime.

ALLOW: 3 hours.
POINTS OF INTEREST
Ocean City State Park
Grays Harbor north jetty
Passenger ferry to Westport

Only three miles south of Ocean City and 1.5 miles north of Ocean Shores, Ocean City State Park is ideally situated as a base camp from which to tour the North Beach Peninsula. As part of the natural sand spit extending southward to form the northern mandible of the mouth of Grays Harbor, the park offers grassy sand dunes and an expansive sandy beach to explore. Small, shallow, marshy lakes attract numerous waterfowl. Dense clumps of wax myrtle provide evergreen beauty in the midst of deciduous alder and willow. Many birds forage among the shrubs and trees, fascinating bird watchers at all seasons of the year. More than 100 tent sites and a few trailer hookups fan out over the campground circles, while a rustic group camp squeezes in between the vegetation, entrance road, and one of the lakes. Restrooms with hot showers complete the amenities.

The platted resort community of Ocean Shores became an incorporated city in 1970. The planned parks and community clubhouses are completed, but many of the residential lots remain vacant. Paved, low-traffic roads crisscross the entire peninsula, while a network of canals connects Duck Lake with Minard Lake and extends throughout the peninsula. Boats may be lifted between the canal-lake system and the bay at the south end marina. Motels, restaurants, inns, and a golf course welcome tourists and convention crowds. The Fog Festival celebration in mid-February always attracts many visitors. Winter storms and minus tides beckon the beachcomber and clam digger to miles of gently sloping sandy beaches.

Traffic along narrow State Route 115 is busy, but disperses when it reaches the business district of Ocean Shores. As the route heads south, homes of all shapes and sizes sprout among the sand dunes. Some are landscaped with lawns, trees, and shrubs, while others are surrounded by dune grasses and driftwood. Nautical themes and decorations appeal to many of the home owners. Habitations decrease at the southern tip of the peninsula, where the north jetty offers an opportunity to view the crashing surf as it slams into the huge man-made breakwater of rocks and boulders.

Near this end of the long sand spit the State of Washington maintains a game refuge, visited occasionally by brown pelicans and yellow-billed loons. Short-eared owls fly low over the dunes by day, looking for mice and other small prey.

The mileage log for this tour takes the cyclist around the perimeter roads of the city of Ocean Shores, but many variations of the route may be made to shorten or lengthen the basic 20.2-mile tour. One such variation incorporates the passenger ferry between Westport and the Ocean Shores marina; operated by Grays Harbor Transit, it is subject to occasional extended interruptions while municipalities haggle over docking fees. Another option (when ferry is operating) is to use Twin Harbors State Park near Westport as a base camp. For the energetic and traffic-hardened cyclist, the loop tour around Grays Harbor via Aberdeen is 50 miles.

MILEAGE LOG

0.0 Picnic area parking lot, Ocean City State Park. Leave parking lot and head for the park entrance.

0.5 Turn right on **State Route 115**. Follow it right as it turns west at mile 1.6.

1.9 Turn left into Ocean Shores on **N. Point Brown Avenue**. Turn right on **Ocean Shores Boulevard N.W.** almost immediately and follow it as it bends south. Proceed along the divided street past motels and through the sparsely settled residential communities.

8.1 Bear left as divided highway ends at a washout at the southwest corner of peninsula. *Note: A quick scramble past the chemical toilets and litter barrels provides access to the protected beach and the rocky north jetty, which stretches 1600 feet out into the ocean.* Road passes sewage treatment plant as it swings north and is named **E. Ocean Shores Boulevard S.W.** Large orange navigation aids appear near the plant. As the road bears left it becomes **Sportsman Way S.W.**

9.6 Right turn on **Greenview S.W.** *Note: Sportsman ends 0.2 mile past Greenview.*

10.5 Right turn on **Marine View Drive S.W.** as Greenview ends. *Note: A bridge over one of the canals goes left on S. Tonquin at mile 11.5; vantage point for viewing ducks and grebes.* A motel, restaurant, grocery, and marina offer services at mile 12.3; passenger ferry to Westport. Road changes name to **Point Brown Avenue S.E.**

12.6 Continue straight on **Discovery S.E.** as Point Brown Avenue goes left. Boat lift here transfers boats between fresh-water canal and salt-water bay.

12.7 Right turn immediately past boat portage on **Catala Avenue S.E.** toward Community Beach Club. Pass the clubhouse at mile 12.9.

13.1 Right turn on **Duck Lake Drive S.E.** and continue north along the eastern edge of the peninsula. Pass Chinook City Park at 14.1. Continue on Duck Lake Drive as Overlake Drive goes left across the lake at mile 15.5. Road name changes to **North Bay N.E.** by airfield as Albatross N.E. crosses at 16.2.

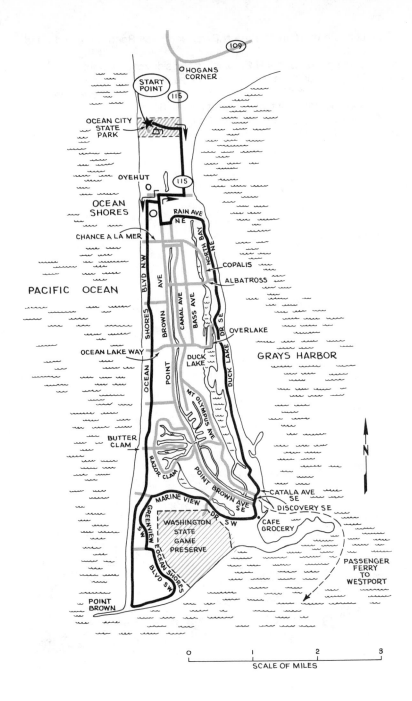

17.1 Left turn on **Rain Avenue N.E.** as North Bay Road is marked Dead End.

17.7 Turn right on **Shoal N.E.**, which is first side road on right.

17.8 Right turn on **Point Brown Avenue** as Shoal ends. Cafe.

18.3 Turn right on **State Route 115** and leave Ocean Shores. Bear left with S.R. 115 as it turns north at mile 18.6.

19.7 Left turn into Ocean City State Park.

20.2 End of tour in parking area.

112 OCEAN CITY STATE PARK–TAHOLAH

STARTING POINT: Ocean City State Park. From the north take exit 104 (U.S. 101) from I-5, continue on State Route 8 and U.S. 12 to Aberdeen, and U.S. 101 to Hoquiam. Continue west on State Route 109 and turn south on State Route 115 to Ocean City State Park. From the south take exit 88B (U.S. 12) from I-5, pick up U.S. 101 in Aberdeen and State Route 109 at Hoquiam. Turn left on State Route 115 to the park. Park in picnic parking area near registration cupola.

DISTANCE: 62 miles.
TERRAIN: Easy hills with some flat.
TOTAL CUMULATIVE ELEVATION GAIN: 1550 feet.
RECOMMENDED TIME OF YEAR: September through May. Avoid minus (clam) tides and Ocean Shores' mid-February Fog Festival.
RECOMMENDED STARTING TIME: 6 to 8 A.M.
ALLOW: 7 to 9 hours.

POINTS OF INTEREST
Ocean City State Park
Pacific Ocean beaches
Quinault Indian Reservation
Cranberry bogs

ELEVATION PROFILE

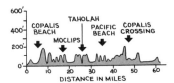

Because Washington State has few roads along its coastline, a bicyclist's exposure to ocean beaches is generally brief and tantalizing. This tour explores one of the longest stretches of seaside road north of Oregon, returning via the inland creek and river valleys of coastal Washington and the northern shores of Grays Harbor.

Fine sand covers miles of Olympic Peninsula beaches and provides the perfect habitat for growth of the much-sought-after razor clam. During the open season between October and June thousands of people line the beaches when tides are low, hoping to harvest their limit of the elusive bivalve. Automobiles are allowed on the beach but must stay above a line marked by tall poles. Gulls keep sharp eyes on the crowds of people, hoping for a chance at their share of the harvest.

Many cabins, resorts, and motels perch along the shoreline and group up in the several small towns catering to the tourists and clam harvesters. After crossing the Copalis River, the route climbs a bluff where tall spruce and cedar trees are sculptured into odd shapes by the westerly winds. The roaring surf comes into view from high atop a steep precipice at a road turnout featuring a dedication to a Weyerhaeuser Company forester. Rolling terrain brings the cyclist onto the beach again, where a state park shares the limited shoreline with the little town of Pacific Beach. Just south of the Quinault Indian Reservation boundary lies Moclips, the last non-Indian town along the northern Washington coast. Indian reservations, an abandoned U.S. Coast Guard Station, and the Olympic National Park claim the remaining 80 miles.

As it enters the Quinault Indian Reservation the route traverses a hill before returning to beach level. Beaches here are marked Tribal Property

No Trespassing, and views of the tumbling waves are blocked by a dense growth of scrub alder and salmonberry. Not until Wreck Creek is reached does the magnificent view of the ocean surf present itself. Big logs float in and out with the wave action in the creek estuary, and surf scoters frolic in and among the breakers.

The pleasant odor of fresh-cut cedar scents the air as the route heads downhill past the Quinault tribal cedar shake mill near the outskirts of Taholah. Lines of floats, marking the locations of gill nets for snaring salmon and steelhead, extend across the Quinault River as it flows past the village; the tribe has its own processing plant on the riverbank. After visiting this isolated cultural center, return along the shoreline to Pacific Beach, where the route heads inland. Cedar, fir, and alder trees form a dense forest, interrupted occasionally by small cedar shingle mills.

Several backroads lead past farms in the valley of the Humptulips. Great blue herons lift from the marshy sloughs. The stump of a giant old spruce tree marks the start of Burrows Road, where the route turns toward the tidal-flat shoreline of the North Bay of Grays Harbor. Red-twigged cranberry bogs spread over many acres of the lowland soil.

The wide shoulder of State Route 109 allows safe pedaling of the several miles to Hogans Corner and the starting point at Ocean City State Park.

MILEAGE LOG

0.0 Ocean City State Park. Leave parking area and proceed to the park entrance.

0.5 Turn left on **State Route 115.**

1.4 Hogans Corner; cafe. Turn left with **State Route 109** as S.R. 115 ends. Pass through Ocean City at mile 3.4 and Copalis Beach at mile 6.1.

6.4 Turn left with State Route 109 and cross the Copalis River as an unmarked county road continues on to Copalis Crossing. Viewpoint and memorial plaque above cliff at mile 10.4; access to beach at mile 12.4. Pacific Beach and Pacific Beach State Park on left at mile 14.7. Pass Moclips beach area at 16.9. Enter Quinault Indian Reservation at 17.6. Moclips-Olympic Highway Road goes right to U.S. 101 at 17.7.

25.7 Road ends at Quinault River in Taholah. Explore village and retrace route through Moclips.

36.8 Bear right at top of hill on old highway into Pacific Beach. State Park, cafe on right at 37.6.

37.7 Cross State Route 109 and continue on **Ocean Beach Road** toward Copalis Crossing, Aloha, and garbage dump.

47.3 Continue on main road toward Hoquiam and U.S. 101 in Copalis Crossing as Copalis Beach Road goes right to ocean beaches. Grocery store at this intersection. Continue straight toward Hoquiam as Copalis Crossing Road goes left to Humptulips and U.S. 101 at mile 48. Cross Humptulips River at 48.7.

49.0 Bear right on narrow, oiled road on dike along Humptulips River. Take first left from dike as old railroad grade appears.

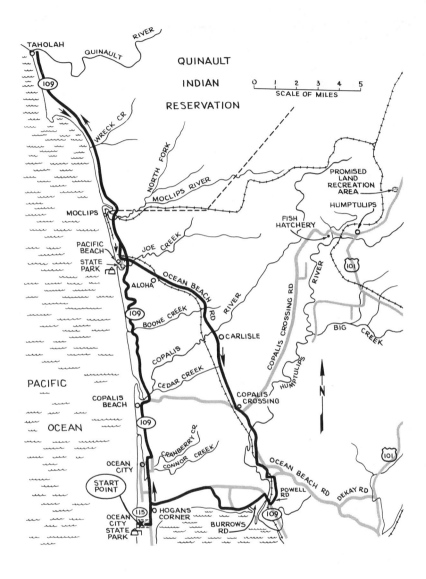

49.4 Right turn on **Ocean Beach Road** again.

50.2 Bear right across old railroad grade on narrow, oiled road. A bend of the Humptulips pulls alongside 0.5 mile beyond.

50.9 Rejoin **Ocean Beach Road** and continue right.

51.1 Turn right on unmarked side road as the highway approaches a bridge over a creek. Side road has two old railroad grade crossings and a bridge over Burg Slough.

52.0 Right turn on **Powell Road** as side road ends.

53.3 Turn right on **State Route 109** and cross Humptulips River.

53.8 Left turn on **Burrows Road** just after crossing bridge. Big spruce tree stump is passed shortly. Cross estuaries of Jessie and Campbell Sloughs. Views of North Bay of Grays Harbor. Cranberry bogs butt up against road.

57.5 Turn left on **State Route 109** and continue along its wide paved shoulder.

60.2 Turn left on **State Route 115** toward Ocean Shores and Ocean City State Park at Hogans Corner.

61.2 Right turn into Ocean City State Park.

61.7 End of tour at picnic area parking lot.

ONE MONTH LATER...

113 ABERDEEN–HOQUIAM–WISHKAH

STARTING POINT: Benn Gymnasium parking lot at Third and F Streets in Aberdeen. From the north take exit 104 (U.S. 101) from I-5 and continue on State Route 8 and U.S. 12 to Aberdeen. Turn right on F Street one block after crossing bridge over Wishkah River. From the south take exit 88B (U.S. 12) from I-5 at Grand Mound and proceed west to Aberdeen. Park in parking lot except when in use by school.

DISTANCE: 29 miles. May be combined with Tour #114 (Wishkah-Wynoochee) for a total of 46 miles.
TERRAIN: Moderate.
TOTAL CUMULATIVE ELEVATION GAIN: 700 feet.
RECOMMENDED TIME OF YEAR: Any season.
RECOMMENDED STARTING TIME: 10 A.M. to 2 P.M.
ALLOW: 4 hours.

POINTS OF INTEREST
Views of Hoquiam and Wishkah rivers

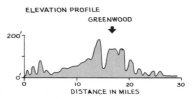

Many are the cyclists who, in attempting to thread their way around the Olympic Peninsula highway loop, have found the section through Aberdeen and Hoquiam particularly hair-raising. This tour presents an entirely different aspect of the area. Rather than braving the dense traffic of U.S. 101, the route follows low-traffic, parallel side streets through the two sister cities. Where the highway is unavoidable for a half mile or so, a sidewalk provides pleasant escape from the traffic. The urban portion, however, is only a small part of the story. The rest is a delightful set of backroads along the placid, slow-moving waters of the Hoquiam and Wishkah rivers. Rows of piling in the estuarial waters, now standing idle, once anchored rafts of sawlogs, which were floated down the river. Now the mills are fed by a fleet of logging trucks thundering their way along U.S. 101, far from these quiet backroads. Two grocery stores at convenient intervals offer the customary refreshments, and their proprietors are always ready to pass the time of day with cyclists. The hills are few and relatively minor, perfect for a good afternoon workout. Just the route for a leisurely Sunday ride!

MILEAGE LOG

0.0 Benn Gymnasium parking lot at Third and F Streets in Aberdeen. Proceed west on **Third Street**.

0.3 Right turn on **K Street** for two blocks.

0.4 Turn left on **Fifth Street**, which descends hill, bends left, and becomes **North Williams Street**.

0.8 Right turn on **Cherry Street**, which bends left after 1.9 miles and becomes **21 Street** in Hoquiam.

2.8 Get up on sidewalk and turn right alongside **U.S. 101**, alias **Riverside Avenue**.

3.1 Turn right on **16 Street** toward East Hoquiam and Woodlawn. Road shortly changes name to **Broadway**.

5.1 Right turn with thoroughfare as **Woodland Street** comes in from left.

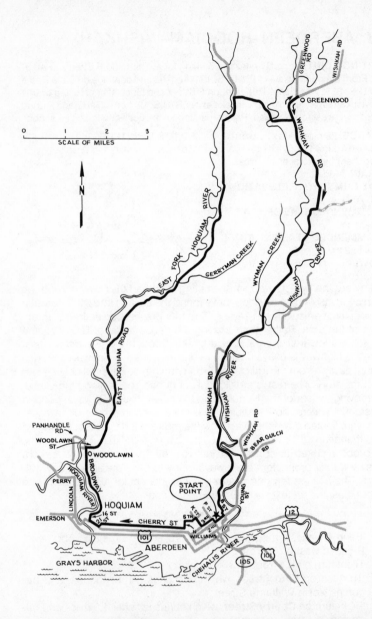

As it leaves Woodlawn, the road is renamed **East Hoquiam Road**.

14.8 Turn right by small grocery store on unmarked road. Cross the Wish-kah River at mile 15.9.

16.5 Turn left at T junction on **Wishkah Road**.

17.2 Small grocery at road fork (Greenwood). Owner allows bicyclists to use small park area behind store for picnic lunch in return for patronage. After lunch, return along Wishkah Road toward Aberdeen. Pass side road toward Hoquiam at mile 17.9. As it enters Aberdeen the road is renamed **B Street**.

28.3 Turn right on **East Second Street** and continue as it jogs left on **E Street**.

28.6 Right turn on **F Street**, then left on **Third Street**.

28.7 Benn Gymnasium parking lot; end of tour.

"*No, you must have made a wrong turn.*"

114 WISHKAH–WYNOOCHEE

STARTING POINT: Benn Gymnasium parking lot at Third and F Streets in Aberdeen. From the north take exit 104 (U.S. 101) from I-5 and continue on State Route 8 and U.S. 12 to Aberdeen. Turn right on F Street one block after crossing bridge over Wishkah River. From the south take exit 88B (U.S. 12) from I-5 at Grand Mound and proceed west to Aberdeen. Park in parking lot except when in use by school.

DISTANCE: 39 miles.
TERRAIN: Moderate with one steep hill; 3.0 miles of gravel road.
TOTAL CUMULATIVE ELEVATION GAIN: 1150 feet.
RECOMMENDED TIME OF YEAR: Any season.
RECOMMENDED STARTING TIME: 10 to 11 A.M.
ALLOW: 5 hours.

POINTS OF INTEREST
Views of Wishkah, Wynoochee, and Chehalis rivers

ELEVATION PROFILE

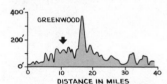

From the busy urban atmosphere of Aberdeen to the quiet estuarial scenery of the Wishkah Valley; the mountainous, rough ridge road; the rushing, clear waters of the Wynoochee; and the swampy sloughs along the Chehalis River, this tour offers variety. It is not, however, for the beginner. Many hills, some steep and some with loose gravel on the curves, require moderate bicycling skill and stamina. For all that, it is an interesting ride. The toot of a logging donkey whistle echoes through the forest, and obscure dirt roads disappear into the trees. A glance over the side of the Wynoochee River bridge brings a glimpse of a clean, gravel river bottom through the clear, rushing waters, an ideal salmon and steelhead spawning area. A fishing access farther down the valley implies that fishermen may think so, too. A bright yellow house with many gables stands out across the valley, inviting conjecture as to its original owners.

Although the great, flowing waters of the Chehalis do not appear until near the end of the ride, their nearness is told by the meandering tidal sloughs along Central Park Drive. This narrow roadway with concrete curbing is out of place in its swampy setting; it would seem more appropriate to an urban residential area. Except for the very occasional automobile, it resembles an exclusive bicycle trail. At the crossing of Higgins Slough a discordant note is struck by remains of automobiles and major household appliances partially submerged in the muck below.

A brief exposure to highway traffic, ameliorated by a wide, paved shoulder, threatens to become unpleasant as the shoulder ahead narrows to extinction. At this point a dead-end side road appears, and as is often the case, bicycles can go where automobiles cannot. By using a short railroad trestle, bicycles can detour on a smooth, blacktopped roadway along the Chehalis River by the Aberdeen water pipeline. When the roadway ends on the highway again, the sidewalks of East Aberdeen relieve the pressure of busy traffic. A wood-decked walkway on the bridge over the Wishkah River provides a bicycle route across the last barrier.

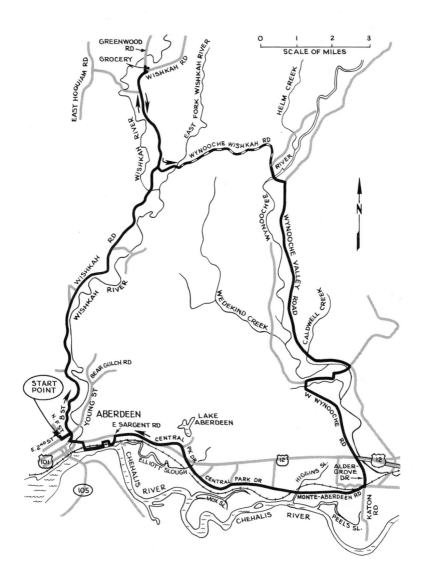

MILEAGE LOG

0.0 Benn Gymnasium parking lot at Third and F Streets. Head south on **N. F Street**, then left on **E. Second Street**. Continue with Second one block later as it jogs left on N. E Street.

0.4 Left turn on **B Street** and pedal out of town along Wishkah River. Road shortly is renamed **Wishkah Road**. Cross Wishkah River at mile 8.0. *Note: Route eventually turns right on side road that goes right toward Wynoochee at mile 8.7, but for lunch facilities continue on Wishkah Road.*

11.5 Greenwood grocery store at road fork. Store owner allows bicyclists to use park area behind store for picnic lunch in return for patronage. After lunch return along Wishkah Road.

14.0 Left turn toward Wynoochee on **Wynooche Wishkah** Road, which descends hill to creek valley, crosses creek on narrow bridge, and climbs steeply on other side, oxalis along roadside. Pavement ends at mile 15.0; summit at mile 16.5, followed by steep descent with loose gravel. Pavement resumes at mile 17.9 at bottom of hill.

18.7 Cross Wynoochee River and turn right on **Wynooche Valley Road** as Wynooche Wishkah Road ends.

24.6 Turn right across bridge over Wynoochee River by fishing access. Many-gabled house on hill; morning glories along road.

25.9 Turn left on **West Wynooche Road** as road ahead is marked Dead End. Cross U.S. 12 at mile 28.5. (On-grade crossing with central left turn island; advise walking bicycles across.) Continue on other side on **Aldergrove Drive**.

29.5 Cross railroad tracks and turn right on **Monte-Aberdeen Road** as Katon Road continues on. Continue through swamp on narrow concrete roadway, crossing Higgins Slough at mile 31.3, where the road is renamed **Central Park Drive**. Small grocery on left in Central Park at mile 32.3.

34.9 Cross U.S. 12 on grade and continue on Central Park Drive toward Lake Aberdeen. Bear left at T junction 0.1 mile thereafter. Lake Aberdeen and Aberdeen Steelhead Hatchery on right at mile 35.1.

35.6 Right turn on **U.S. 12** and continue along wide shoulder. Beware of broken glass.

36.8 Turn left across highway just past Entering Aberdeen sign and proceed downhill on **East Sargent Road** toward Junction City and Juvenile Facility. Cross railroad tracks and keep right past warehouses as road narrows, and degenerates to a narrow gravel path. Get up on railroad grade, cross railroad trestle, and bear left to blacktopped roadway along water pipeline. Continue around iron gate at mile 37.6.

38.0 Cross U.S. 12 as road ends in East Aberdeen. Continue left (west) on sidewalk.

38.5 Cross Wishkah River on bridge walkway and bear right with sidewalk on other side. Cross East Market and continue on **N. E Street**.

38.7 Left turn on **E. Second Street**, then right on **N. F Street**.

38.8 Back at parking lot.

115 ELMA–SCHAFER STATE PARK

STARTING POINT: Corner of Third and Young Streets in Elma. From the north take exit 104 (U.S. 101) from I-5 and continue on State Route 8 and U.S. 12 to the second Elma exit. From the south take exit 88B (U.S. 12) from I-5 at Grand Mound. Take the second Elma exit to Third Street in Elma. Park on side streets in downtown Elma.

DISTANCE: 36 to 45 miles, including 3 miles of unpaved road.
TERRAIN: Flat to moderate with optional hilly side trip.
TOTAL CUMULATIVE ELEVATION GAIN: Basic tour, 700 feet; side trip, 550 feet.
RECOMMENDED TIME OF YEAR: Any season. April features many spring flowers.
RECOMMENDED STARTING TIME: 9 A.M.; Sunday recommended for Satsop Nuclear Plant side trip.
ALLOW: 5 to 6 hours.

POINTS OF INTEREST
Washington Public Power Supply
   System Satsop Nuclear Plant site
Schafer State Park

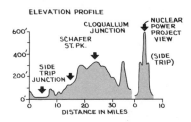
ELEVATION PROFILE

Being self-propelled, bicyclists are particularly conscious of personal energy production and conservation. Other forms of energy are generally of little interest, but the opportunity to view such a major energy-transforming project as the Satsop Nuclear Power Project is too interesting to pass. To gain the view, energy must be expended to boost the masses of bicycles and bicyclists 500 feet in altitude to the parking lot next to the project. From here, the heat exchanger convection tower dwarfs the viewer with its sheer magnitude. Other nearby buildings and their spacings, viewed close up, give forcible impressions of the project's size. On the return down the hill, bicyclists recover the potential energy stored in their vigorous climb.

The tour begins in Elma and follows the Chehalis River flood plain for several miles before reaching the turnoff for the side trip to the nuclear plant. The road is narrow and somewhat rough as it runs through a dairy farmyard with a milking barn on one side and riverside pastureland on the other. Jersey cows on their way to pasture stare at the two-wheeled intruders, but a few spoken words will calm them as they amble along the road. Another dairy employs the zero pasture system of feeding their Holstein-Friesian cows; served "breakfast in bed" with daily rations of freshly mowed green pasturage, the cows lounge about in their big open shelter.

The delightful rural character continues along the Satsop River, where beef cattle and horses replace the dairy herds. Several small streams flow down hillsides, cross the meadow, and empty into the meandering Satsop.

Mason County claims Schafer State Park, one of Washington State's older parks. To honor the memory of their parents, the children of John and Anna Schafer, pioneers of 1870, presented the land to the state in 1924. Huge bigleaf maple, Douglas fir, western red cedar, and western hemlock trees make the park a truly pristine setting. The large leafy foliage of the lobaria pulmonaria lichen drapes the tree branches, occasionally falling to decorate the ground underneath. Water ouzels dip and bob their way over rocks and stones of the rushing East Fork of the Satsop River, which borders the park. The handsome thick masonry walls of the comfort stations display artistry of design with smooth river stones.

Wildflowers of many shapes and colors grow in profusion along the Satsop-Cloquallum Road. Especially numerous are the spring-flowering varieties, including white spring beauties, pink bleeding hearts, white trillium, yellow skunk cabbage, and green carpets of large shamrock-leafed wood sorrel with white blossoms. Foxglove, beadruby, and false solomon's seal display their blooms in summer. The fruit of red elderberry and devil's club lend color to the forest in late summer and early fall.

Cloquallum Creek wanders through bright green pastures where black Angus cattle keep company with robins and blackbirds. Isolated homesteads, new and old, play hide-and-seek behind the forest vegetation. The route bursts upon the edge of urbanization shortly before returning to the starting point in downtown Elma.

MILEAGE LOG

0.0 Downtown Elma. Mileage log begins at the intersection of North Third Street with W. Young Street. Head south on **North Third Street**. Cross W. Main Street with traffic light at 0.1. Cross U.S. 12 on an overpass at 0.4 mile.

0.7 Turn right toward Elma airport on **Wenzel Slough Road**. Road bends left at mile 1.8; airport is to the right. Route crosses a small creek, follows the Chehalis River, and proceeds through a dairy farm milking Jersey cows. The Watch For Cattle Crossing road sign applies to bicyclists as well as autos.

5.1 Turn right on **Keyes Road** as Wenzel Slough Road ends. *Note: For a side trip to the Satsop Nuclear Plant site, turn left, crossing the Chehalis River after 0.7 mile, then ride uphill on Keyes Road for 3.1 miles to the plant parking lot. Return to this corner.* Keyes Road bends right (north) and crosses U.S. 12 on grade at mile 6.0 to enter Satsop.

"Road Hazards"

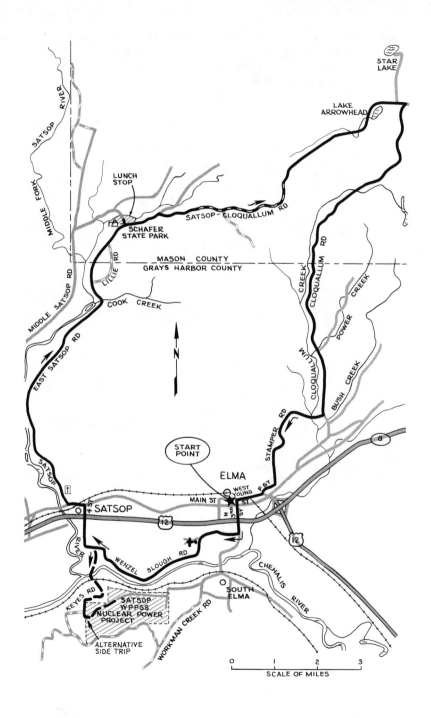

6.2 Left turn on old highway from Fourth Street in Satsop. Acute-angled railroad tracks at 6.4.

6.8 Right turn on **East Satsop Road** and start uphill. Pass cemetery at 7.1. Road surface varies from new blacktop to a rough, patchy oiled surface. Satsop River flows along on the left. Enter Mason County at mile 13.3

14.4 Keep left toward Schafer State Park as Satsop-Cloquallum Road goes right.

14.6 Right turn into Schafer State Park. Picnic area has tables beside the East Fork Satsop River, among the trees, and in a covered rustic shelter. The camping area on the opposite side of the road from the picnic area has 44 campsites and hot showers. After lunch return to the Satsop-Cloquallum Road intersection. (Mileage log allows 0.7 mile for touring the state park.)

15.5 Left turn on **Satsop-Cloquallum Road**. Many spring-blooming wild-flowers grow along this road. Pavement ends at mile 17.4, but gravel road is firm and smooth.

17.6 Keep left as side road goes right. Begin a gentle climb. Pavement resumes at mile 20.1. Forest, meadows, and old farmhouses. One ranch raises creamy white Charolais beef cattle. Platted development around Lake Arrowhead begins at mile 22.7; clubhouse at 23.3.

23.8 Bear right at a wye on **Cloquallum Road** (paved) toward Elma. Cross Cloquallum Creek several times. Green pastures, black Angus cattle. Enter Grays Harbor County at mile 28.6.

32.1 Bear right on unmarked road at a wye (first right turn). No road signs, but mailboxes identify it **Stamper Road**. Top a ridge at mile 33.6 and start a rapid descent. Cross railroad tracks at the bottom of the hill at mile 35 as signs of civilization appear.

35.2 Road bends left, then right, and is renamed **Oakhurst Drive** and **North F Street** in succession.

35.7 Right turn on **East Young Street** as F Street ends, and cross railroad tracks on an overpass.

35.9 End of tour at starting point on North Third Street in downtown Elma.

116 ELMA–OAKVILLE

STARTING POINT: Corner of Third and Young Streets in Elma. From the north take exit 104 (U.S. 101) from I-5 and continue on State Route 8 and U.S. 12 to the second Elma exit to Third Street in Elma. From the south take exit 88B (U.S. 12) from I-5 at Grand Mound and proceed west to the second Elma exit to Third Street in Elma. Park on side streets in downtown Elma.

DISTANCE: 46 miles.
TERRAIN: Flat with one minor hill.
TOTAL CUMULATIVE ELEVATION GAIN: 500 feet.
RECOMMENDED TIME OF YEAR: Any season.
RECOMMENDED STARTING TIME: 8 to 10 A.M.
ALLOW: 5 to 6 hours.

POINTS OF INTEREST
Old steam locomotive in McCleary's Beerbower Park

ELEVATION PROFILE

Elma's only traffic signal turns green, and bicycles roll down the hill, across the freeway overpass, and out into open farm country. The road is built up on fill to keep it above the not infrequent floodwaters from the Chehalis River. Previous meanderings of the river are evident in the many oxbow lakes about the landscape. Soon the river flows by underneath as the route enters the community of South Elma. Railroad tracks parallel the road through dairy farms interspersed with stretches of forest. Red-winged blackbirds sing and display their brilliant orange epaulets, ducks flush from oxbow puddles, and cattle with bright red ear tags stare as bicycles whisper along. Old orchards, now serving as pasture, are neatly trimmed at cow-head height. Occasional large-wheeled irrigation systems keep the fields green for pasture and for replenishing the occasional pungent silage pile.

A carefully tended cemetery and a grange hall (the conversion of an old schoolhouse) are the only evidence of the former community of Sharon. A family-style, oyster-and-ham dinner beginning at noon on the first Saturday in April is an annual event at the Sharon Grange. As the tour continues, swampland shrubbery closes in, and hanging lichens festoon the branches. At the second crossing of the Chehalis, the route makes a brief traverse of the Chehalis Indian Reservation, and the town of Oakville appears with a shady city park for a picnic lunch. Enhancement of the lunchtime menu may be obtained from the town's grocery store and cafe on Pine Street.

After lunch, the route returns to bucolic settings by way of the backyard of a shingle mill with the delicate aroma of fresh-sawn cedar. The mighty Chehalis rolls by, its banks occasionally penetrated by fishermen's trails. A brief reappearance of valley farms is cut short by increasing proximity of the river to the edge of the valley, whereupon the only remaining bicycle route lies along the broad shoulder of the highway. Soon another escape route presents itself as a backroad wending its way up Mox Chehalis Creek. A diamond-shaped highway warning sign with a black cow silhouette gives wordless warning of possible road hazards. Power lines hum briefly over-head as cattle ranches march up the hillsides.

In McCleary's Beerbower Park, an old wood-burning steam locomotive and fire pumper inject a nostalgia theme. During McCleary's Bear festival in July the nostalgia turns to festive celebration, featuring bear stew. Automotive traffic picks up again until another escape route is found leading into Elma via the back door by the Grays Harbor Fairgrounds. A few blocks of side streets are all that remain of this tour through the Chehalis Valley.

MILEAGE LOG

0.0 Starting from the corner of North 3rd Street and West Young Street in Elma, head south on **North 3rd Street** and cross U.S. 12 on over-pass. Continue across valley and over the Chehalis River.

1.9 Cross railroad tracks and turn left with **South Bank Road** in South Elma as Workman Creek Road goes right to Satsop Power Plant.

7.3 Bear right at a wye with South Bank Road. Sharon Grange is on the right at 7.9, and Sharon Cemetery on the left at mile 8.1.

15.9 Bear left as Garrard Creek Road goes right. Cross Chehalis River and continue through Chehalis Indian Reservation.

17.2 Bear left with main thoroughfare at four-way intersection. As it enters Oakville the road is named **State Street**. Oakville city park on right at mile 17.8.

17.9 Turn left on **Pine Street (U.S. 12)** by grocery store in Oakville.

18.2 Turn right on old concrete highway across from drive-in cafe as Park Street goes left. Skirt a cedar shingle mill.

18.7 Bear right on **U.S. 12**, then cross shortly and continue on a narrow, oiled road along Chehalis River. This is **Elma Gate Road**.

23.3 Join **U.S. 12** as Elma Gate Road ends. Cross and continue on shoulder, which varies from 2 to 6 feet. Grocery in Porter on right at mile 26.0.

27.7 Cross Mox Chehalis Creek and turn right by grocery in Malone. Con-tinue up creek valley on **Mox Chehalis Road**. Power lines overhead at mile 30.8.

35.6 Bear left with Mox Chehalis Road as Mox Chehalis Road E. goes right. Cross State Route 8 at mile 36.3.

36.5 Left turn on **William McCleary Road** and continue over hill into Mc-Cleary as road is renamed **3rd Street**.

37.1 Turn left on **Simpson Avenue (State Route 108)**. Beerbower Park on right. Cafe, grocery, bakery.

38.1 Continue straight toward Whites on **Elma McCleary Road** as S.R. 108 goes left to Olympia, Elma, and Aberdeen.

38.3 Continue straight on **Church Road** as Elma McCleary Road bends left by grocery and auto repair shop.

38.8 Bear left on **Elma Hicklin Road** as Church Road ends.

40.0 Cross railroad tracks and bear right on **Elma McCleary Road** as Elma Hicklin Road ends.

41.6 Turn left on **Heise Road** and cross Wildcat Creek. Cross State Route 8 on grade at mile 42.0 and continue past highway rest area.

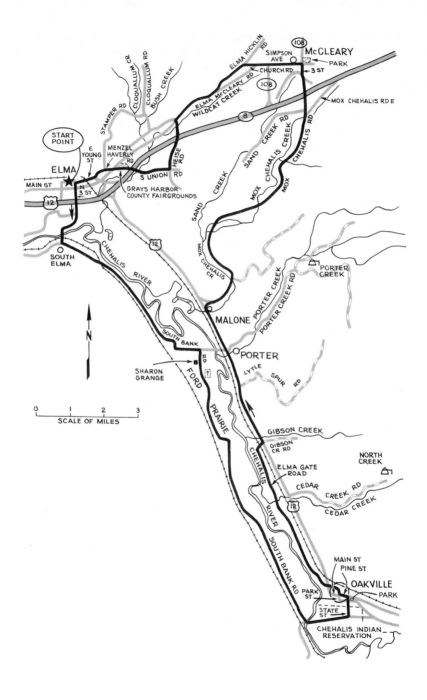

42.9 Right turn on **S. Union Road** as Heise Road is marked Dead End. Cross State Route 8 again and continue on **Fairground Road** past Grays Harbor County Fairgrounds.

44.6 Cross Elma-Oakville Road and continue on **Menzel Haverly Road** as Fairground Road ends.

44.9 Turn left on **Stamper Road** as Menzel Haverly Road ends. Road executes several bends threading its way through residential area, and is renamed **Oakhurst Drive** and **North F Street** in succession.

45.6 Turn right on **East Young Street** as F Street ends.

45.9 End of tour at North 3rd Street in Elma.

"I CAN CLIMB ANY HILL WITH THIS!"

117 OAKVILLE–BROOKLYN–MONTESANO

STARTING POINT: City park by corner of Main and State streets in Oakville. Take exit 88B (U.S. 12 West) from I-5 to Oakville. Park on side streets near city park.

DISTANCE: 73 miles.
TERRAIN: Mountainous to flat, with 9 miles of gravel road.
TOTAL CUMULATIVE ELEVATION GAIN: 1400 to 2000 feet.
RECOMMENDED TIME OF YEAR: Avoid snow or spring thaw; otherwise, any season.
RECOMMENDED STARTING TIME: Start early enough to allow sufficient daylight to complete tour.
ALLOW: 8 to 10 hours or overnight.
POINTS OF INTEREST
Ridge crest scenery
Brooklyn Tavern
WPPSS nuclear site

ELEVATION PROFILE

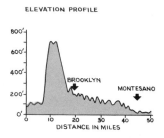

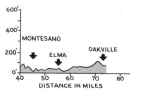

Logging, one of the principal industries in Grays Harbor County, began soon after the arrival of early settlers in the 1850s. The great forests of Douglas fir, hemlock, and cedar echoed with the sounds of "timbe-r-rr," as one giant tree after another crashed to the forest floor. Today, the virgin stands of timber are gone and even much of the second growth has been harvested. Douglas fir, which grows so well in the mild wet climate of the Pacific Northwest, is now a valuable crop, planted with care and harvested on a regular basis.

Lumberjacks of yesteryear lived lonely, isolated lives: the logging camps, with rude bunkhouses and few comforts, sprang up close to the working area, and only occasionally did the loggers get out for a night on the town. Things are different today as loggers live with their families in small towns and commute many miles to work, just as urban dwellers do. Most of the old logging camps disappeared completely many years ago, but an occasional small community still clings to life. Nestled in the valley of the North River in the Willapa Hills east of Raymond, Brooklyn is still home to a few families. It can even boast of a school for approximately 90 children in grades K through 12. But the old bunkhouses and other buildings associated with early logging either have been dismantled or lie buried beneath a tangled growth of brambles. The last remaining business establishment is an old tavern that has been in continuous operation since 1933. The base of its bar has the unusual feature of a metal gutter entitled "snoose creek" because running water washes away tobacco wastes and deposits them outside the building. Doubling as the town's only cafe, Brooklyn Tavern offers real hamburgers.

Although involving several miles of gravel roads, this tour into the hills east of Brooklyn offers the bicyclist a close look at a well-managed forest replanted to Douglas fir. Deer roam the hillsides, seeking the browse offered by the young forest. Views from the long, narrow ridge crest include Mt. Rainier and vapor plumes from the steam electric power plant at Centralia.

Along the road beside the North River, traffic is almost nonexistent. Red-tailed hawks survey the parklike setting of alders, bigleaf maples, and green grass, while ruffed grouse flush from clumps of brush. Homes are few and far between. Forested scenery continues along State Route 107 with increasing traffic density as Montesano and Elma are approached. Lake Sylvia State Park, just up the hill from motels in Montesano, boasts a fine swimming beach, secluded campsites, and a comfortable group camp area available by reservation with the park manager.

Once past Elma, the route branches on rural roads along the Chehalis River, where pastureland and dairy farms spread across the valley. Stunted Garry oak trees, growing in the area that was once an Indian campground, give their name to the little town of Oakville on the edge of the Chehalis Indian Reservation.

MILEAGE LOG

0.0 Oakville city park by corner of Main and State streets in Oakville. Head south (away from highway) on **State Street**.

0.5 Bear right at road junction and proceed through Chehalis Indian Reservation.

1.9 Cross Chehalis River and turn left on **Garrard Creek Road** across bridge over railroad cut.

5.3 Bear right toward Brooklyn as Garrard Creek Road bends left toward Centralia. Pavement ends at mile 6.9, becoming very rough and loose for 1/4 mile, but smoothing out and firming up thereafter. Climb steep hill, gaining summit ridge at about mile 10.4. Pavement resumes at mile 16.2. Brooklyn Tavern at mile 18.4.

19.7 Bear right toward Aberdeen and Highway 101 as left road fork (Smith Creek Road) continues to Raymond. Riverbank by bridge over North River offers possible picnic site at mile 20.4 as road enters Grays Harbor County.

32.8 Turn right on side road as main road approaches new concrete bridge over North River.

35.1 Bear right on **U.S. Highway 101** by Artic Grocery and Tavern.

36.9 Right turn at traffic light on **State Route 107** toward Montesano, just past highway weighing station. Cross Chehalis River at mile 44.0. Beware of dangerous railroad grade crossing after leaving bridge. Short road leads sharp right to fishing access with toilets. As it enters Montesano, the road is named **Main Street**.

45.0 Turn right on **Pioneer Avenue** at traffic light in Montesano. Motel, cafes, bakery. *Note: For an overnight stay at Lake Sylvia State Park, turn left here, then right and uphill on Third Street; 2 miles and 250-foot elevation gain to the park.*

47.1 Right turn on **Montesano-Brady Road**, cross U.S. 12, and bear left

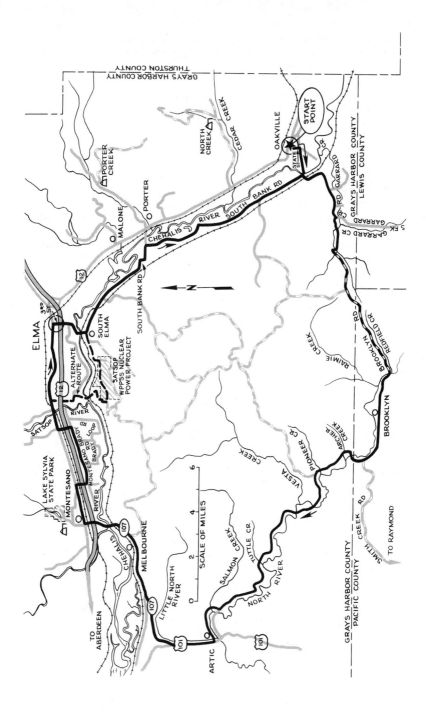

with main thoroughfare at T junction as a dead end road goes right.

49.7   Turn left toward Brady. Cross U.S. 12, cross railroad tracks, and bear right past grange hall.

50.2   Bear right on old highway. Cross Satsop River at mile 50.8. Continue through Satsop to Elma. *Note: Alternate route goes right at mile 51.5 in Satsop on 4 Street, continuing on Keyes Road uphill past WPPSS mothballed nuclear power plant, left toward Elma at stop sign at bottom of hill, rejoining route at mileage log 57.2. Adds 1.2 miles and a 600-foot elevation gain.* Drive-in restaurant in Elma at mile 55.1.

55.4   Right turn toward freeway on **Third Street** at traffic light. Cross U.S. 12 on overpass and continue across valley.

57.2   Cross Chehalis River and railroad tracks, and bend left on **South Bank Road** as side road goes right to Satsop Power Plant.

62.6   Bear right with South Bank Road as steel truss bridge appears ahead. Sharon Cemetery on the left at mile 63.4.

71.2   Bear left toward Oakville as Garrard Creek Road goes right to Brooklyn. Cross Chehalis River and continue through Chehalis Indian Reservation.

72.5   Bear left with main thoroughfare at crossroads.

73.1   End of tour by city park in Oakville.

"YOU GO ON – I'M STAYING HERE TONIGHT."

THURSTON COUNTY

118 STEAMBOAT ISLAND

STARTING POINT: Take exit 104 (U.S. 101) from I-5 at Olympia. Follow U.S. 101 7.7 miles to Steamboat Island Road exit. Park in Griffin Elementary School parking area (nonschool days only), just off Steamboat Island Road on 33 Avenue N.W.

DISTANCE: 25 to 31 miles.
TERRAIN: Hilly.
TOTAL CUMULATIVE ELEVATION GAIN: 900 feet.
RECOMMENDED TIME OF YEAR: Any season.
RECOMMENDED STARTING TIME: 9 to 10 A.M.
ALLOW: 3 to 5 hours.
POINTS OF INTEREST
Puget Sound waterscapes

ELEVATION PROFILE

The name for this ride is derived from a diminutive mound of earth at the end of a long peninsula jutting into the southern end of Puget Sound. A one-lane concrete causeway across a gravel bar provides access from the mainland to the island, where houses crowd each other wall-to-wall for a piece of the highly prized waterfront. Although the island itself is of only passing interest to cycle tourists, the views across the sheltered waters to nearby islands and other peninsulas are unusual. Quiet, moderately hilly backroads offer leisurely cycling. A 90-acre tract of land at Frye Cove, acquired several years ago by Thurston County for a public park, is currently undeveloped. It has no picnic tables, drinking water, or toilet facilities. Even so, the park has a relaxing atmosphere and a peaceful beach where crumbs from the lunch sack may be shared with aquatic crabs and barnacles. With winter's high tides, loons and cormorants surface close to shore, scolding loudly as they complain about the humans occupying their secluded beach and cove. A side trip to Oyster Bay adds several miles and another view of one of Puget Sound's extremities to this short, 25-mile tour. For the bicycle tourist not looking for a marathon spectacular, this is a leisurely ride.

MILEAGE LOG

0.0 Parking lot of Griffin Elementary School. Proceed out of school yard on **33rd Avenue N.W.** to **Steamboat Island Road N.W.** and turn right. Grocery on left at mile 4.8. Cross bridge to Steamboat Island at mile 9.1. Continue on **Steamboat Island Loop N.W.**

9.5 Road doubles back at north end of island by Olympia Outdoor Club Park (private). Continue around loop and back across bridge onto **Steamboat Island Road N.W.**

12.1 Go straight on **Urquhart Road N.W.** past fire station and Rignall Hall.

12.2 Bear right at wye and continue on **81st Avenue N.W.** Cross Steamboat Island Road N.W.

12.8 Road bends left and is renamed **Howe Street N.W.**

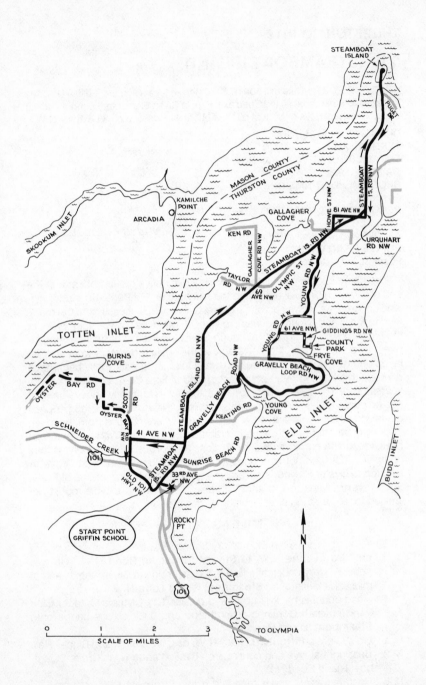

STEAMBOAT ISLAND

PUGET

MASON COUNTY
THURSTON COUNTY

KAMILCHE POINT

ARCADIA

GALLAGHER COVE

SKOOKUM INLET

KEN RD

COVE RD NW

STEAMBOAT 15 RD NW

HOWE ST NW

81 AVE NW

15 RD NW

STEAMBOAT 15 RD NW

URQUHART RD NW

TAYLOR RD NW

69 AVE NW

OLYMPIC ST NW

YOUNG RD NW

TOTTEN INLET

BURNS COVE

OYSTER BAY RD

SCOTT RD

OYSTER BAY RD NW

41 AVE NW

STEAMBOAT ISLAND RD NW

GRAVELLY BEACH Road NW

KEATING RD

YOUNG RD N W

61 AVE NW

GIDDINGS RD NW

COUNTY PARK

FRYE COVE

GRAVELLY BEACH LOOP RD NW

YOUNG COVE

ELD INLET

BUDD INLET

SCHNEIDER CREEK

101

STEAMBOAT 15 RD NW

SUNRISE BEACH RD

33 RD AVE NW

OLD 101 HWY NW

START POINT GRIFFIN SCHOOL

ROCKY PT

N

101

TO OLYMPIA

0   1   2   3
SCALE OF MILES

13.1 Rejoin **Steamboat Island Road N.W.**

13.3 Bear left on **Young Road N.W.** Pavement ends at mile 14.9.

15.5 Left turn on **61st Avenue N.W.** Road descends to creek bottom, climbs steeply on other side, bends right at 16.1, and is renamed **Giddings Road N.W.**

16.2 At park welcome sign, take bicycles down driveway and bear left on footpath to beach. Have a quiet picnic lunch, pack up all trash, and return to Young Road.

17.3 Turn left on **Young Road N.W.** as 61st Avenue N.W. ends.

17.9 Left turn on **Gravelly Beach Loop N.W.** on blacktop pavement as Young Road ends. Continue around point over a series of hills and dales.

21.2 Turn left on **Gravelly Beach Road N.W.** as the loop road ends. End of Young Cove appears on left.

22.8 Bear left on **Steamboat Island Road N.W.** by power substation, then immediately turn right on **41st Avenue N.W.**

23.8 Left turn on **Oyster Bay Road N.W.** as 41st Avenue ends. *Note: For an interesting side trip, turn right on Oyster Bay Road 3.0 miles to end of road and return.*

24.2 Cross U.S. 101 and continue on **Old 101 Highway N.W.** as it bends left.

25.0 Cross U.S. 101 again and turn left on **Sexton Drive N.W.**

25.1 Bear right with thoroughfare on **Steamboat Island Road N.W.**

25.2 Turn right on **33 Avenue N.W.**, then left into school yard. End of tour.

"Good thing it was a tree he hit—he didn't have his helmet on."

119 PRIEST POINT–TOLMIE STATE PARK

STARTING POINT: Priest Point Park in Olympia. Take exit 105B (Olympia) from I-5 and continue through city center on Plum Street, which changes its name to East Bay Drive as it leaves metropolitan area. Park entrance is 2 miles from I-5 exit and appears on the right about 50 yards before park road overpass. Park cars by county shops behind picnic shelter.

DISTANCE: 37 miles plus 12 miles of optional side trips.
TERRAIN: Hilly.
TOTAL CUMULATIVE ELEVATION GAIN: 1750 feet plus optional side trips totaling 350 feet.
RECOMMENDED TIME OF YEAR: Any season.
RECOMMENDED STARTING TIME: 9 A.M.
ALLOW: 5 to 7 hours.

POINTS OF INTEREST
Thurston County's Burfoot Park
Tolmie State Park

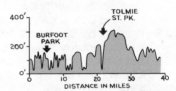

ELEVATION PROFILE

Numerous, long fingerlike projections of land reach into southern Puget Sound to form many inlets, bays, and passages. Olympia, the capital city of Washington State, stands at the end of one of the larger inlets, Budd Inlet. Olympia's Priest Point Park fronts the inlet with forested hillside picnicking areas, and is the starting point for this tour. Thurston County's Burfoot Park on Budd Inlet is a day-use park featuring nature trails, picnicking, and beach access. Several walk-in campsites with a communal fire circle are available for overnight group camping by reservation with the park manager.

Other seascapes dot this tour. At Boston Harbor, a marina and small grocery cater to the boating fraternity. At Woodard Bay, mud flats are in a continuous state of flux as the tides ebb and flow into the long, narrow bay. Great blue herons frequent the shallow waters, while gulls make regular inspection flights.

Fronting on Nisqually Reach, Tolmie State Park offers views toward Anderson Island and Longbranch Peninsula in Pierce County. Although the park has no overnight camping, it offers two separate picnic areas, each with its own restroom and kitchen shelter. The kitchen facilities are equipped with stainless steel sinks, hot and cold running water, and coin-operated electric hot plates. The hillside picnic area features secluded picnic sites overlooking the sound. The beach-level shelter stands on a small knoll with paved paths down to the high-tide mark. Scuba divers find the extensive shallow beach a prime area for their sport.

Automobile traffic along most of this tour is minimal, the only busy traffic occurring on Marvin Road where it crosses I-5 and becomes State Route 510. Scenery for the most part is semirural-suburban. Evergreen huckleberry, growing in the forest edge along some of the roads, is a relatively uncommon bush, but most of the other flora are typical of the western Washington region.

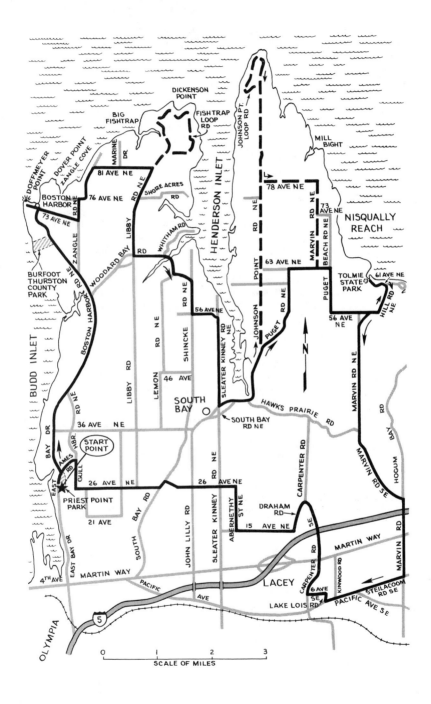

Commerce and industry are also represented on this tour, which includes a mushroom farm at the corner of Marvin Way and Steilacoom Road, where large piles of baled straw surround the windowless buildings. Sand and gravel companies mine the valuable aggregates just north of I-5 on Carpenter Road, but their trucks usually do not operate on weekends.

Suburbia briefly takes over as the tour approaches Olympia's city limits, to be followed by dense forest along Ames Road. A short stretch marked "Bike Route" returns the tour to the starting point at Priest Point Park.

MILEAGE LOG

0.0 Parking area behind picnic shelter in Olympia's Priest Point Park. Cross park overpass and bear right on drive on other side.

0.1 Bear left on sidewalk along **East Bay Drive**.

0.3 Cross East Bay Drive as Ames Road intersects on the right. Continue north along East Bay Drive on marked bikeway, which proceeds 0.3 mile to end at city limit, where the road is renamed **Boston Harbor Road N.E.** Continue on wide, paved shoulder. *Note: Tour may be shortened by 8 miles by turning right on Woodard Bay Road at mile 3.5.* Thurston County's Burfoot Park on the left at mile 4.8.

5.3 Turn left on **73rd Avenue N.E.** for a view off Doffmeyer Point. Grocery and marina. Return to Boston Harbor Road and continue on 73rd Avenue N.E.

6.6 Left turn on **Zangle Road N.E.** as 73rd Avenue ends by fire station. Road bends right and left and is renamed **76th Avenue N.E.** and **Zangle Road N.E.**

7.6 Turn right on **81st Avenue N.E.** as Zangle is marked Dead End.

8.7 Right turn on **Libby Road N.E.** *Note: Turning left here provides optional 3.8-mile side trip around Fishtrap Loop Road on Dickenson Point.*

10.4 Turn left on **Woodard Bay Road N.E.** Bear left with Woodard Bay Road as Lemon Road goes right at mile 11.1.

11.5 Bear right on **Shincke Road N.E.** as it comes in from a dead end on the left.

12.1 Left turn on **56th Avenue N.E.**, which rounds a bend 0.4 mile farther and is renamed **Sleater Kinney Road N.E.**

14.1 Turn left on **South Bay Road N.E.** (busy, but has wide, paved shoulders). As it rounds the end of Henderson Inlet it is renamed **Johnson Point Road N.E.**

15.5 Turn right on **Puget Road N.E.** *Note: Tour may be extended by 8.3 miles by continuing on Johnson Point Road, going around the loop on Johnson Point, and proceeding via 78th Avenue N.E. and Marvin Road to rejoin main tour at mile 17.6.*

17.1 Right turn on **63rd Avenue N.E.** as Puget Road ends.

17.8 Turn right on **Puget Beach Road N.E.**, which bends left 0.8 mile farther and is renamed **56th Avenue N.E.**

19.0 Continue on 56th Avenue N.E. as main thoroughfare turns right and is renamed Marvin Road N.E. 56th Avenue soon bends left and is renamed **Hill Road N.E.**

20.0 Bear left toward Tolmie State Park on **61st Avenue N.E.**, which enters park boundary in 0.2 mile. For a visit to beach area, do not turn into upper-level parking lot, but continue on main thoroughfare down steep hill.

20.5 End of road and trail system at beach; suggested lunch stop. Restrooms and picnic shelter facilities at both upper and lower levels of park. Views of Case Inlet, Key Peninsula, and Anderson Island. Return via entrance route along **61st Avenue, Hill Road N.E.**, and **56th Avenue N.E.** to Marvin Road intersection.

22.0 Left turn on **Marvin Road N.E.** at wye. I-5 roars underneath at mile 25.9; restaurants. Drive-in cafe at Martin Way crossing at mile 26.3 as road name changes to **Marvin Road S.E.** and **State Route 510** signs appear.

27.0 Turn right on **Steilacoom Road S.E.**

27.9 Merge with **Pacific Avenue S.E.** and continue on broad, paved shoulder.

28.4 Turn right on **Lake Lois Road** about 0.1 mile past tavern. Road bends left and is renamed **6th Avenue S.E.**

28.9 Right turn on **Carpenter Road S.E.** as 6th Avenue ends. Cross Martin Way on grade and I-5 on overpass.

30.5 Bear left with main thoroughfare on **Draham Road N.E.** as Carpenter Road N.E. bends right. As Draham Road rounds a bend 0.5 mile farther it is renamed **15th Avenue N.E.**

32.1 Turn right on **Abernethy Street N.E.**

32.8 Left turn on **26th Avenue N.E.** as Abernethy ends.

34.1 Turn left on **South Bay Road N.E.** as 26th Avenue ends, then right again on **26th Avenue N.E.**

35.7 Right turn on **Gull Harbor Road N.E.** as 26th Avenue is marked Dead End.

36.1 Turn left on **Ames Road N.E.** as Gull Harbor road starts down a short hill. Olympia city limits.

36.5 Cross **East Bay Drive**, turn left, and continue on marked bikeway.

36.7 Bear right on drive into Priest Point Park. Cross overpass and continue to parking area by county shops to complete this tour.

120 MILLERSYLVANIA–DELPHI–OLYMPIA

STARTING POINT: Millersylvania State Park. Take exit 95 (State Route 121, Maytown, state park) from I-5. Follow signs to Millersylvania State Park, 3.5 miles east of the freeway. Park in the picnic area parking lot.

DISTANCE: 43 miles.
TERRAIN: Moderate.
TOTAL CUMULATIVE ELEVATION GAIN: 1200 feet.
RECOMMENDED TIME OF YEAR: Any season.
RECOMMENDED STARTING TIME: 9 to 10 A.M.
ALLOW: 5 to 6 hours.
POINTS OF INTEREST
McLane Creek Nature Trail
Capitol Lake Park
Olympia Brewery

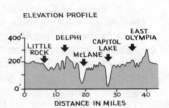

ELEVATION PROFILE

Tour #47 (Millersylvania-Olympia) in *Bicycling the Backroads Around Puget Sound* also begins at Millersylvania State Park and touches some of the same places as this tour, but the two routes are quite different. This tour is seven miles longer and proceeds through the town of Little Rock and the small communities of Delphi and McLane as well as the Evergreen State College campus. The route then goes through some of Olympia's residential areas, skirts its business district, continues past Capitol Lake and the Olympia Brewery, and out into the countryside of East Olympia before returning to the state park.

The McLane Creek Nature Trail, managed by the Department of Natural Resources (DNR), winds through a portion of a forested lowland valley. It gives the visitor a chance to study some of the things that occur in the wild to influence and change the environment: the flooding of a creek valley, the construction of beaver dams, and forest fires. Capitol Lake and the surrounding park, on the other hand, show how man alters the environment by changing the course of a river, damming it up, and forming a lake. Marshy areas formed around the edge of the lake attract waterfowl to feed and eat. Parks built on the dredged landfill boast picnic tables, restrooms, and green lawns, where coots, mallards, widgeons and sea gulls frequently forage. Man also has introduced a run of Chinook salmon that makes its annual pilgrimage through Capitol Lake and up the Deschutes River to spawn.

A series of artesian wells dots the golf course near the Deschutes River at Tumwater Falls, providing the many gallons of water needed for the Olympia Brewery's operation. Interesting guided tours take the public through the different operations in the plant. Several cemeteries along Cleveland Avenue in Tumwater beautify the environment with carefully maintained and land-scaped memorial grounds and gardens.

Only small stands of evergreen trees remain in the fields and pastures of East Olympia. Not until the boundary of Millersylvania State Park is approached can the cyclist realize how the area must have appeared to the

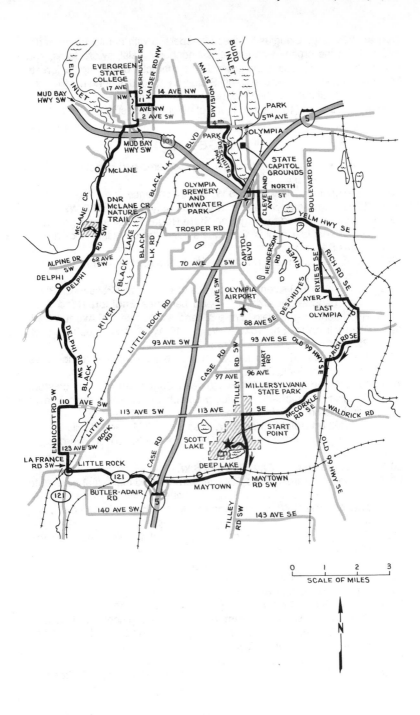

SCALE OF MILES

N

early settlers: large Douglas fir trees interspersed with hemlock and cedar tower above the brushy vine maple, salmonberry, salal, sword ferns, and many wildflowers carpeting the ground. The character of the original forests has been preserved at Millersylvania State Park, because John L. Miller, the original owner of most of the land, did not clearcut the forests as did many of his neighbors, and thus left a legacy of tall timber for succeeding generations to enjoy.

MILEAGE LOG

0.0 Head out park entrance road from picnic area parking lot of Millersylvania State Park.

0.2 Turn right on **Tilley Road S.W.** at park entrance.

1.0 Cross railroad tracks and turn right on **Maytown Road S.W.**

3.6 Go under I-5 and turn right on **State Route 121** at stop sign. Wide, paved shoulder begins. Continue straight through Little Rock at mile 6.5 as S.R. 121 swings left.

6.6 Cross railroad tracks and immediately turn right on **La France Road S.W.**

7.2 Left turn on **123 Avenue S.W.** as La France ends. Cross Black River. Road bends right at mile 7.4 and becomes **Endicott Road S.W.** Road bends right again at mile 8.8 and is renamed **110 Avenue S.W.**

9.3 Turn left on **Delphi Road S.W.** as 110 Avenue changes to gravel. Pass through Delphi at mile 13.5.

15.7 Left turn on drive into McLane Creek Nature Trail recreation area (Washington State DNR).

16.2 End of road in parking lot by trail head. Suggested picnic lunch stop. Pit toilets, picnic tables, guiding pamphlets for trail around beaver pond. Return to Delphi Road.

16.7 Turn left on **Delphi Road S.W.** Pass through McLane at mile 18.1.

18.7 Bear right as truck route goes left. Cross U.S. 101 on overpass at mile 20.2.

20.6 Turn right on **Mud Bay Highway S.W.**

20.7 Go past Evergreen State College entrance and turn left at bike route sign across street from fire hall. Continue left with bike route sign on **2nd Avenue S.W.**, which ends at bike trail head. Continue on bike trail.

21.5 Turn right at stop sign on roadway. No street name sign here, but this is **17 Avenue N.W.**

21.8 Right turn on **Overhulse Road N.W.**

22.2 Turn left on **11 Avenue N.W.**

22.7 Left turn on **Kaiser Road N.W.**

22.9 Turn right on **14 Avenue N.W.** by power substation.

24.5 Right turn on **Division Street**. Bicycle lane along shoulder. Bike lane ends 0.5 miles farther as road changes from two to four lanes. Cross Harrison Avenue at traffic light at mile 25.3.

25.4 Turn left on **4th Avenue** and proceed down a hill.

26.0 Bear right on **Olympic Way** and continue down the hill. Sidewalk available.

26.4 Turn sharp right on **5th Avenue N.** *Note: Turning left here goes into Olympia business district. Capitol grounds, stores, cafes.* As it proceeds around Capitol Lake, 5th Avenue changes name to **Deschutes Parkway.** Capitol Lake Park south area on left at mile 27.0; picnic tables, toilet facilities. Crosby House Museum on left at mile 28.3.

28.6 Left turn at stop sign and flashing red light by Olympia Brewery. Cross bridge over Deschutes River.

28.8 Turn right on **Custer Way** and continue uphill. *Note: Drive leads right at 28.9 to Olympia Brewery visitors' entrance; guided tours of brewery.*

29.1 Cross Capitol Way and take next right turn on **Cleveland Avenue** toward Yelm and Rainier. Views of golf course with brewery artesian wells on right, Oddfellows Cemetery on left. Road bends left and is renamed **Yelm Highway S.E.** Wide shoulder.

31.9 Turn right on **Rich Road S.E.** toward East Olympia.

32.8 Go straight on **Rixie Street S.E.** and cross railroad tracks as Rich Road bends left. Road zigzags and is renamed **78 Avenue S.E.**, **Ayer Street**, and **83 Avenue S.E.** in quick succession.

35.1 Right turn on **Rich Road S.E.** by East Olympia Store and post office. Cross railroad tracks. Cross Deschutes River at mile 37.4.

37.7 Turn left on **Old 99 Highway S.E.** as Rich Road ends.

38.6 Right turn on **McCorkle Road S.E.**, which executes a bend after 0.4 mile and becomes **113 Avenue S.E.** Crank over a hill.

41.2 Turn left on **Tilley Road S.W.**

42.2 Right turn into entrance of Millersylvania State Park.

42.4 Picnic area parking lot; end of tour.

"CHAAARGE!"

121 BLACK RIVER

STARTING POINT: Millersylvania State Park. Take exit 95 (State Park, Maytown, State Route 121) from I-5 and follow signs to the state park, 3.5 miles east of the freeway. Park in picnic area parking lot.

DISTANCE: 30 miles.
TERRAIN: Flat.
TOTAL CUMULATIVE ELEVATION GAIN: 300 feet.
RECOMMENDED TIME OF YEAR: Any season; May and June best for flowers.
RECOMMENDED STARTING TIME: 10 A.M.
ALLOW: 4 to 5 hours.
POINTS OF INTEREST
Spring flowers
Historical monuments
Scatter Creek Game Range

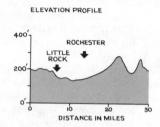

ELEVATION PROFILE

The soil south of Olympia and north of Centralia between the Willapa Hills and Cascade foothills contains the rocky debris left by the once huge glaciers that plunged down Mt. Rainier in ages past. Trees grow well in this stony soil, but the usual thick underbrush of the Puget Sound forest is missing. In its place are flowers and plants, many not common to other places around western Washington. Camas lily, a deep-seated bulb, blooms April to June with predominantly blue, hyacinthlike flowers, though white ones also occur. Its bulb was an important food in the diet of the Western Indians. A poisonous white-flowered bulb, resembling the camas and appropriately called the death camas, also grows in the same area, its showy flowers forming a tight terminal raceme rather than the loose one of the blue camas.

The prairie north of Rochester becomes a scene of many colors in springtime as wildflowers put on their show: orange honeysuckle, lavender vetch, blue campanula, red columbine, blue-eyed grass, pink kinnikinnick, yellow cinquefoil, blue lupine, pink roses, and yellow balsam root.

Brush and flowers preferring a moist and shady habitat thrive along the slowly moving Black River. The young purplish red twigs of the western dogwood add a touch of color to the tangle of branches along the stream. Steeple bush produces soft pyramidal clusters of bright pink flowers in the midst of the thicket. By spring the berries of the osoberry have already formed and hang in sparkling orange-red bunches among pale green leaves. The small pink blossoms of the brushy snowberry give off a sweet fragrance, particularly when wet with rain. Their large white berries hang on the bushes until late in winter.

Bright canary yellow monkey-flowers line many of the moist ditches across the prairie, while purple iris prefer a dry area. Brilliant yellow Scotch broom invades much of western Washington, and the well-drained stony ground of this tour in Thurston County is no exception. Their pungent odor fills the air until late spring.

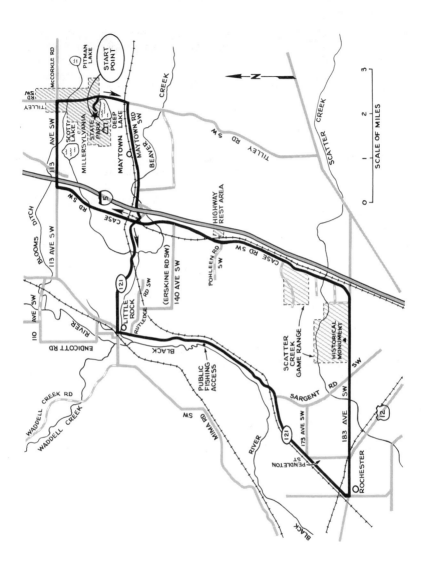

Birds that make their summer home in western Washington begin arriving early in the spring. By May and June the western tanager sings from the tall firs, and the bright yellow warbler flits from bush to bush. Resident song sparrows render their lovely song again and again. Spring is the ideal time for this tour into the prairie land of southwestern Thurston County.

MILEAGE LOG

0.0 Go out park entrance road from picnic area parking lot of Millersylvania State Park and turn right on **Tilley Road S.W.**

1.0 Right turn on **Maytown Road S.W.**

3.6 Go under I-5 and turn right on **State Route 121** toward Little Rock. Wide shoulder, bicycle route signs.

6.5 Turn left with S.R. 121 in Little Rock by grocery. Public fishing access at mile 8.5.

13.9 Left turn on **U.S. 12** in Rochester. Grocery and cafes.

14.8 Continue straight on **183 Avenue S.W.** as U.S. 12 bends right. Fieldstonemasonry pedestal at corner. Masonic monument, historical monument marking the location of Fort Henness, and cemetery at mile 17.6.

18.7 Left turn on **Case Road S.W.** Entrance to Scatter Creek Game Range on left at mile 20.3; pit toilets. *Note: Conservation license required to use game range facilities.* Cross Maytown Road S.W. (State Route 121) at mile 24.5.

26.7 Turn right on **113 Avenue S.W.** as Case Road ends.

28.5 Right turn on **Tilley Road S.W.**

29.4 Turn right into entrance of Millersylvania State Park.

29.6 Picnic area parking lot; end of tour.

122 RAINIER–CLEAR LAKE

STARTING POINT: Town of Rainier. From the north take I-5 to exit 127 (State Route 512) toward Puyallup and Mt. Rainier. Turn right on State Route 7 toward Mt. Rainier and Tacoma and right again on State Route 507 to Rainier. From the south take exit 88A (Grand Mound) east to Tenino and follow State Route 507 to Rainier. Park in parking area on Dakota Street by Rainier City Hall, fire station, and school.

DISTANCE: 37 miles.
TERRAIN: Moderate.
TOTAL CUMULATIVE ELEVATION GAIN: 850 feet.
RECOMMENDED TIME OF YEAR: Clear Lake fishing access open mid-April to mid-July. Avoid opening weekend of lake fishing; otherwise, any season.
RECOMMENDED STARTING TIME: 9 to 10 A.M.
ALLOW: 5 hours

POINTS OF INTEREST
Groves of oak and aspen trees
Camas lilies May through June

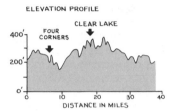

ELEVATION PROFILE

Snow began to fall, lightly at first, then more heavily, covering the countryside with a soft, white blanket. Our narrow bicycle tires bit through to the blacktop pavement. Muffled sounds seemed distant, yet close at hand. The twittering of the juncos and scolding of the winter wrens lost some of their usual intensity, and even the jets overhead could not disturb the peaceful solitude. Unconcerned by the falling snow, with their warm breath forming a misty fog, furry-coated horses stood calmly under huge, spreading oaks. The expressions of a power line crew, eating lunch in their big truck, showed utter disbelief that anyone would ride a bicycle in such weather. The old Clackamas schoolhouse and gymnasium, a relic of days gone by, stood empty and forlorn. Evening grosbeaks made cracking noises as they opened the seedpods still hanging on the bigleaf maple trees. Fences with closed gates surrounded the residential community of Clearwood; no one was looking at homesites on that snowy day.

A deserted, white field sloped from the road down to the shores of Clear Lake, marking the Department of Wildlife boat-launching ramp, but it was not exactly the time of year for a picnic by the lake. Snow began sticking to the roads and packing up under the bicycle fenders before our return to Rainier. A wintry day was a fascinating time for a tour of the backroads in Thurston County, but a ride need not be postponed for these conditions; this tour would be a different but pleasant scene in any other season.

MILEAGE LOG

0.0 Starting from parking area on Dakota Street in Rainier, head east, paralleling school grounds.

0.1 Turn right at stop sign on **Algyer Road**. Name changes to **148th Avenue S.E.** at mile 3.1 as Runyon Road S.E. goes right.

3.9 Left turn on **Martinson Road S.E.**, which after 0.5 mile bends right and becomes **143rd Avenue S.E.**

5.3 Turn left on **Vail Road S.E.** by Deschutes Grange Hall No. 222 as 143rd Avenue ends.

8.6 Right turn on **Bald Hill Road S.E.** Four Corners Grocery here has deli bar.

12.2 Bear left at wye with **Bald Hill Road** as Smith Prairie Road S.E. continues on. Grocery on left at mile 17.7.

18.4 Left turn into Clear Lake Public Fishing Access. Toilet facilities, ducks to feed, view of lake, lunch stop. *Note: Conservation license required*. Return along **Bald Hill Road**.

21.5 Turn left on **Longmire Road S.E.** as Bald Hill Road prepares to dive down a steep hill.

22.5 Bear right with **Neat Road S.E.** as Longmire turns to gravel and is marked Dead End. Glimpses of Deschutes River.

24.6 Left turn on **Lawrence Lake Road S.E.** as Smith Prairie Road goes on. Deschutes River rolls by on the left.

26.7 Turn left on **153 Avenue S.E.**

27.5 Left turn on **Lindsay Road S.E.** by fire station #22, "Wildbunch." *Note: Alternate lunch break at Lawrence Lake fishing access, 1.1 miles left on Pleasant Beach Road as Lindsay Road bends right at mile 28.5.*

29.0 Turn left on **Vail Road S.E.** Cross Deschutes River at mile 29.8.

31.7 Continue on **Vail Cutoff S.E.** as Vail Loop S.E. goes left. Cross Deschutes River and climb hill.

33.4 Bear right at stop sign with Vail Cutoff S.E. Olympic Pipeline Co. pump station at mile 34.9.

35.6 Right turn on shoulder of **State Route 507** as Vail Cutoff ends.

36.2 Turn right on **Minnesota Avenue** in Rainier and bear left on diagonal street toward school parking lot.

36.3 End of tour.

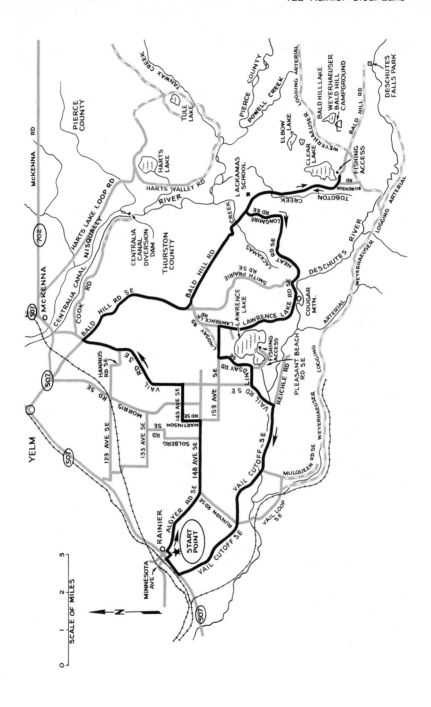

123 McKENNA–RAINIER

STARTING POINT: McKenna Elementary School at junction of State Route 702 with State Route 507 just north of McKenna. From the north take I-5 to exit 127 (State Route 512) toward Puyallup and Mt. Rainier; turn right on State Route 7 toward Rainier and Tacoma and right again on State Route 507 through Roy to McKenna. From the south take I-5 to exit 88A and head east to Tenino. Pick up State Route 507 and continue northeast to McKenna. Park in parking area at north end of school complex.

DISTANCE: 31 to 42 miles.
TERRAIN: Flat to moderate.
TOTAL CUMULATIVE ELEVATION GAIN: 700 to 1000 feet.
RECOMMENDED TIME OF YEAR: Any season.
RECOMMENDED STARTING TIME: 8 to 10 A.M.
ALLOW: 4 to 6 hours.
POINTS OF INTEREST
Centralia City Light Power Canal Headworks
Views of Mt. Rainier

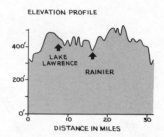

This tour along relatively traffic-free roads of Thurston County lies due west of Mt. Rainier, with magnificent views of the mountain from every twist and turn. Glaciers covered with snow embrace the massif and give it a perpetual blanket of white. During the summer months, after the snow has melted from the rocks and steep cliffs, the two outer peaks of the seemingly three-peaked giant appear jagged and smeared with brown. Columbia Crest alone remains smooth and unblemished.

Early settlers to Washington Territory claimed the natural prairie lying between the Nisqually and Deschutes rivers southeast of Olympia for their homesteads. Later owners brought water from the Nisqually River for irrigation, to increase the production of crops on the stony but fertile soil. A canal dug along the hillside above the river extended across the prairie from two miles below the mouth of Ohop Creek all the way to Yelm. Competition from an expanding agriculture eventually altered the economics of this farming area, and the irrigation system was abandoned. Today only a few operating dairy farms and chicken ranches survive. Owners of homes and acreage make their living elsewhere, but small garden plots and pastures still produce bountifully when carefully watered and tended.

Centralia City Light Power Project, begun in 1928, still diverts water from the Nisqually River and sends it via a canal to a power generating plant near Yelm. A visit to this diversion dam requires permission from the Centralia City Light power plant manager, preferably at least two days in advance. Write to Centralia Light Department Superintendent, 1102 N. Tower, Centralia, WA 98531, or call 736-7611. Civil engineering buffs will find the facility fascinating. The State Fisheries Department requires the river to be maintained above a minimum flow, and thus the amount of water diverted into the canal varies from season to season. Control gates and spillway form one end of a steel-and-concrete basin. A double set of fish screens, mandated by the Fisheries Department in 1955, stretches across the head of the basin. Completely automated, the screens slowly move up and down in succession as a water spray washes leaves and debris into a gutter leading back to the river's main channel. The screens are expensive to replace and can be damaged if trash is allowed to build up against them and create a differential pressure. A backup hydraulic power supply system for operating the screens stands ready. Once a year the screens receive a thorough hand-scrubbing.

Barn swallows find the concrete ledges around the basin to be ideal nesting sites. Happy chatter accompanies their continuous search for insects on the wing. Swooping low over the water, they skim the surface with an occasional splash. An osprey, or fish hawk, makes regular patrols, periodically plunging into the river to emerge with a fish clutched in its talons. Shaking the water from its feathers as it gains altitude, the hawk soon disappears over the trees. Great blue herons wait patiently along the bank of the river for itinerant fish. With a quick jab of a long sharp beak, the heron acquires a meal.

A boat-launching site maintained by the State Department of Wildlife offers public access to picturesque Lake Lawrence. Canoeists paddle quietly along a bit of marshland of the mushroom shaped lake, while fishermen move slowly about in their motorized boats. Water-skiers crisscross the lake, stirring up the water. Mt. Rainier rises above them all, casting a reflection on the sun-drenched scene.

Logging of the forested hillsides south of the Deschutes River continues to be important to the economy of the little town of Rainier. Once a Weyerhaeuser Company town site with rows of homes for employees, the old town of Vail is gone. Employees now commute to the remaining logging headquarters and rail transfer yard.

MILEAGE LOG

0.0 Parking lot of McKenna Elementary School by junction of State Route 702 with State Route 507. Head south on **S.R. 507** toward McKenna. Continue through McKenna, crossing Nisqually River into Thurston County at mile 0.5.

0.7 Cross Centralia Power Canal and turn left on **Vail Road S.E.** toward Lawrence Lake, Clear Lake, and airport. *Note: Cook Road goes left at mile 1.3 to Centralia City Light Power Canal Headworks; round trip 8.2 miles, 1.5 miles gravel road each way. See text (pages 122-123) for tour of headworks.*

1.6 Turn left on **Bald Hill Road** by grocery store.

5.1 Go straight at wye on **Smith Prairie Road S.E.** as Bald Hill Road swings left, then immediately turn right on **Lawrence Lake Road S.E.**

6.2 Turn right on **153rd Avenue S.E.**

7.0 Left turn on **Lindsay Road S.E.** by fire station #22, "Wildbunch." *Note: Optional side trip goes left at mile 8.0 on Pleasant Beach Road*

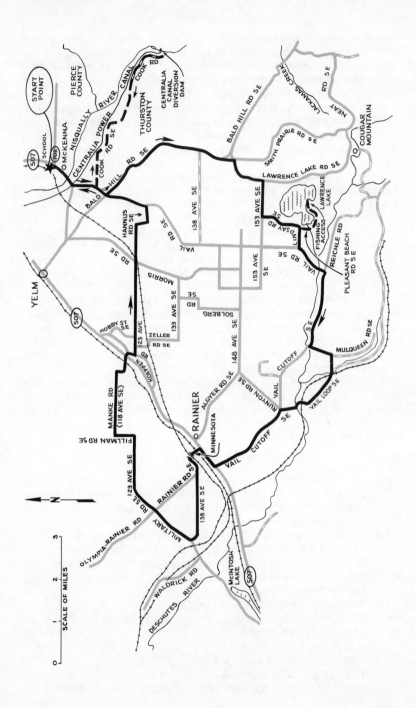

S.E. to public fishing access on Lawrence Lake, 2.2 miles round trip. Possible picnic lunch site; pit toilets.

8.5 Turn left on **Vail Road S.E.** Cross Deschutes River at mile 9.2, and continue with thoroughfare as it is renamed **Vail Cutoff S.E.**

11.2 Left turn with **Vail Loop S.E.** as Vail Cutoff continues across bridge. Cross logging road and railroad tracks at mile 12.1. Site of previous town of Vail on right at mile 12.4. Cross railroad tracks and Deschutes River at mile 13.3.

14.7 Continue on **Vail Cutoff S.E.** as Vail Loop ends.

16.0 Turn right on **State Route 507** toward Tacoma. As it enters Rainier it is named **Binghampton Street**. Drive-in cafe in Rainier.

16.5 Left turn (north) on **Minnesota Street** toward East Olympia in Rainier. Cross one set of railroad tracks, go under a trestle, and climb hill. Road changes name to **Rainier Road S.E.**

17.4 Go straight on **138th Avenue S.E.** as Rainier Road swings right.

18.9 Turn right on **Military Road S.E.** as 138 Avenue ends. Road name changes to **123rd Avenue S.E.** at mile 20.6.

21.9 Left turn on **Fillman Road S.E.** as 123 Avenue is posted Dead End. The road makes two successive right turns and is renamed **118th Avenue S.E.** and **Manke Road S.E.**

24.3 Cross railroad tracks and State Route 507. Continue right with thoroughfare at wye on **Koeppen Road S.E.**

24.4 Turn left on **123rd Avenue S.E.** Watch for dangerous railroad crossing at mile 26.9. Road is renamed **Hannus Road S.E.** as it bends right and left through green irrigated fields.

28.5 Left turn on **Vail Road S.E.** Cross Bald Hill Road by grocery store at mile 29.6.

30.5 Right turn on **State Route 507** and cross the Nisqually River into Pierce County. Continue through McKenna.

31.2 McKenna Elementary School; end of tour.

124 CENTRALIA–LINCOLN CREEK– OAKVILLE

STARTING POINT: Fort Borst Park in Centralia. Take I-5 to exit 82. The park is one block southwest of the interchange. Park in the park office parking lot, across from the ball diamond.

DISTANCE: 50 miles.
TERRAIN: Moderate to flat.
TOTAL CUMULATIVE ELEVATION GAIN: 750 feet.
RECOMMENDED TIME OF YEAR: Mid-May best for camas; otherwise, any season.
RECOMMENDED STARTING TIME: 9:30 A.M.
ALLOW: 6 hours.
POINTS OF INTEREST
Fort Borst blockhouse
Chehalis Indian Reservation

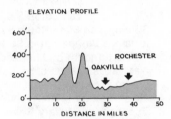

The territory around Centralia was one of the earliest to be settled in Washington State. Much of the farm and prairie land covered in this tour was originally settled under the Donation Land Claim Act of 1850, by which a married couple could stake a claim to 640 acres of land and a single person could claim 320 acres. Although the local Chehalis Indians continued to be friendly and took no part in skirmishes, the Indian Wars of 1855–56 interrupted the firming up of these claims as families took refuge at Fort Henness near Rochester. The blockhouse at Fort Borst Park was used as a secure granary to supply troops in the White and Puyallup valleys. Originally located at the junction of the Chehalis and Skookumchuck rivers, the blockhouse was moved to its present location in 1923 and presented to the city of Centralia as a memorial to early-day settlers by a descendant of the original donation land claim owners, Mary Adeline and Joseph Borst. Only a granite monument marks the location of Fort Henness (see Tour #121).

The natural prairies and bottom lands along the Chehalis and Skookumchuck rivers had already been spoken for when settlers began to locate along Lincoln Creek. Stands of huge virgin timber, felled and stacked in gigantic piles, burned for days and nights as the clearing job continued. The logging industry was yet to come, and the trees were only a nuisance.

Deer, bear elk, grouse, and tremendous flocks of ducks and geese provided easy pickings for cougars, incoming settlers, and the coastal Indian residents. Game was plentiful, and fish were there for the catching in the many lakes, streams, and rivers.

Chances are still good for seeing a wild animal or two along the backroads of this tour. Winter and early spring bring the best sightings of the elusive tundra swan or the ubiquitous mallard and striking pintail. The distant, very low hooting of a blue grouse lends an eerie quality to the woodland summits. Occasionally a red-shafted flicker or Harris woodpecker plays a staccato accompaniment on an old resonant snag, and swallows of

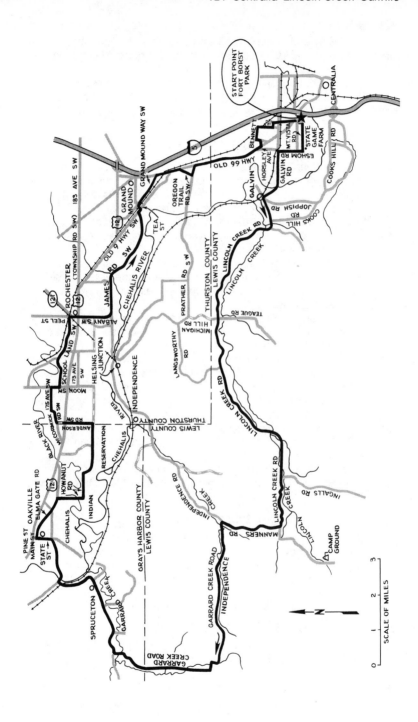

many varieties fly and swoop over fields all summer. Meadowlarks sing all year. The blue camas lily, once a staple in the diet of the Chehalis Indians, blooms profusely along the roads of this tour.

This bicycle tour nudges the mind to visions and sounds of the past with miles of traffic-free roads, then brings it up short and back to the present on the return to Fort Borst Park alongside noisy I-5.

MILEAGE LOG

0.0 Fort Borst Park, Centralia. Leave west entrance of park and proceed west through the junior high school parking lot past the tennis courts. Go around end of school yard fence next to tennis court, through gateway in second fence, and continue on **Mt. Vista Road**.

1.0 Right turn on **Eshom Road** past Centralia High School.

1.9 Turn left on **Galvin Road** and travel into the countryside past a large dairy farm. Cross Chehalis River at 2.6.

3.2 Follow left with the main thoroughfare in Galvin as the road is renamed **Lincoln Creek Road**. Continue along the valley for several miles. Houses, orchards, and farm buildings hug the hillside along the edge of the valley.

15.1 Turn right and uphill on **Manners Road** toward Independence as the valley of Lincoln Creek narrows to its end. Top a summit and coast down into Independence Creek Valley.

17.0 Turn left on **Garrard Creek Road**; cross Independence Creek and follow along its banks. Road at first is narrow and rough but widens out as it climbs to a summit at mile 20.0. Descend into another valley and pass a small fire station. Enter Grays Harbor County at mile 23.5.

24.5 Keep right toward Oakville as sign points left to Brooklyn.

28.2 Cross railroad tracks on overpass, turn right at stop sign, cross Chehalis River, and continue through the Chehalis Indian Reservation.

29.6 Bear left with main thoroughfare at crossroads and enter Oakville on **State Street**. City park at corner of State and Main streets at mile 30.0. Grocery store, drive-in, and restaurant along U.S. 12 (Pine Street).

30.0 Head east out of Oakville on **Main Street**. As it leaves town the road is renamed **Elma Gate Road**. This is an old concrete highway with blacktop overlay. Many oak trees in the yards and pastures.

31.5 Turn right on **Howanut Road**, which crosses the Black River at mile 32.1 and bends left. Chehalis Indian Reservation Tribal Center on the right at the top of a rise.

34.7 Left turn on **Anderson Road S.W.** This is the county line between Grays Harbor and Thurston counties.

35.6 Cross U.S. 12 and continue on Anderson. Endure 0.3 miles of gravel.

35.9 Right turn on **McCormick Road S.W.** as Anderson ends and enter Thurston County. Road bends left, then right, and becomes 175 **Avenue S.W.**

36.9 Right turn on **Moon Road S.W.**

37.2 Left turn on **School Land Road S.W.** Black River rolls slowly along on the left.

39.4 Road bends right and becomes **Albany Street S.W.**

39.5 Cross railroad tracks and enter Rochester as **State Route 121** joins from the left. Cross U.S. 12 at 39.6; drive-in and grocery. Continue out of Rochester on Albany Street.

40.7 Bear left on **James Road S.W.** as it joins from the right. Pass several dairy farms.

44.2 Join **Old 9 Highway S.W.**, bear right, then immediately turn left on **Tea Street S.W.** Cross railroad tracks and turn right on **Grand Mound Way S.W.** State of Washington Maple Lane School is on the right across railroad tracks and Old 9 Highway.

45.3 Right turn on **Old 99 Highway S.W.** as Grand Mound Way ends.

45.7 Continue on Old 99 Highway as Old 9 comes in from the right.

46.0 Right turn on **Oregon Trail Road S.W.** for a short diversion away from the traffic on Old 99 Highway.

46.4 Left turn on **Prather Road S.W.**

46.7 Right turn on **Old 99 Highway S.W.** by gas-grocery. Enter Lewis County at mile 47.2 as rough, oiled shoulders along this busy old concrete highway give way to smooth blacktop.

48.8 Left turn on **Horsely Avenue** by antique shop.

49.0 Left turn on **Foron Road**.

49.1 Right turn on **Bennett Road** and follow it as it turns right at mile 49.4 and becomes **Van Wormer Street**.

49.9 Turn left through a cemetery. Turn right on **Johnson Road** on the other side. Cross railroad tracks and continue south to Fort Borst Park.

50.4 End of tour at parking lot in Fort Borst Park.

125 CENTRALIA–BUNKER CREEK–INDEPENDENCE

STARTING POINT: Fort Borst Park in Centralia. Take I-5 to exit 82. The park is one block southwest of the interchange. Park in the park office parking lot, across from the ball diamond.

DISTANCE: 48 miles.
TERRAIN: Moderate to hilly.
TOTAL CUMULATIVE ELEVATION GAIN: 900 feet.
RECOMMENDED TIME OF YEAR: Any season.
RECOMMENDED STARTING TIME: 9:30 A.M.
ALLOW: 6 hours.
POINTS OF INTEREST
Fort Borst blockhouse
Claquato historic sign

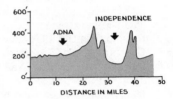

Although claimed by U.S. settlers over a century ago, the valleys of Lewis County are still sparsely settled in comparison to the neighboring counties of Pierce and King to the north. The Donation Land Claim Act of 1850 and the Homestead Act of 1862 allowed early farmers to acquire land with minor capital outlay, providing that it be brought under cultivation. Names of the original settlers are reflected in street and place names.

Crops of corn, barley, and oats flourish in the bottom land along the Chehalis River. Fields of lush green grass provide summer grazing for the many dairy herds as well as pungent silage for the winter months. During the rainy season, low-lying areas flood as they did a century ago, receiving upland silt to add to soil fertility and providing wintering sites for flocks of ducks and occasional swans. Deer appear near edges of pastures but vanish into the forest as bicycles approach.

Virgin forest long ago gave way to the axes and saws of settlers and lumberjacks, who cleared the valleys and denuded the hills. Rivers provided the original transportation arteries, but as farming and lumbering moved inland, railroads made their way up the valleys. In Lincoln Creek Valley remnants of the railroad, which operated into the 1930s, still protrude from creekbanks. As the roads were poor or nonexistent, railroads became the sole means of transportation. Household goods, supplies, and crops were moved by handcar along the rails, and children walked to and from school along the tracks. Eventually the trees were all cut and many of the railroads abandoned. Roads were built and gradually improved. All of the rural roads now are paved, providing delightful bicycle routes.

From the valleys Mt. St. Helens is visible on the southeastern horizon. As the bicyclist of today climbs to the summit of Michigan Hill and gazes eastward, Mt. Rainier presents its everlasting snow-covered and glaciated face as it did to the settler of yesteryear. Peaceful rural farmlands, pleasant forest settings, and expansive mountain vistas guarantee an enjoyable bicycle tour.

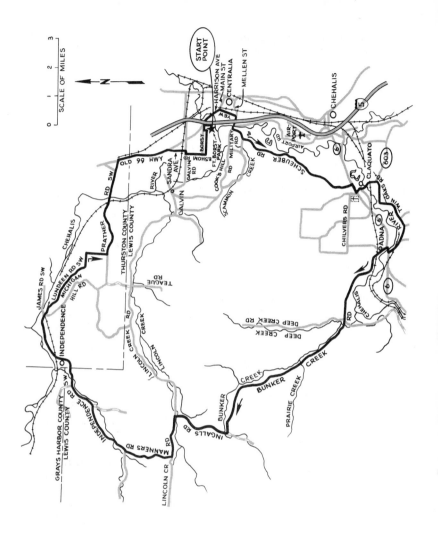

MILEAGE LOG

0.0 From the parking lot head east through the park past the ball field and around the park loop road, observing the one-way traffic regulations.

0.3 At the northeast corner of the park take sidewalk right toward I-5 underpass and continue right on **Harrison Avenue**. A ramped sidewalk is available here. Bear left with thoroughfare at mile 1.1 as it changes name to **W. Main**.

1.2 Right turn on **Yew Street**.

1.7 Turn right on **Mellen Street** and again go under the freeway. Cross the Chehalis River at mile 2.1.

2.2 Turn left on **Military Road.**

2.9 Another left turn on **Scheuber Road** as it heads into the countryside. Views of Mt. Rainier and Mt. St. Helens as the road undulates.

7.7 Right turn on **State Route 6** as Scheuber Road comes to an end. Interesting historical sign at Claquato at 7.9.

8.0 Turn left on **State Route 603** and cross the Chehalis River.

8.7 Right turn on **Twin Oaks Road.** Although the original oaks are gone, two sets of twin oaks remain to justify the name. Pedal through acres of cultivated cropland.

12.3 Turn right on **State Route 6** and cross the Chehalis River.

12.6 Turn left on **Bunker Creek Road** and enter Adna. Grocery store on the left. Continue out of town along Bunker Creek and into valley farmland.

23.0 Turn right on **Ingalls Road** as Bunker Creek Road goes left to a dead end. Route begins to climb out of the valley, topping a summit at mile 24.0.

25.3 Cross Lincoln Creek, then immediately turn left on **Lincoln Creek Road.** Small single-engine fire station at mile 26.

26.8 Right turn on **Manners Road** and climb over a hill.

28.7 Keep right with **Independence Road S.W.** toward Rochester as Garrard Creek Road goes left to Oakville. Cross Independence Creek at mile 29.0; possible lunch stop. Pedal into rolling farmland, entering Thurston County at mile 32.8. Cross railroad tracks at 33.6 and ride along the Chehalis River.

35.4 Turn right on **Michigan Hill Road S.W.**, duck under a low railroad trestle, then turn left on **Lundeen Road S.W.** and start climbing a steep hill. Views of Chehalis Valley and Mt. Rainier at mile 36.4. *Note: Continuing on Independence Road leads to Rochester and food services.*

39.2 Turn left on **Prather Road S.W.** as Lundeen Road ends. Begin a gradual descent. Cross railroad tracks at mile 41.3 and the Chehalis River at 41.4.

42.9 Turn right on **Old 99 Highway S.W.** at stop sign by gas-grocery. Reenter Lewis County at mile 43.3.

44.8 Turn right on **Sandra Avenue.**

45.5 Turn right on **Galvin Road**, then left on **Eshom Road.**

46.2 Left turn on **Borst Avenue.**

47.2 Right turn on **Belmont Avenue** at entrance to Fort Borst Park.

47.5 End of ride.

126 HANAFORD VALLEY

STARTING POINT: Fort Borst Park in Centralia. Take I-5 to exit 82. The park is one block southwest of the interchange. Park in the park office parking lot, across from the ball diamond.

DISTANCE: 38 miles.
TERRAIN: Some hilly, some flat.
TOTAL CUMULATIVE ELEVATION GAIN: 1050 feet.
RECOMMENDED TIME OF YEAR: May is recommended for spring flowers.
RECOMMENDED STARTING TIME: 9:30 A.M.
ALLOW: 5 hours plus time for optional steam plant tour.
POINTS OF INTEREST
Centralia Steam Electric Project

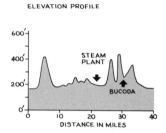

ELEVATION PROFILE

The botanist, the bird watcher, and the electric power engineer all will find features of interest in this tour. In spring the wild blue camas lily, a native of the Chehalis Valley, provides large masses of color. Its onionlike bulb was an important food to the coastal Indians, and camas fields were tribal property jealously guarded against trespassers. The lavender tough-leaved wild iris decorates the roadside along cuts and fills. Serviceberry bushes, some growing to a height of 15 feet, add clouds of white blossoms to the scene. The white plumes of the false solomon's seal and the delicate twin white bells of the Oregon fairy bells arch from the banks along the road. Later on, berries replace the blossoms. In the Hanaford Valley, virtually pure stands of timber-sized Oregon ash trees (a hardwood forest is unusual in western Washington), plus common inhabitants of the montane forest, such as sword fern and bleeding heart, make this tour a botanist's delight.

The roadside terrain, alternating between valley, prairie, and forest, offers opportunities for seeing and hearing a wide variety of birds. The savannah sparrow and the goldfinch share the prairie with the robin, meadowlark, swallow, and red-shafted flicker. Buteos soar the thermal updrafts along the hillside. In the forest, the winter wren spews out his high-pitched rapid-fire aria. Vireos, kinglets, and warblers stay high in the trees, only their distinctive songs revealing their presence. Add to this the display of exotic pheasants at the game farm close to the starting point, and you have a tour for the bird freak.

As the bicyclist rounds a bend in the Hanaford Valley, Mt. Rainier shows its three peaks, then the Centralia Steam Electric Plant with its two tall smokestacks comes into view. On the right, four banks of evaporative cooling towers send billows of fog shooting into the air. Alongside the plant a large blue rectangular lake forms a surge reservoir for cooling water. Entrance to the green lawns and parking lot beside the Visitors Center is through a guarded fence. Guided plant tours, available July through March, must be arranged beforehand by contacting the plant supervisor, Route 2,

Box 42, Centralia, WA 98531. At the Visitors Center interesting pictorial displays explain coal mining, power production, and ecological restoration projects.

The Centralia Steam Electric Project went on line in 1971, the culmination of more than a decade of planning and development work by the electric-power industry of the Pacific Northwest. Large low-sulfur soft coal reserves that provide the fuel for this plant are mined by economical surface methods, and the land is rehabilitated to productive uses as the mining progresses.

Next to the plant a giant machine gnaws at huge piles of coal, reminding one of a big gold-mining dredge as it sits between the morainelike coal piles, swinging its huge bucket-toothed wheel, gulping up coal, and sending it to the furnace via a network of covered, inclined beltways. A road overpass allows enormous trucks to haul the coal from the mine to the processing plant.

Views of the open-pit mine areas from the hill roads east of the old town site of Tono are impressive: whole mountains have been gnawed away. A brisk dash down the final hill is followed by a crossing of the Skookumchuck River at the edge of the old historic town of Bucoda, the site of the first territorial prison, whose inmates worked in the adjacent coal mine.

Traffic picks up on State Route 507 as the route winds through Waunch Prairie and follows the Skookumchuck River back to Centralia.

MILEAGE LOG

0.0 Fort Borst Park in Centralia. Leave the west entrance of the park, proceed through the junior high school parking lot past tennis courts. Go around end of schoolyard fence next to tennis court, go through gateway in second fence, and continue on **Mt. Vista Road**. Lewis County Game Farm displays pens of pheasants. Road bends right by Centralia High School and is renamed **Eshom Road**.

1.6 Turn left on **Galvin Road** as Eshom ends, and proceed past dairy farms. Cross Chehalis River at mile 2.6.

3.1 Turn left on **Joppish Road** in Galvin and proceed out of town. Enjoy the flora and fauna as this delightful traffic-free road leaves the valley and winds through the forested hillside to upland pasture areas.

4.9 Turn left on **Cooks Hill Road** as Joppish Road ends at the summit of the hill. Descend hill and enter Centralia on a broad, concrete road. Pass Centralia General Hospital and continue under I-5, where the road name changes to **Mellen Street (State Route 507)**. Follow S.R. 507 as it is marked **Alder Street** and **S. Cherry Street** in succession.

8.7 Right turn on **S. Silver Street** as a traffic light appears one block ahead on Cherry.

9.1 Turn left on **Summa Street**, cross railroad tracks and both one-way lanes of State Route 507, and head out into an open green valley, where the road is renamed **E. Summa Street** and finally **Salzer Valley Road**.

12.9 Bear left with main thoroughfare as Reinke Road (dead end) goes on. Climb a short, gentle hill, then tackle a longer, steeper one.

15.0 Don't miss this left turn on **Little Hanaford Road** as L. Hanaford Road continues on. Go past a dip in the road and immediately turn right on **Teitzel Road**, which shortly emerges into the valley of South Hanaford Creek.

16.7 Turn left with Teitzel Road as Teitzel Road E. goes right.

19.5 Turn right on **Big Hanaford Road**. Mt. Rainier visible at the end of the valley. Soon the twin smokestacks of the Centralia Steam Electric Plant come into view.

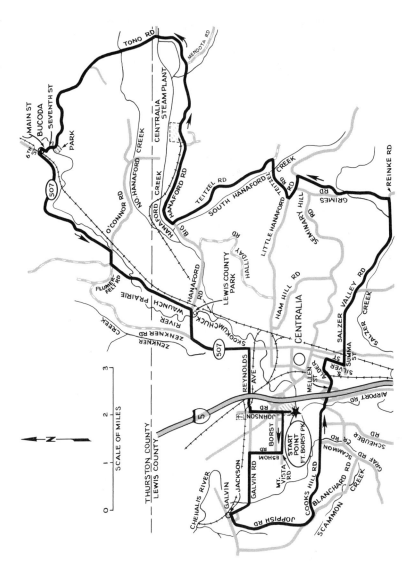

21.4   Left turn into steam plant's main office entrance drive. *Note: If a guided tour has been arranged, report to the security gate.* Permission should be requested for a short snack break on the front steps or lawn. Return out the entrance gate and continue left on Big Hanaford Road past the power plant and coal piles.

24.4   Turn left on **Tono Road S.E.** after crossing Hanaford Creek. The road traverses two summits with a creek valley between. As the road descends from the second summit, the gigantic excavation of the open-pit coal mine comes into view. Bucoda Volunteer Park appears on the left just before the road crosses the Skookumchuck River. Park has tables and a shelter. Children swim in the placid river by the park. Cross bridge and enter Bucoda on **7th Street**.

28.4   Turn right on **Main Street**. Tavern, grocery, and post office. Turn left on **6th Street**, then left on **State Route 507** toward Centralia. Cross Skookumchuck River at 32.3 as Waunch Prairie broadens out. Enter Lewis County at 33.0.

33.8   Bear right with highway and cross the Skookumchuck River as Hanaford Road goes left to the steam plant. Lewis County Schafer Park on east bank of the river. Enter Centralia on **Downing Street**, which bends left by grocery and becomes **N. Pearl Street**.

35.7   Turn right on **Reynolds Avenue** shortly before Pearl Street crosses railroad tracks and steel bridge over the Skookumchuck. Cross railroad tracks under I-5 viaduct at mile 36.7. Bear left and right with Reynolds over more tracks at 36.9.

37.1   Turn left on **Johnson Road**. Cross Harrison Avenue at light at 37.5.

37.8   Back at parking lot in Fort Borst Park.

127 CENTRALIA–CHEHALIS

STARTING POINT: Fort Borst Park in Centralia. Take I-5 to exit 82. The park is one block southwest of the interchange. Park in the park office parking lot, across from the ball diamond.

DISTANCE: 25 miles.
TERRAIN: Mostly flat (two hills).
TOTAL CUMULATIVE ELEVATION GAIN: 600 feet.
RECOMMENDED TIME OF YEAR: Any season. Roads may be under water during spring floods.
RECOMMENDED STARTING TIME: 9 A.M. to 2 P.M.
ALLOW: 3 to 4 hours.
POINTS OF INTEREST
Claquato Cemetery
Claquato Church
Alexander Park

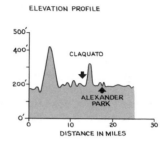

ELEVATION PROFILE

This 25-mile loop tour between Centralia and Chehalis follows the backroads of the Chehalis River Valley west of I-5. A climb up to the summit of Cook Hill comes near the start of the ride to give the bicyclist a short workout. When joined with Millersylvania-Centralia (#51), Morton-Millersylvania (#50), Chehalis–Lewis and Clark State Park (#128), or Rainbow Falls–Seaquest (#132), this tour provides a vital link in north-south backroad bicycle routes of western Washington State.

Dairy and beef cattle graze the pastures near the Chehalis River as the route leaves Centralia and touches the southeastern tip of the valley of Lincoln Creek. Leaving the valley, the route climbs the forested hillside to upland pastures before plunging back downhill into the outskirts of Centralia and heading south. Mt. St. Helens, with its abruptly truncated volcanic cone, appears on the southeastern horizon. Views into the past history of early Lewis County are offered by a side trip up the Claquato Cemetery hill.

Alexander Park provides a pleasant spot for the summer picnic lunch, where a beach on the Chehalis River invites swimmers. For cold-weather bicycle tourists, restaurants in downtown Chehalis are easily reached via the sidewalk under I-5 near State Route 6. The fragrant aroma of peppermint announces the closeness of the Chehalis industrial district; the I. P. Callison and Sons plant is one of the major processors of peppermint oil, extracting the flavoring from freshly mowed peppermint leaves brought by the truckload over the Cascades from the Yakima Valley.

Numerous oxbow lakes along the airport road attract several varieties of ducks, while the osprey, or fish hawk, occasionally dives in to garner his share of the aquatic population.

Always interesting and often provocative, the Hamilton Farms signboard to the right of Airport Road near I-5 signals the return to Centralia and the end of an enjoyable bicycle tour.

MILEAGE LOG

0.0 Fort Borst Park in Centralia. Leave the west entrance of the park, proceed through the junior high school parking lot past tennis courts. Circumvent end of schoolyard fence next to tennis court, go through gateway in second fence, and continue on **Mt. Vista Road**. Lewis County Game Farm displays pens of pheasants.

1.0 Right turn on **Eshom Road** past Centralia High School.

1.9 Left turn on **Galvin Road** and pass a dairy farm. Cross Chehalis River at mile 2.6.

3.1 Turn left on **Joppish Road** in Galvin and proceed out of town. Enjoy the flora and fauna as this delightful traffic-free road leaves the valley and winds through the forested hillside to upland pastures.

4.9 Left turn on **Cooks Hill Road** as Joppish Road ends. This is the summit; continue downhill into Centralia. Centralia General Hospital on right at mile 7.4.

7.7 Turn right on **Military Road**.

8.4 Left turn on **Scheuber Road** as it heads into the countryside. Views of Mt. Rainier and Mt. St. Helens on the southeastern horizon.

13.2 Right turn on **State Route 6** as Scheuber Road comes to an end. Interesting historical sign about Claquato at 13.3. *Note: A 0.5-mile side trip uphill on Stearns Road leads to Claquato Cemetery, down Water Street to historic church with bronze bell, and continues downhill to S.R. 6.*

13.5 Left turn on **State Route 603** and cross Chehalis River. Cross two sets of railroad tracks before heading up a very steep hill. Top a summit at mile 14.6.

14.7 Turn left on **Tune Road** and plunge downhill.

16.3 Left turn on **Shorey Road**. Cross Newaukum River and more railroad tracks at mile 16.5, where the road is renamed **S.W. Newaukum Avenue**.

16.8 Turn left on **Sylvenus**.

16.9 Left turn on **Riverside Drive** and cross footbridge to Alexander Park, suggested lunch stop at 17.1. The park has a snack bar, kitchen shelters, playground equipment, and access to the Chehalis River. After lunch recross the footbridge, turn right on **Sylvenus**, then left again on **S.W. Newaukum Avenue**. *Note: A sidewalk goes right and under I-5 to cafes in downtown Chehalis at 17.9.* Cross State Route 6 and continue on **N.W. Louisiana Avenue**.

18.4 Left turn on **N.W. Airport Road** as N.W. West Street goes right over I-5 to downtown Chehalis. Pass Riverside Golf Course at mile 18.6. Several oxbow ponds attract ducks and osprey at 20.7. Hamilton Farm signboard is on right along I-5.

22.2 Right turn on **Mellen Street (State Route 507);** go under I-5 and into Centralia.

22.5 Left turn on **Yew Street**.

23.1 Left on **W. Main Street**.

23.2 Bear right as thoroughfare changes name to **Harrison Avenue** and ducks under I-5.

24.1 Turn left on **Belmont Avenue** and enter Fort Borst Park. Turn right by restrooms toward ball field.
24.3 Back to parking lot; end of ride.

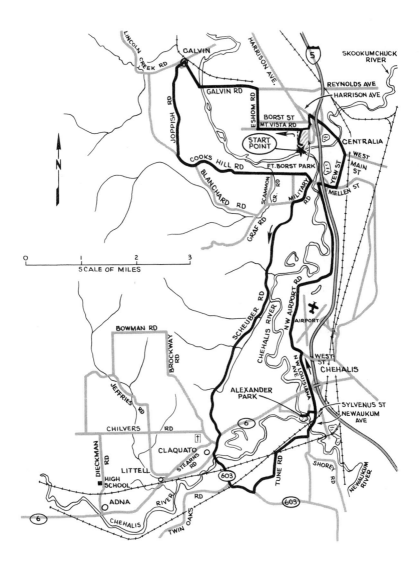

128 CHEHALIS–LEWIS AND CLARK STATE PARK (Newaukum Valley)

STARTING POINT: Public parking lot in downtown Chehalis. Take I-5 to exit 77 (State Route 6). Turn east and enter Chehalis on Main Street. Parking lot is at corner of Main Street and Railroad Avenue next to railroad tracks.

DISTANCE: 34 miles.
TERRAIN: Easy to moderate.
TOTAL CUMULATIVE ELEVATION GAIN: 750 feet.
RECOMMENDED TIME OF YEAR: Any season.
RECOMMENDED STARTING TIME: 9 A.M. to 2 P.M.
ALLOW: 4 hours.
POINTS OF INTEREST
Chehalis Recreation Park
Jackson Prairie School
Jackson Courthouse Historic Site
Lewis and Clark State Park

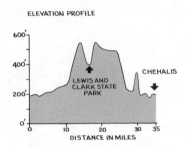

ELEVATION PROFILE

Lewis County dates back to 1845, when the area lying north of the Columbia River to latitude 54° 40' and west of the Cowlitz River to the Pacific Ocean was designated as separate from Vancouver County. All of this happened before the Oregon Territory was created in 1848 and before the boundary between the United States and Canada had been finalized. By the time Washington Territory became a fact of life in 1853, Pacific, Thurston, King, Pierce, Jefferson, and Island counties had been carved from Lewis County. The remaining counties west of the Cascade Mountains evolved from these and all were in existence by the time Washington entered the union in 1889. Chehalis has been the Lewis County seat since 1872, when the honor was snatched away from the declining little town of Claquato. (Attracting the Northern Pacific Railroad to Chehalis helped to swing the decision.)

Today, Claquato is marked by a historical sign along State Route 6, while Chehalis is a modern, thriving city. The residents of Chehalis are proud of its history and display two important monuments of the past in their recreation park: an old logging steam railway engine of the Mikado 2-8-2 type which was built by the Baldwin Company in 1917 and pulled thousands of logs during its active years; and the McKinley Stump, which was cut near Pe Ell in 1901, boasts a pagoda roof, and was erected for President McKinley's reception of that year. President Theodore Roosevelt also spoke from this stump in 1903. The production of lumber is still an important industry in and around Chehalis.

This bicycle tour also touches another famous landmark. The Jackson Prairie Courthouse near U.S. Highway 12 at Mary's Corner is the oldest standing building used for courthouse purposes in the State of Washington. It was built as a private home in 1850 and became an important stopping place for travelers in Washington Territory.

History of a different sort is evident at the Lewis and Clark State Park. Columbus Day 1962 brought a storm of hurricane proportions to the State of Washington. Many big trees were toppled in the high winds, and the camping area in this state park was devastated. A young Douglas fir forest now surrounds the rebuilt campground. Amazingly enough, the big trees along the extensive nature trail in the park were not blown over and present an interesting and informative two- to three-mile hike.

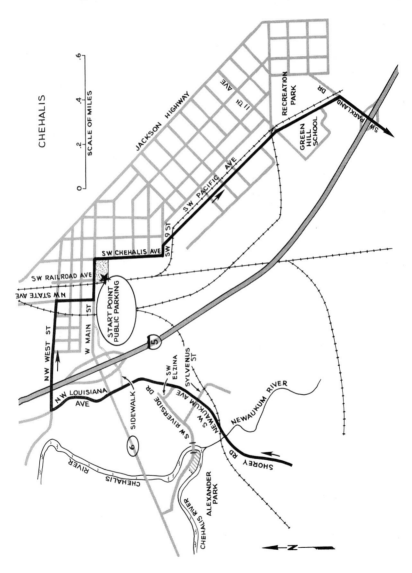

MILEAGE LOG

0.0 Chehalis public parking lot. Head east on **W. Main Street** from **S.W. Railroad Avenue**, then turn right on **S.W. Chehalis Avenue**. Road bends left at 0.8 and becomes **S.W. 9th Street**.

0.9 Right turn on **S.W. Pacific Avenue**. Washington State's Green Hill School on the right.

1.3 Turn right on **S.W. Parkland Drive**. Chehalis Recreation Park is on the left; old steam locomotive and McKinley Stump.

1.6 Cross I-5 on overpass and ride out into farmland along the Newaukum River. Chehalis's Stan Hedwall Park at mile 1.7 has camping, picnic shelters, and playground. Road name changes to **Rice Road**.

4.0 Left turn on **LaBree Road** as Rice Road ends.

4.4 Right turn on **Hamilton Road** as LaBree Road turns left.

5.8 Turn right with Hamiton Road as Hamilton Road North goes left.

6.5 Turn left under freeway on **Rush Road**, and immediately turn right on **Kirkland Road**. Cross Newaukum River at mile 7.0.

9.0 Left turn on **Forest Napavine Road E.** as Kirkland Road ends.

10.2 Turn right on **Jackson Highway**. Lewis County Road Department Central Shop is on the right. Good five-foot-wide paved shoulders. Cross State Route 508 at mile 11.7 and proceed up moderate grade. Jackson Prairie School, built in early 1900s, now houses an antique shop on the right at 13.8. Matilda Jackson Roadside Park on right at mile 13.9; picnic shelter with tables surrounded by many large fir trees. *Note: Tour may be shortened by 4.5 miles by turning right on Avery Road at mile 14.0.*

14.3 Cross U.S. 12 at Mary's Corner. Jackson Courthouse Historic Site just beyond on the left.

15.9 Right turn into Lewis and Clark State Park; picnic area with shelters, camping sites, and nature trail. Allow 0.5 mile for bicycling around the park.

16.4 Leave park entrance and turn left on Jackson Highway. Cross U.S. 12 at Mary's Corner at mile 18.2.

18.5 Turn left on **Avery Road East** by Loggers World.

20.5 Turn right on **U.S. 12** and cross I-5; delicatessen and two cafes.

21.5 Turn right on **N. Military Road** at stop sign.

22.5 Left turn on **Koontz Road** as Military Road ends. As it enters Napavine, the road is renamed **E. Washington Street**.

23.9 Right turn on **2nd Avenue East** in Napavine by grocery. Mayme Shaddock Park on left at 24.4. Second Avenue becomes **Rush Road** as it leaves Napavine and descends a long hill.

25.8 Left turn on **Newaukum Valley Road** just before Rush Road crosses the Newaukum River. Road traverses the hillside along the edge of the valley, providing nice views of the farms.

28.6 Turn left and uphill on **Rogers Road**. Cross Burlington Northern main-line tracks at mile 29.6 and continue up a short, steep hill.

29.9 Right turn on **Shorey Road** and coast down hill. Shorey Road becomes **S.W. Newaukum Avenue** just after crossing the Newaukum River at mile 32. Alexander Park is to the left on Sylvenus Street and

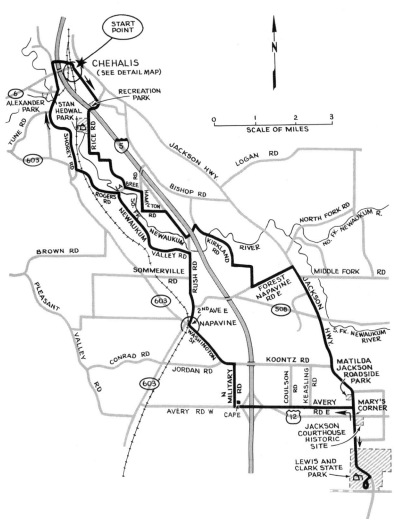

across bridge closed to motor traffic. This day-use-only park has picnic facilities, swimming beach on the Chehalis River, and a food concession open during summer months. *Note: To shorten tour by 0.5 mile, turn right on sidewalk under I-5 to Main Street at mile 32.6.* Cross State Route 6 at mile 32.7 and continue on **N.W. Louisiana Avenue.**

33.1 Turn right on **N.W. West Street** as N.W. Airport Road goes left, and cross I-5 on overpass.

33.6 Right turn on **N.W. State Avenue** just past first set of railroad tracks.

33.9 Turn left on **W. Main Street**, cross railroad tracks, and return to parking lot at mile 34.0.

129 LEWIS AND CLARK STATE PARK– ONALASKA

STARTING POINT: Lewis and Clark State Park. Take exit 68 from I-5, then U.S. 12 east 2.7 miles to Mary's Corner. Turn right (south) on Jackson Highway and proceed 1.6 miles to the park entrance. Park in the picnic area parking lot.

DISTANCE: 45 miles.
TERRAIN: Some hilly, some flat.
TOTAL CUMULATIVE ELEVATION GAIN: 1450 feet.
RECOMMENDED TIME OF YEAR: Any season. September through November best for salmon hatchery tour, last Sunday in August for Steam Threshing Bee.
RECOMMENDED STARTING TIME: 9 to 10 A.M.
ALLOW: 6 to 8 hours.
POINTS OF INTEREST
Lewis and Clark State Park
Jackson Courthouse Historic Site
Cowlitz Salmon Hatchery
Cowlitz Trout Hatchery
Cowlitz Mission

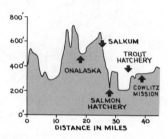

ELEVATION PROFILE

During the years in which the Hudson's Bay Company traded in the Pacific Northwest, it operated a farming subsidiary called the Puget Sound Agricultural Company. Some of the most productive land was the natural prairie north of the Cowlitz River near Toledo in Lewis County. Although the Cowlitz Prairie is no longer a major producer of hay and grains, it still offers the wide horizons of an open prairie, cultivated by "gentleman farmers" and grazed by a few operating dairy farms. An interesting historic attraction is the St. Francis Xavier (Cowlitz) Mission, which staked one of the early donation land claims on the prairie. Founded in 1838, the mission is the oldest in the northwest and the first Catholic Church in Washington State. The nearby cemetery is a link to the past.

To attend the Steam Threshing Bee, held the last Sunday in August at the Robert Herren Ranch on the prairie, is to step back in time. Steam-engine buffs come hundreds of miles to operate and exhibit their steam tractors. Coupled to threshers by long, twisted, flat belts, the big wood-burning engines make quick work of piles of wheat sheaves. Other steam tractors roll over the pastureland, entertaining the crowds with their shrill whistles and distinctive chuffing and hissing sounds. A steam tractor also powers a buzz saw to cut wood for the boilers. The Cowlitz Prairie is only one of the features of a bicycle tour that explores the valleys of the Newaukum and Cowlitz rivers and the ridges separating them.

The early settlers seldom lacked food, as the rivers produced a bountiful supply of fish. The Cowlitz River was one of the major sources of salmon and trout. When Tacoma City Light planned its huge hydroelectric project on the Cowlitz, it put as much planning and money into protecting and producing fish as into equipment for generating electricity. The Cowlitz Salmon Hatchery, now operated by the Washington Department of Fisheries, is the world's largest. The trout hatchery raises and releases thousands of steelhead, sea-run cutthroat, and rainbow trout into the Cowlitz River. Visits to these facilities top off this vigorous and scenic bicycle tour.

"It's called Usnea Longissima, Charlie... Charlie?"

MILEAGE LOG

0.0 Picnic area parking lot, Lewis and Clark State Park. Follow park road to exit and turn left on **Jackson Highway**. Jackson Courthouse Historic Site on right at mile 1.7. Cross U.S. 12 at mile 1.8; Matilda Jackson Roadside Park on left 0.4 mile farther. Head downhill and cross State Route 508 at mile 4.3.

5.4 Turn right on **Middle Fork Road** and cross South Fork Newaukum River at 5.8.

6.1 Left turn on **Rosebrook Road**. North Fork Newaukum appears on right as road bends left.

7.6 Right turn on **North Fork Road** as Rosebrook ends. Cross the North Fork Newaukum River on a one-lane bridge and enter a lovely wide valley. Although frequently bathed in clouds and fog, Mt. Rainier sometimes looms over the pastoral greensward.

11.2 Turn right on **Centralia Alpha Road** and cross North Fork Newaukum River. Start up a long hill through dense second-growth forest of alder and fir. Long, yarnlike strands of lichen (*Usnea longissima*) hang from the tree branches. Top a summit at mile 13.0, dive downhill, cross a creek, and climb to a second summit, where the road levels out.

15.0 Right turn on **Beck Road**.

16.3 Right turn on **Middle Fork Road** as Beck Road ends.

17.2 Turn left on **Deggler Road** toward Onalaska. Plunge downhill and into a broad, open valley. A tall smokestack marks the location of an old lumber mill as Mt. St. Helens comes into view on the southern horizon. Road name changes to **Carlisle Avenue** as it enters Onalaska. A small park is on the left by the high school; a diminutive drive-in on the right. Cross State Route 508 at mile 18.9 and continue on **Leonard Road;** grocery and cafe on left. Cross South Fork Newaukum River at 19.2.

19.8 Turn left on **Burchett Road** and proceed uphill past small farms and woodlots.

22.3 Right turn on **Fred Plant Road** at bottom of a downhill grade.

23.5 Left turn on **Gore Road** as Fred Plant Road ends. Road winds through hay fields before heading down a short, steep hill.

25.6 Turn right on **Stowell Road** as Gore Road ends, and enter Salkum.

25.9 Turn right on **Salkum Road;** Salkum Drive-in at mile 26. Cross U.S. 12 at mile 26.1 and continue through pastureland on **Fuller Road** as it descends toward the river.

27.3 Left turn on **Spencer Road** as Fuller Road ends on a cliff overlooking the Cowlitz River. Descend 0.7 mile to the Cowlitz Salmon Hatchery for an interesting, self-guided tour of this facility. Guided tours may be arranged by contacting Public Relations, Tacoma Department of Public Utilities. After touring the hatchery, return to Spencer Road and proceed along the high bluff above the Cowlitz River. Long strings of pale green lichen, some eight to ten feet long, decorate the trees.

33.9 Turn left 0.3 mile to visit the Cowlitz Trout Hatchery and Visitors

Center, hours 8 A.M. to 5 P.M. Tour the hatchery and landscaped visitors center, then return to Spencer Road.

34.5   Turn left and continue uphill on **Spencer Road**. The road dips into a small creek valley and emerges on the broad, cultivated Cowlitz Prairie. The horizon broadens to the Olympic Mountains in the west, Mt. Rainier in the east, and Mt. St. Helens in the south. At mile 39.0 pass the Robert Herren Ranch, location of the annual Steam Threshing Bee. The Cowlitz Mission sits atop a hill at mile 39.8. St. Mary's Center shares the panoramic site.

40.1   Right turn on **Jackson Highway**. Pass the Toledo-Winlock Airport at mile 40.7.

43.9   Turn left into Lewis and Clark State Park. Follow park road traffic pattern past the restrooms to the picnic area parking lot. End of ride at mile 44.3.

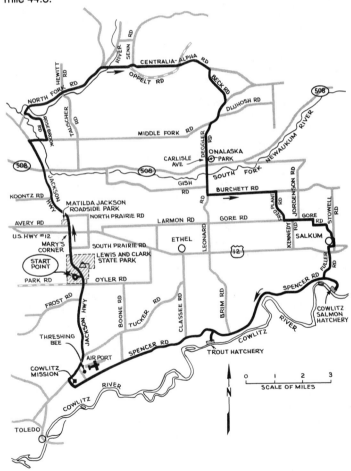

130 ADNA–LEWIS AND CLARK STATE PARK

STARTING POINT: Back Memorial Lewis County Park in Adna. Take I-5 to exit 77 (State Route 6). Turn west, proceed 4.5 miles to Adna, turn right on Bunker Creek Road, right on Dieckman Road, then right again into park. Gate is locked at 8 P.M.

DISTANCE: 48 miles.
TERRAIN: Half hilly, half flat; 5 miles of steep gravel road.
TOTAL CUMULATIVE ELEVATION GAIN: 2000 feet.
RECOMMENDED TIME OF YEAR: August through October for best condition of gravel road.
RECOMMENDED STARTING TIME: 8 to 9:30 A.M.
ALLOW: 5 to 7 hours.
POINTS OF INTEREST
Winolequa Park, Winlock
St. Urban Church
Lewis and Clark State Park
Jackson Courthouse Historic Site

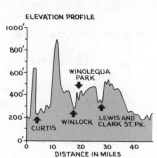

This 48-mile tour in Lewis County covers many different types of terrain, giving the bicyclist a chance to observe and experience several changes of scenery. After a very short stretch of the Chehalis Valley, the route heads steeply up the hill toward Curtis. Acres of neatly sheared Christmas trees cover much of the countryside, while young Douglas fir forests cling to the steeper slopes and give promise of continued timber harvests in years to come. Oak and ash trees mingle with alder, willow, fir, and maple as the route follows the valley along Lake Creek. Several old homesteads, long abandoned, nestle among vines and shrubs that almost engulf them. Other old homes present a picture of continued interest and intensive care.

The route follows a steep gravel road as it traverses the ridge northwest of Winlock and winds uphill through dense second-growth forest of fir and cedar. Pavement again covers the road surface as habitations lay claim to isolated clearings.

Open grassy fields, ringed with fir and cedar trees, identify Grand Prairie east of Winlock. A short side trip leads to Winlock's delightful Winolequa Park, which derives the latter half of its name from adjacent Olequa Creek. A large, well-equipped kitchen shelter serves the many picnic tables scattered among the trees. After a short meander along the rolling plateau, the route dips to the valley again, where thick stands of Oregon ash, oak, and aspen trees present an unusual display of deciduous hardwood forest. A two- to three-mile nature trail in Lewis and Clark State Park offers an opportunity to view virgin fir and cedar trees and to identify many other lowland flora such as devil's club, hazelnut, vine maple, and the unusual inside-out flower. As the tour climbs to the plateau again and continues across Jackson Prairie, gladioli thrive in the soil, presenting a colorful display during summer months.

Fields of wheat, oats, corn, and grass cover the fertile mouth of Pleasant Valley all summer long. Sprinkler irrigation systems provide added moisture to ensure a bountiful harvest. Peas are an important early crop.

Varied scenery, low-traffic roads, and occasional views of both Mt. Rainier and Mt. St. Helens add the crowning touch to an enjoyable bicycle tour.

MILEAGE LOG

0.0   Back Memorial Park parking lot. Go out entrance road and turn left on **Dieckman Road**.

0.3   Left turn on **Bunker Creek Road**.

0.5   Turn right on **State Route 6** and cross the Chehalis River. Grocery. Watch for acute-angled railroad tracks at mile 1.0.

1.6   Turn left on **Curtis Hill Road**. Proceed steeply uphill past several homes. Huge old English walnut trees hang over fences near the summit at mile 3.3. Plunge downhill past a Weyerhaeuser clearcut (winter 1976–77) that has been replanted to Douglas fir trees.

4.9   Left turn on **Lake Creek Road**. Downtown Curtis, 0.1 mile farther on Curtis Hill Road, consists of a store, service station, and post office all in one building; closed on Sundays.

6.0   Turn left on **King Road** as Lake Creek Road ends. Wind past old homesteads, some in mint condition, others in disrepair and covered with vegetation. At mile 7.7 the pavement ends. The road passes several farms and woodlots before narrowing, entering forest, and topping a summit at mile 11.4. Pavement resumes at mile 12.8. Occasional homes and clearings among the trees.

18.3   Bear left across creek on **W. Fir** in Winlock. Cross State Route 603.

18.4   Cross main-line railroad tracks and turn left on **First Street**. *Note: Cafe and grocery, half block to the right on First Street, are open all week.* Follow First Street uphill and around corner, and continue on **Rhoades Road** as it joins from the right. Mt. Rainier and Mt. St. Helens appear on the southeastern horizon as Rhodes Road wanders back and forth across upland pastures.

19.3   Continue on **Rhoades Road North** (dead end) as Rhoades Road turns right. Enter Winolequa Park at mile 19.7. Constructed by Winlock Jaycees and concerned citizens, this park was dedicated to the Vietnam veterans in 1975. A well-equipped kitchen shelter may be reserved for group usage; contact Winlock City Hall for reservations. Return to Rhoades Road intersection.

20.0   Turn left (east) on **Rhoades Road** from Rhoades Road North.

21.2   Left turn on **Minkler Road** as Rhoades Road ends.

22.3   Bear right on **Sargent Road** as Minkler Road ends. St. Urban Church of the Assumption, built 1891, on the right at mile 23.3. Cross I-5 on an overpass at mile 23.7.

24.3   Right turn on **Meier Road** as Park Road goes on.

25.3   Left turn on **Hart Road** and head down into a valley.

26.3   Continue on **Frost Road** as it joins from the right. Large grassy field surrounds a clump of oak, aspen, and ash trees.

27.9   Turn left on **Jackson Highway**. Wide, paved shoulder.

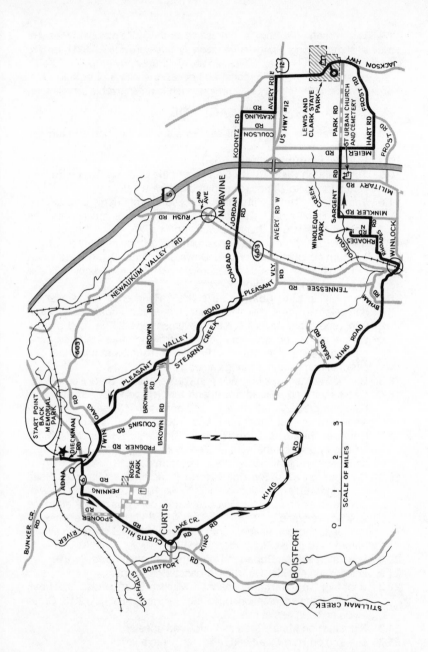

28.8   Left turn into Lewis and Clark State Park; camping, picnicking, kitchen shelters, and nature trail. Follow the loop drive around the park.

29.3   Leave park and turn left on **Jackson Highway**. Jackson Courthouse Historic Site on right at 31.0. Cross U.S. 12 at mile 31.1.

31.4   Left turn on **Avery Road East** by Loggers World sign.

32.4   Turn right on **Keasling Road**.

33.4   Left turn on **Koontz Road** as Keasling ends. Roadside nurseries display fields of gladioli and other floral attractions. Cross I-5 on an overpass at mile 35.0.

35.7   Left turn on **Jordan Road**. Cross main-line railroad tracks and State Route 603 at mile 37.1; continue on **Conrad Road** and coast downhill through forest. Vine maple adds a touch of brilliant color during a fall tour.

39.1   Turn right on **Pleasant Valley Road**. Enjoy six miles of delightful, relaxing riding.

45.4   Left turn on **Twin Oaks Road** as Pleasant Valley Road ends.

46.9   Turn right on **State Route 6** and cross the Chehalis River.

47.1   Turn left on **Bunker Hill Road** and enter Adna.

47.3   Right turn on **Dieckman Road**.

47.5   Turn right into Back Memorial Park; end of tour.

131 TOLEDO–TOUTLE

STARTING POINT: Toledo Community Park in Toledo. From the north take exit 63 from I-5, head east on State Route 505 for 2.6 miles to the Jackson Highway, and turn right (south) toward Toledo. Keep right on Fifth Street and turn right on Cedar Street, following signs to the park. Park entrance is on Sixth Street. From the south take exit 60 from I-5, head east on State Route 505 for 3.5 miles, then turn right on Fifth Street in Toledo. Keep right with Fifth Street and follow signs to the park as above. If park entrance is closed, park in elementary school parking lot (nonschool days only) two blocks north on Sixth Street.

DISTANCE: 47 miles.
TERRAIN: Hilly.
TOTAL CUMULATIVE ELEVATION GAIN: 1500 feet.
RECOMMENDED TIME OF YEAR: Any season.
RECOMMENDED STARTING TIME: 8 to 9 A.M.
ALLOW: 6 to 8 hours.
POINTS OF INTEREST
Lone Hill Cemetery
Toutle River flood damage
Volcano Interpretive Center

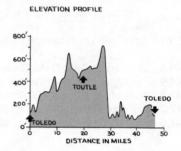

ELEVATION PROFILE

This tour may be taken at any season of the year, but a bright, clear sunny day enhances the majestic appearance of Mt. Rainier and Mt. St. Helens, which command the horizon from many points along the way. Mt. Rainier dominates the northeastern Cascades as the tour follows the valley near the Cowlitz River. Mt. St. Helens joins the skyline as the route climbs to the plateau above the river. Lone Hill Cemetery provides an excellent vantage point for enjoying the splendor of the scene. Perched atop a narrow ridge above the Cowlitz River, this old cemetery dates back to the 1850s, when Washington Territory was first penetrated by settlers. A monument at the cemetery entrance proclaims the friendship between the early pioneers and the Cowlitz Indians, who hunted the nearby prairie. Today the prairie is fenced and plowed, and supports Christmas trees and cattle.

Oak and ash trees line the edges of Layton Prairie as the route joins State Route 505. Viewed from two successive road summits, the distant hillsides resemble a patchwork quilt pattern of browns and greens, the result of many years of clearcut logging operations. Summertime slash fires fill the air with the smell of smoke, as areas are being readied for replanting of forest with tiny fir seedlings.

Tall firs line the road as the route heads west along the North Fork Toutle River. Suddenly the road bursts out of the forest, and the devastation of the Toutle River Valley appears. The eruption of Mt. St. Helens in May 1980 sent a wall of water and gray volcanic ash mud down this valley, sweeping everything in its path. The valley is still a wasteland of mounds of volcanic ash, but young alder trees have begun the process of reclaiming the edges of the valley to forest.

Numerous ducks frequent the marshy edges of Silver Lake west of the little town of Toutle. Eagles soar over the foothills near Seaquest State Park. As the route climbs to the top of one of these hills, Mt. St. Helens emerges then disappears again, and the road plunges downhill toward I-5, where huge draglines, resembling gigantic geese with their necks outstretched, line the tops of tall mounds of dredged-up volcanic ash.

Mt. Rainier puts in one last appearance as the route briefly leaves the Cowlitz River lowland and runs along a side valley. As the route recrosses the Cowlitz River it is not difficult to picture the old sternwheeler *Toledo* chuffing its way up from Longview to the upper landing and trading post that were the beginnings of the present town of Toledo.

MILEAGE LOG

0.0 Toledo Community Park. Leave park and head east on **Cedar Street** for several blocks.

0.2 Left turn on **Second Street**.

0.4 Turn right on **Cowlitz Street (State Route 505)**. Cross Cowlitz River on narrow, two-lane bridge. Continue uphill on S.R. 505 as Jackson Highway goes right at mile 1.0.

1.4 Left turn on **Collins Road**. Descend to the valley along the Cowlitz River. The road zigs and zags across the valley before climbing steeply uphill.

3.8 Bear left at unmarked wye, pedal uphill, and merge with **Eadon Road** (unmarked) at stop sign. Lone Hill Cemetery on the left at mile 5.6; magnificent views of Mt. St. Helens and Mt. Rainier.

6.4 Turn right on **Layton Road** as Eadon Road ends.

7.3 Left turn on **State Route 505** and pedal through prairie land. Cross Cedar Creek at 9.7 and climb to a summit at mile 10.5. Descend into a valley, cross Salmon Creek at 12.6, and top another summit at 14.7.

15.3 Bear right toward Toutle at wye, merge with **State Route 504**, and wind through a canyon of trees. Cross the South Fork Toutle River at mile 19.0.

19.5 Go through downtown Toutle; grocery store, post office, drive-in cafe, and restaurant. Cross marshy area at end of Silver Lake at mile 22.1 near Lakeside Cafe. Silver Lake Store at mile 24.6. Seaquest State Park at mile 24.9; picnicking and camping with hot showers, Mt. St. Helens Volcano Interpretive Center.

26.4 Right turn on **Schaffran Road** and pedal uphill to views of Mt. St. Helens.

29.1 Bear left on **Tower Road** as Schaffran Road ends.

29.2 Right turn on **State Route 504** and descend a long hill.

31.0 Turn right on **Pacific Highway North** just before S.R. 504 crosses I-5. Cross Toutle River and I-5 at miles 33.5 and 33.8; road now marked **Barnes Drive**. Cowlitz River and main-line railroad tracks on the left.

37.0 Left turn on **Imboden Road** as Barnes Drive turns right and ascends a long hill.

37.1 Left turn on **Mickler Road** for a visit to public fishing access on the

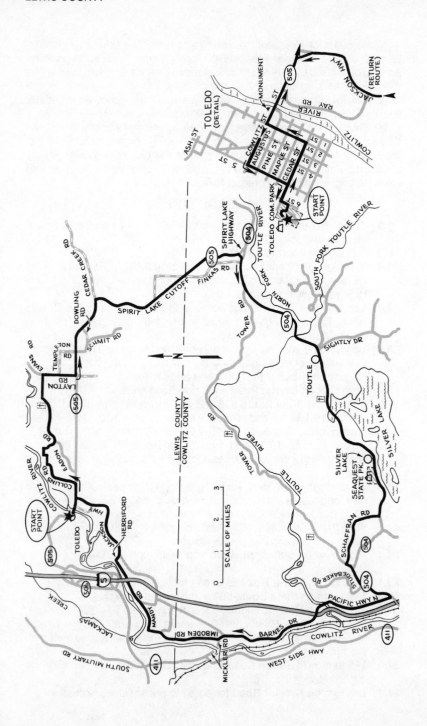

Cowlitz River at mile 37.4; remains of old bridge abutments on both sides of river. Return to Imboden and turn left. Road is renamed **Mandy Road** as it enters Lewis County at 39.1.

39.8 Turn left with Mandy Road as Rogers Road continues on. I-5 crosses overhead at mile 42.1; fishing access along the Cowlitz River has chemical toilets.

42.6 Left turn on **Herriford Road** as Mandy heads up a short hill.

43.2 Turn left on **Jackson Highway**. Mt. Rainier looms over the countryside.

46.0 Left turn on **State Route 505** toward Toledo. Cross Cowlitz River and enter Toledo at mile 46.3.

46.5 Bear left on **Cowlitz Street** as S.R. 505 bends right and uphill.

46.6 Left turn on **Fifth Street** as Cowlitz ends.

46.7 Right turn on **Cedar Street**.

46.8 End of tour at Toledo Community Park.

"NAW – THAT HAPPENS ONLY ONCE EVERY THOUSAND YEARS."

132 RAINBOW FALLS STATE PARK– SEAQUEST STATE PARK

STARTING POINT: Rainbow Falls State Park. Take I-5 to exit 77 (State Route 6), turn west, and proceed 16 miles to state park. After checking with park manager, leave cars in picnic area parking lot.

ALTERNATIVE STARTING POINT: (Reduces tour by 18 miles.) Back Memorial County Park in Adna, 4.5 miles west of I-5 on State Route 6. Turn right on Bunker Creek Road, then right on Dieckman Road to the park entrance.

DISTANCE: Total, 45 to 105 miles: first day, 34 to 50 miles; second day, 32 to 55 miles.
TERRAIN: Hilly.
TOTAL CUMULATIVE ELEVATION GAIN: 500 to 3500 feet: first day, 900 to 1900 feet; second day, 1200 to 1600 feet.
RECOMMENDED TIME OF YEAR: Any season, but road summits may be icy in winter.
RECOMMENDED STARTING TIME: 9 A.M.
ALLOW: 6 hours to 2 days.
POINTS OF INTEREST
Pe Ell covered bridge
Nostalgic Burma Shave signs
Historical Monument in Toledo
Volcano Interpretive Center

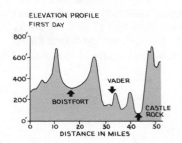

ELEVATION PROFILE
FIRST DAY

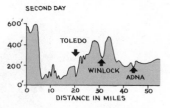

SECOND DAY

This tour utilizes the facilities of several conveniently located parks. As the tour leaves Rainbow Falls State Park on the Chehalis River, it follows backroads and State Route 6 into the valley near Pe Ell, where a side trip beckons covered bridge buffs. Small farms contribute their part to the local economy, but it is the forested hillsides that produce the main crop of trees for the forest products industry. Logging roads take off right and left as the route climbs to a 600-foot summit before descending into the picturesque South Fork Chehalis River Valley. Another forested summit must be conquered before the route descends to Cougar Flats along Stillwater Creek. Freshly painted Burma Shave signs nudge the memories of those over 40. Blades spin on a brightly decorated windmill, its wind power generating little but pleasure for the beholder.

The little town of Vader supplies the needed calories to generate pedal power for continuing the tour south along the Cowlitz River. After another fuel stop at the bakery in Castle Rock, several miles of backroad hill-climbing stand between the cyclist and the camping destination of Seaquest State Park, where the new U.S. Forest Service Volcano Interpretive Center entertains visitors. Motels along the highway in Castle Rock offer alternative accommodations.

The return route to Rainbow Falls State Park runs along the eastern bank of the Cowlitz River to the next upstream bridge at Toledo, another alternative overnight target. Close inspection of the river shows several miles of fishing access provided by the State Game Department. A broad, freely flowing river as it joins the Columbia at Kelso-Longview, the Cowlitz River provided the main means of transportation into the prairies and forest of Washington Territory. Sternwheelers plied the river upstream to the historic Cowlitz Landing near the present town of Toledo, which was named after one of the riverboats. A monument near the bridge commemorates the convention held in 1851 that drafted a petition to Congress to divide up Oregon Territory and establish a separate territory for the land north of the Columbia River.

Leaving Toledo, the bicycle route continues over prairie land that was claimed through the Donation Land Claim Act of 1850. Magnificent views of Mt. Rainier and Mt. St. Helens greeted the settlers of yesterday as they do bicycle tourists of today.

As are other towns along this tour, Winlock is situated deep in a valley, along the banks of King and Olequa creeks. A steep hill separates it from the Napavine Prairie. The route climbs this hill and traverses a bit of the

prairie before following the pleasant valley of Stearns Creek to join the Chehalis Valley at Claquato. Acres of oats, wheat, corn, and peas flourish in the fertile soil near Adna, terminus of one of the shorter versions of this tour.

Busy traffic along State Route 6 complicates the climbing of the last hill of this tour, but a viewpoint lined with old masonry guardrails offers a break shortly before a backroad route leaves the highway toward the back gate of Rainbow Falls State Park.

MILEAGE LOG

FIRST DAY

0.0 Rainbow Falls State Park. Proceed north through the park, around the back gate, and turn left on **Leudinghaus Road**. *Note: For alternate starting directions from Adna, see end of mileage log.*

1.0 Left turn on **Chandler Road** and cross the Chehalis River.

1.3 Turn right on **Doty Dryad Road** (unmarked) just before Chandler intersects highway.

2.7 Left turn on **Stevens Road** at stop sign in Doty as Doty Dryad is marked Dead End.

3.0 Right turn on **State Route 6**. Road shoulder is smooth and generous as it turns and climbs over the hill into the Pe Ell Valley.

6.4 Bear left on **Mauerman Road** as S.R. 6 continues to Pe Ell.

7.4 Left turn on **Pe Ell-McDonald Road** as Mauerman Road ends. *Note: One mile right into Pe Ell, then one mile left out of Pe Ell on Third Street, then one mile right on graveled Muller Road leads to an iron-pipe gate mounted in large rubber tires. Below the gate is the Pe Ell covered bridge.* Road follows the valley and heads uphill to a summit at mile 10.3. Road continues through forest and rolling countryside. Pass Boistfort Lions Club Park on the right at mile 13.8; picnic shelters and pit toilets.

16.1 Right turn on **Wildwood Road** by Boistfort grocery. Route passes farms of the South Fork Chehalis River Valley before climbing uphill. Top a summit at 25.7.

28.0 Turn left on **State Route 506** toward I-5 as a directional sign points right 1.5 miles to Ryderwood (grocery/cafe). Watch for Burma Shave signs and gaily painted windmill. *Note: Winlock-Vader Road goes left to Winlock at 32.1; cuts 42 miles off full tour.* Pass through Vader at mile 32.4; grocery and cafe. Cross main-line railroad tracks.

33.1 Right turn on **State Route 411** at top of steep hill with tremendous view of Mt. Rainier and Mt. St. Helens (see note below). On a clear day a small section of Mt. Adams shows up behind the distant foothills. Enter Cowlitz County at mile 34.2. *Note: Mickler Road goes left at mile 35.2 to old bridge abutments on Cowlitz River; 1.4 miles round trip.* Climb a short hill and cross main-line railroad tracks at mile 35.5. Route follows Cowlitz River for several miles. *Note: To shorten this tour by 30 miles, do not turn right on S.R. 411, but continue on S.R. 506 and S.R. 505 into Toledo. See detail map of Tour #131 for directions to Toledo Community Park.*

42.5 Left turn toward Castle Rock at blinking red light by grocery. Pass Castle Rock Fairgrounds, cross Cowlitz River, and enter Castle Rock on **A Street**.

43.2 Left turn on **Front Street**. Bakery, cafe, and grocery in downtown Castle Rock. Continue on **Huntington Road** as it joins from the right, and climb out of town along the river. Cross I-5 and continue uphill past motels on wide shoulder of **State Route 504 (Spirit Lake Highway)**.

46.0 Left turn on **Tower Road** by gas-grocery. Immediately bear right on **Schaffran Road** and continue uphill. Views of Mt. St. Helens at summit.

48.7 Turn left on **State Route 504**.

50.2 Left turn into Seaquest State Park; Camping, picnicking, shelters, group camp, Volcano Interpretive Center.

SECOND DAY

0.0 Leave Seaquest State Park entrance and turn right on **State Route 504**.

5.5 Right turn on **Pacific Highway North** just before S.R. 504 crosses I-5. Cross Toutle River and I-5 at miles 8.0 and 8.3. Road now named **Barnes Drive**. Cowlitz River and main-line railroad tracks appear on the left.

11.5 Left turn on **Imboden Road** as Barnes Drive ascends a long hill.

11.6 Turn left on **Mickler Road** for a visit to the public fishing access on the Cowlitz River at mile 11.9. Notice old bridge abutments on either side of the river. Return to Imboden intersection.

12.1 Left turn on **Imboden Road**. Road enters Lewis County at 13.6.

14.3 Turn left with **Mandy Road**. I-5 crosses overhead at mile 16.6. Fishing access along Cowlitz River has chemical toilets.

17.1 Left turn on **Herriford Road** as Mandy heads up a short hill.

17.7 Left turn on **Jackson Highway**. Mt. Rainier on the eastern horizon.

20.5 Turn left on **State Route 505** toward Toledo. Cross Cowlitz River and enter Toledo at mile 20.8.

21.0 Keep right with S.R. 505 as Cowlitz Street goes left. Toledo Community Park is 0.3 mile from this intersection at Cedar Street and Sixth Street. See detail map, Tour #131.

21.1 Continue on **Fifth Street** as it joins from the left. Signs point back on Fifth Street toward Community Park, 0.5 mile.

21.3 Turn left on **Ash Street** by grocery–fishing tackle store toward Vader and Ryderwood. (This is a branch of S.R. 505.) Climb up to open prairie.

22.0 Right turn on **Drew's Prairie Road**.

23.4 Turn left with Drew's Prairie Road as Camus Road goes right. Descend a short hill, go under I-5 at mile 24.0, and climb up to the prairie again.

24.1 Right turn at top of hill on **Knowles Road** toward Winlock. I-5 traffic dashes past on the right. Road pulls away from I-5 and starts uphill through forest at mile 25.4. Note huge ant hill on the left at mile 26.5.

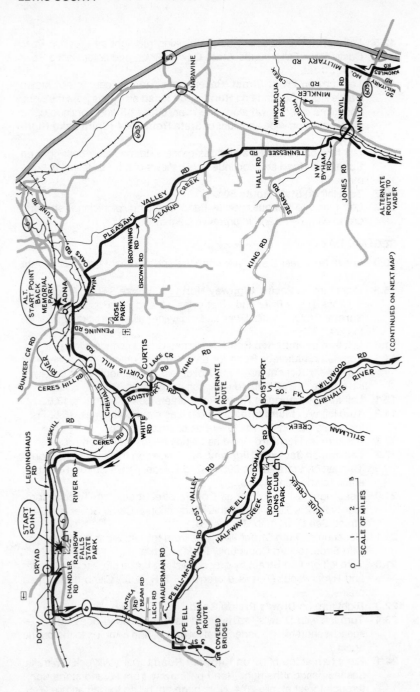

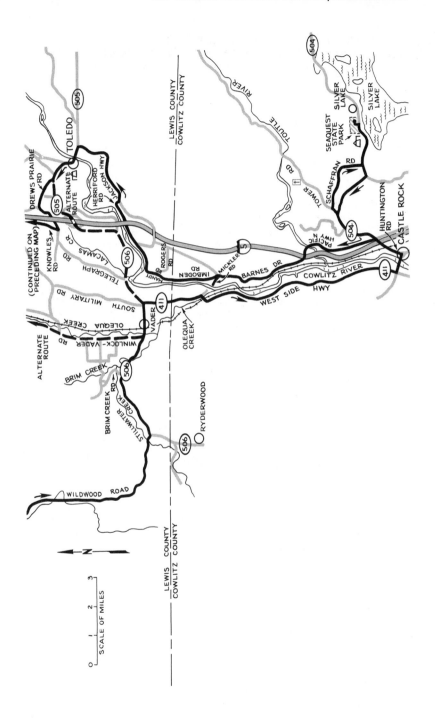

26.6   Left turn at stop sign on **State Route 603**.

26.9   Right turn on **N. Military Road** toward Mt. St. Helens High School.

27.7   Left turn on **Nevil Road** just past the high school. Acres of sheared Christmas trees.

29.8   Rejoin **State Route 603** at Winlock city limits. Cross N.E. First Street; cafe and grocery one block right on First.

30.0   Cross railroad tracks and continue on **W. Walnut Street** as S.R. 603 goes right.

30.1   Cross Olequa Creek and turn right on **N.W. Arden Avenue**.

30.3   Continue on **N.E. King Road** at crossing of **Fir Street**.

30.4   Bear right on unmarked road past Lewis County Public Works as N.E. King Road continues uphill. Road later signed **N.W. Dexter Avenue**.

30.5   Left turn with thoroughfare as it is renamed **N.W. Byham Road**.

30.7   Turn right on **Tennessee Road**, cross King Creek, and head uphill.

34.0   Left turn on **Pleasant Valley Road** as Tennessee ends.

41.4   Left turn on **Twin Oaks Road** as Pleasant Valley Road ends.

42.8   Left turn on **State Route 6**. Traffic will pick up along this road. Cross South Fork Chehalis River at mile 46.5. *Note: For Adna return, turn right on S.R. 6, cross bridge, turn left into Adna on Bunker Hill Road, then right on Dieckman Road to Back Memorial Park.*

49.6   Right turn on **River Road**. Old stone guardrails along the road next to river.

51.9   Turn right across the Chehalis River on **Meskill Road**, then immediately left on **Leudinghaus Road**.

54.5   Left turn into Rainbow Falls State Park back entrance, marked by closed, white-painted log gate.

54.6   End of tour by picnic area.

ALTERNATIVE STARTING POINT MILEAGE LOG

0.0   Head out of Back Memorial Park on entrance road and turn left on **Dieckman Road**.

0.2   Left turn on **Bunker Creek Road**.

0.4   Turn right on **State Route 6** and cross the Chehalis River. Watch for acute-angled railroad tracks at mile 0.9.

4.4   Cross the South Fork Chehalis River and turn left on **Boistfort Road**.

10.2   Continue on **Wildwood Road** as Pe Ell McDonald Road goes right. Continue on main mileage log at mile 16.1.

PACIFIC COUNTY

133 LONG BEACH PENINSULA

STARTING POINT: Fort Canby State Park. From the north, take exit 104 (U.S. 101) from I-5 in Olympia and continue on State Route 8 and U.S. 12 to Montesano. Follow State Route 107 to rejoin U.S. 101 and continue south to Ilwaco. Prominent signs direct the traveler to Fort Canby State Park. From the south take exit 39 (State Route 4) from I-5 in Kelso. Follow State Route 4 to where it joins U.S. 101. Continue south to Ilwaco and Fort Canby State Park.

DISTANCE: 43 miles.
TERRAIN: Flat with one hill.
TOTAL CUMULATIVE ELEVATION
GAIN: 520 feet.
RECOMMENDED TIME OF YEAR:
Any season.
RECOMMENDED STARTING TIME:
9 A.M.
ALLOW: 6 hours.
POINTS OF INTEREST
Lewis and Clark Interpretive Center
Fort Canby State Park
Old homes in Oysterville
Cranberry bogs

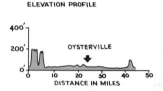

ELEVATION PROFILE

From its junction with the mainland at the mouth of the Columbia River, the Long Beach Peninsula extends its narrow finger north for 25 miles, protecting the calm waters of Willapa Bay from the frequently storm-tossed waters of the Pacific Ocean. Cape Disappointment, the peninsula's southern extension, forms the high bluff of forested land where the Columbia River flows into the Pacific Ocean. It was first charted in 1775 by Spanish explorers but received its name from the British fur trader John Meares, who tried but failed to find a navigable channel into the mouth of the great river in 1788. American explorer Captain Robert Gray succeeded in crossing the bar in 1792 and entered the river, naming it after his ship. In the fall of 1805 the Lewis and Clark expedition, having traveled westward from the Mississippi River, viewed the Pacific Ocean from atop Cape Disappointment. The history of this most successful of American explorations is presented in interesting detail at the Interpretive Center in Fort Canby State Park. Cape Disappointment was selected as the site of a lighthouse in 1850, and the light went into operation in 1856. A second lighthouse went up on North Head in 1898, and both are still important aids to navigation. The area was proclaimed a military reservation in 1852 and officially named Fort Canby in honor of General Edward Richard Sprigg Canby in 1875.

Over the years, barracks and fortifications with mortars and rifles have been installed and removed; even a minefield was activated during World War II. Remains of the concrete bunkers are still in evidence today. In 1947 Fort Canby was declared surplus property and placed in the custody of the Corps of Engineers. During the next year 491 acres were transferred to the

Coast Guard, while the Washington State Parks and Recreation Commission leased and purchased land for a state park.

Crossing the Columbia Bar has always been a difficult maneuver for ships, and many have run aground or capsized in the stormy waters. The Coast Guard maintains a lifeboat station east of the North Jetty with a motor-lifeboat surf school for training coastguardsmen. Visitors to the state park may have a chance to observe these young people learning their trade as their boats are tossed by the waves breaking over the bar.

Several towns dot the Long Beach Peninsula. Ilwaco, at the south end, supports the commercial and charter fishing industries while Seaview and Long Beach are oriented toward beach tourism and summer and retirement homes. Nahcotta, on the Willapa Bay side of the peninsula, is an important center for the propagation and harvesting of oysters. Nearby cranberry bogs cover many acres and represent an important part of the cranberry industry in Washington State. Oysterville, founded in 1854 near the northern end of the peninsula, has been placed on the National Register of Historic Places. Several houses and a church built before 1900 remain as fine examples of the architecture of that era. The excellent restoration and maintenance of these buildings bear testimony to the pride and industry of today's Oysterville townspeople.

Leadbetter Point State Park (undeveloped) on the northern tip of the peninsula and nearby Willapa National Wildlife Refuge offer important natural habitats for waterfowl such as the black brant goose and Caspian tern.

MILEAGE LOG

0.0 Fort Canby State Park parking area by restrooms. Proceed out of park past park office and turn left up the hill toward Ilwaco.

0.6 Bear left on unmarked road as sign points right toward Ilwaco.

1.1 Left turn toward North Head.

1.9 Turn left down gravel path to North Head Lighthouse. Sweeping views of beach and surf toward the mouth of the Columbia River. Return to the road.

2.4 Turn left again to a viewpoint. Trails lead around the fort's old lookout bunkers. Return to main road.

3.4 Turn left on main road and head downhill.

4.5 Left turn on **Willows Road** and continue downhill.

5.5 Left turn on **L Place** in Seaview.

7.0 Left turn on **10 South Boulevard** as L ends, then right on next right side road and enter Long Beach.

7.6 Jog right, then left, and continue north on **N Street**. Main access to the proclaimed World's Longest Beach is to the left through an archway. Long Beach shopping area to the right; bakery, cafes.

8.9 Turn right on **95 Street**, then left on **State Route 103**. Entrance to Loomis Lake State park is on the left at mile 13.2.

17.1 Continue on **Vernon Avenue** as S.R. 103 ends in Ocean Park. Entrance to Pacific Pines State Park is on the left at mile 17.8.

18.6 Left turn on **Joe Johns Road**, then right at stop sign on **N Street**, which bends left and is marked **295 Street**. Road bends right at 19.4

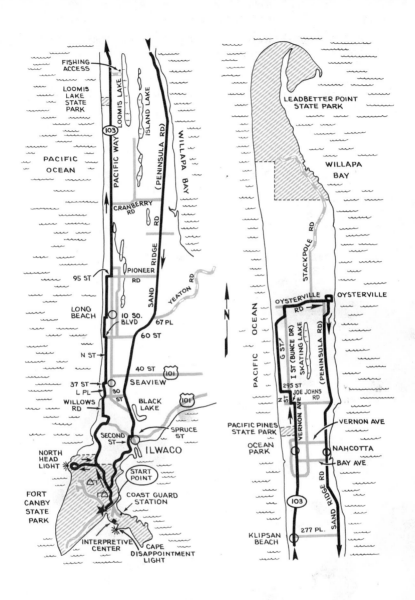

and becomes **G Street**. Pedal through Surfside Estates.

21.8 Left turn on **I Street** at stop sign.

22.0 Turn right on **Oysterville Road** and pedal over sand ridge. *Note: At mile 22.9 Stackpole Road goes left 4.8 miles to Leadbetter Point State Park.* Oysterville Store and Post Office (oldest post office in Washington State) on the right at mile 23.1.

23.2 Cross Pacific Street in Oysterville and follow around loop past oyster company buildings.

23.7 Cross Oysterville Road and continue on **Pacific Street**. Signs date old homes, schoolhouse, and church in Oysterville.

24.5 Bear left on **Sand Ridge Road**. Ark Restaurant on the left in Nahcotta at mile 27.1; reservations advised. Oyster farming facilities nearby. Cranberry warehouse and bogs on right at mile 34.6. Cross U.S. 101 at mile 39.0.

40.0 Join **U.S. 101** as it merges from right, and pedal past Ilwaco municipal water supply (Black Lake). Memorial to World War II casualties.

40.6 Turn right on **Spruce Street** in Ilwaco, then immediately left on **Second Street** as sign encourages tourists to continue on Spruce to Fort Canby State Park.

42.4 Left turn at stop sign.

42.9 Right turn by Fort Canby park office.

43.1 End of tour at picnic area parking lot.

"You know, I have never seen a bird in this area."

CLARK COUNTY

134 LEWIS RIVER

STARTING POINT: Parking area along back fence behind police station in Woodland, near corner of Bozarth and Goerig. Permission granted for use of parking area weekends and bank holidays only. Take exit 21 from I-5 (Woodland, Lake Merwin) into Woodland. Turn right on Bozarth, left behind city hall, and park along fence behind police station.

ALTERNATIVE STARTING POINT: Port of Kalama Marina parking lot; extends ride by 29 miles. See Tour #135.

DISTANCE: Total, 56 miles: first day, 20 miles; second day, 36 miles. Alternative starting point, 85 miles: first day, 39 miles; second day, 46 miles.
TERRAIN: Hilly
TOTAL CUMULATIVE ELEVATION GAIN: 2150 feet: first day, 1350 feet; second day, 1800 feet.

RECOMMENDED TIME OF YEAR: March through October.
RECOMMENDED STARTING TIME: 9 to 10 A.M.
ALLOW: 7 to 8 hours; 1 to 2 days.
POINTS OF INTEREST
Views along Lewis River
Battle Ground Lake State Park

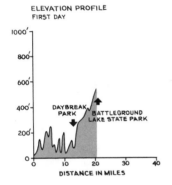

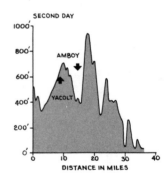

When traced back from its junction with the Columbia River near Woodland, the Lewis River retreats quickly into a series of wild canyons and hydroelectric reservoirs. Steep canyon walls discourage extensive development of recreational property, and timber interests control much of the adjoining countryside, keeping traffic density low on the many county roads. With the bonus of the relatively unspoiled scenery, this is a great backcountry tour.

Several parks line the course of this tour. Horseshoe Lake Park in Woodland takes the name of a lake formed when a bend in the Lewis River was bypassed. Although the river now flows straight past the town, the county boundary still follows the original river course through this oxbow lake. When the east fork of the river is crossed, Clark County's Daybreak Park of-

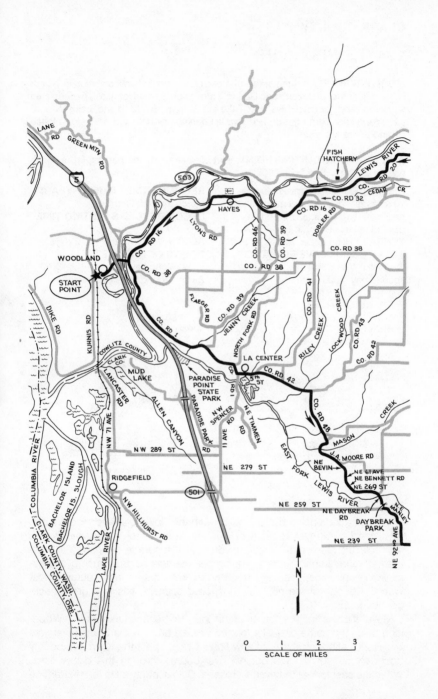

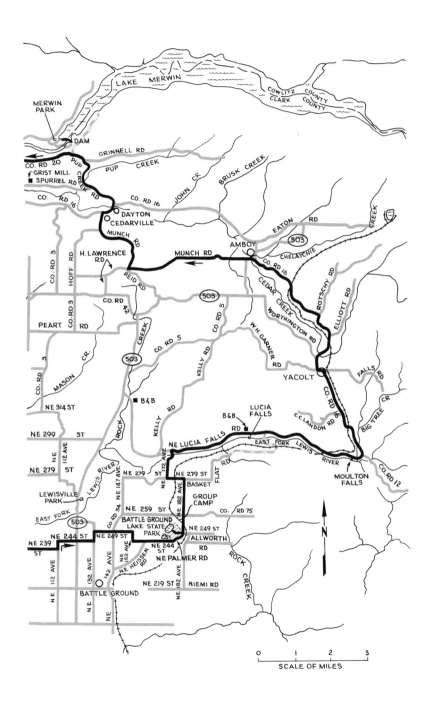

SCALE OF MILES

0   1   2   3

fers a delightful setting for relaxing along the rippling water. A private resort at Lucia Falls has long been available to the motoring public, while farther up the river the county has acquired extensive river frontage by Moulton Falls. These parks, although of interest, are secondary to the main objective of this tour—Battle Ground Lake State Park. The lake occupies the basin of a crater with no surface tributary or outlet: underground springs and sinks keep the water clear and fresh for enjoyable swimming. Park trails and entrance road climb the rim of the crater and descend to the water's edge. Drive-in and walk-in campsites, coin-operated hot showers, and kitchen shelters in the central park area provide facilities for a wide range of activities. A group camp, available by reservation with the park manager, offers Adirondack shelters, tables, fire pits, and the environmental benefits of an adjoining railroad. For cyclists not interested in camping, two nearby bed-and-breakfast opportunities offer more luxurious accommodations. (See B & B index.)

Although hills abound on this ride, the scenery makes them all worthwhile. The wild rapids and falls of the pea green Lewis River and its tributaries, rippling and splashing their way through dense forests, are a favorite habitat of the water ouzel. Wintering tundra swans, their cries sounding like children at play along the water, fly up from a quiet bend of the river. Acres of daffodils identify bulb farms along the main fork of the Lewis River, and herds of deer graze the pastures and roadsides. The countryside is slow to change, making this a delightful tour.

MILEAGE LOG

FIRST DAY

0.0 Parking area along back fence by Woodland Police Station and Old National Bank in Woodland. Proceed out to **Goerig Street** and turn left. Continue under I-5 at mile 0.3.

0.5 Turn right toward La Center and Amboy and cross Lewis River.

0.8 Bear right with **County Road 1** on far side of bridge.

6.0 Turn left on **E. 5th Street** toward Amboy and continue through La Center; grocery. As it leaves La Center, road is renamed **County Road 42**.

6.4 Bear right with County Road 42 as County Road 41 forks left.

8.2 Right turn on **County Road 48** at the top of a steep hill. View of Mt. St. Helens.

9.5 Bear right at a wye on **J.A. Moore Road** as County Road 48 goes left.

10.8 Continue on N.E. Bevin as N.E. 284 Street goes left. As the road executes several bends it is renamed **N.E. 61st Avenue, N.E. Bennett Road,** and **N.E. 269th Street**.

12.4 Bear right on **N.E. Daybreak Road** toward Battle Ground and cross the East Fork Lewis River. Daybreak Park is on left at mile 12.6 as road is renamed **N.E. 82 Avenue**.

13.0 Turn left on **N.E. 259th Street**. As the road bends, it is renamed **N.E. Manley Road**. At top of hill, road is renamed **N.E. 92nd Avenue**.

14.3   Left turn on **N.E. 239th Street**.

15.3   Turn left on **N.E. 112th Avenue** as N.E. 239th Street ends. Road bends right and becomes **N.E. 244th Street**. Cross N.E. Lewisville Highway (State Route 503) at mile 16.0.

16.5   Left turn on **N.E. 132nd Avenue** as N.E. 244th Street ends.

16.8   Turn right on **N.E. 249th Street** by Sacred Heart Cemetery as N.E. Dublin Road (dead end) continues. Road executes right and left bends and is renamed **N.E. 152nd Avenue, N.E. 244th Street, N.E. Palmer Road**, and **N.E. 182nd Avenue**.

19.6   Turn left on **N.E. 249th Street** into Battle Ground Lake State Park. *Note: To visit group camp, do not turn on N.E. 249th Street, but continue on N.E. 182nd Avenue for 0.5 mile, turn left on N.E. 259th Street, cross railroad tracks, and turn left into group camp entrance road.* See index for bed-and-breakfast telephone numbers. Nearest grocery is 1.8 miles into next day's ride; next nearest is in Battle Ground.

SECOND DAY

0.0   Leave Battle Ground Lake State Park entrance on **N.E. 249th Street** and turn left (north) on **N.E. 182nd Avenue**.

1.5   Left turn on **N.E. 279th Street** as 182nd Avenue ends. Grocery at mile 1.8.

1.9   Turn right with thoroughfare on **N.E. 172nd Avenue**. Cross East Fork of Lewis River at mile 2.5.

2.6   Right turn on **N.E. Lucia Falls Road**. *Note: Bed-and-breakfast locations 2.5 miles either way on N.E. Lucia Falls Road.* Falls Cafe at mile 5.0, Clark County Moulton Falls Park at mile 8.1. Road name changes to **County Road 16** as County Road 12 goes right at mile 8.3, and to **Railroad Avenue** as it enters Yacolt at mile 10.5.

10.9   Left turn on **W. Yacolt Road** in Yacolt as Railroad Avenue ends, then immediately turn right toward Amboy. Road is eventually renamed **County Road 16**.

15.3   Turn left on **State Route 503** by tavern in Amboy. Cross creek and climb short hill.

15.8   Go straight on **Munch Road** by cafe and grocery as S.R. 503 swings left.

19.1   Turn right with Munch Road as H. Lawrence Road continues.

21.4   Right turn toward Amboy on **County Road 16** at base of hill. Cross Cedar Creek and turn left on **Pup Creek Road** toward Merwin Dam and Green Mountain.

24.1   Continue with **County Road 20** as it enters from right (gravel) from vicinity of Merwin Dam. County Road 32 merges from left at mile 28.5.

28.9   Bear right on **County Road 16** as County Road 20 ends.

34.8   Bear right at wye toward Woodland and cross Lewis River as County Road 1 continues left.

35.1   Turn left on **State Route 503** into Woodland. As it enters town the road becomes **Goerig Street**.

35.6   Right turn on **Bozarth** and left into lot behind city hall. End of tour.

135 KALAMA–WOODLAND

STARTING POINT: Port of Kalama Marina parking lot in Kalama. Take exit 30 from I-5 into Kalama, 2.5 hours driving time from Seattle. Turn right at west end of overpass and follow signs to marina along Hendrickson Drive.

DISTANCE: 34 miles.
TERRAIN: Flat to moderate.
TOTAL CUMULATIVE ELEVATION GAIN: 300 feet.
RECOMMENDED TIME OF YEAR: Any season.
RECOMMENDED STARTING TIME: Not critical.
ALLOW: 2 to 6 hours.
POINTS OF INTEREST
Historical monuments in Horseshoe
Lake Park
Views along Columbia and Lewis
rivers

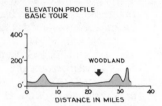

ELEVATION PROFILE
BASIC TOUR

In April of 1976, the Washington State Highway Commission instituted a six-month trial of a bikeway along the shoulder of Interstate 5 between the Dike Road Interchange north of Woodland and the Todd Road Interchange south of Kalama. The experiment proved successful (no reported casualties), and this bikeway is now available to bicyclists as are most of the rural interstate shoulders in Washington. Bikeway rules include use of the right-hand shoulder in daylight hours only and conformity with bike route regulations. Experiences using this bikeway have been surprisingly nontraumatic. Compared to shoulderless secondary highways, it is almost idyllic, the traffic noise being the only major liability.

Noises of the freeway are left far behind when the route descends to Dike Access Road and heads across the delta to the Columbia River. Levees and pumping stations along the river keep the fertile land from flooding. Oat and wheat stubble provides winter forage for large flocks of Canada geese as well as for smaller flocks of tundra and trumpeter swans. Large herds of dairy cattle graze the lush green pastures and stare at unfamiliar two-wheeled intruders. Meadowlarks flush from alongside the roads, singing as they fly away. Red-winged blackbirds seek out nesting sites in the cattails. A red-tailed hawk carefully surveys the territory from his perch atop an old piling.

Fishermen's shacks, with oil-drum stoves to provide warmth on cold days, dot the sandy beach along the Columbia River. Wide doorways on the shelters reduce trampling casualties when the little bells attached to the tops of fishing poles ring, signaling a strike.

Big ocean-going ships, decks piled high with container freight, move slowly through the broad waters of the Columbia on their way up the river to Portland as tugs push sawdust-piled barges down the river. A pulp mill across the river in St. Helens, Oregon, sends plumes of fog into the atmosphere.

Groves of cottonwood and alder trees line many of the delta-land roads, while swamp dogwood, snowberries, blackberry vines, and horsetails fill in the wet spots. Garry oak thrives around Horseshoe Lake in Woodland, where a city park provides picnicking and swimming. Restaurants and grocery stores are nearby.

The rapid return trip to Kalama via the five miles of freeway brings no surprises except a corpse or two of small animals such as opossum, raccoon, and barn owl. Energetic cyclists who elect to climb over Green Mountain are rewarded with a spectacular view of the Woodland-Kalama delta area, including the giant heat exchanger of the Trojan Nuclear Power Plant with its strobe-light warning beacon rising high above the Columbia River near Rainier, Oregon.

MILEAGE LOG

0.0 Parking lot by Port of Kalama Marina office in Kalama. Leave parking area and follow exit road around lagoon.

0.2 Right turn between boat sales office and sewage treatment plant toward RV Park.

2.3 Turn right up **I-5** access ramp and continue along shoulder marked for bicycles.

7.9 Bear right with bicycle route signs on exit ramp and leave freeway. Turn right on **Dike Access Road** at foot of ramp.

"NO THANKS, I THINK I'D RATHER WALK IT."

9.8 Bear left at wye on **Dike Road**. Fishing access on right with toilet facilities and sandy beach along Columbia River at mile 10.5; fishermen's shelters. Road bends left alongside railroad tracks at mile 16.3 and becomes **Kuhnis Road**.

17.9 Turn right on **Whalen Road** and cross railroad tracks as Kuhnis ends.

18.4 Bear right at wye on **South Pekin Road** by apex of Horseshoe Lake.

20.5 End of paved road by State Department of Wildlife fishing access on Lewis River. *Note: Signed conservation park; conservation license required for use of facilities.* Pekin Road continues on other side of river, inaccessible by bicycle. Turn around and go back along Pekin Road.

22.4 Turn right on **Pinkerton Drive** and pedal past ends of Horseshoe Lake. Road name changes to **Lake Shore Drive** by second arm of lake. Horseshoe Park (city of Woodland) on left at 23.5. A memorial plaque is dedicated to a friendly Indian named Zack.

23.6 Turn right on **Goerig Street** and follow main thoroughfare out of town toward La Center. As it goes under I-5, road is designated **State Route 503**. Continue on S.R. 503 past Oak Tree Restaurant.

24.7 Continue past end of high retaining wall along Lewis River and turn left on **N. Goerig Street**. Ignore an earlier Goerig turnoff by drive-in. *Note: For the adventuresome and hardy, Green Mountain Road goes right at mile 25.4 up long, very steep hills, eventually leading back to Kalama; additional elevation gain 1000 to 2000 feet. For this you are on your own.*

25.9 Turn right with bike route signs onto approach to **I-5** and proceed along marked shoulder.

30.7 Exit freeway with bike route signs, turn right on **Robb Road**, then left on **Todd Road (Old 99, Co. Rd. 377)**. Enter Kalama on **First Street**.

33.3 Left turn under I-5 on **Elm Street** at south edge of Kalama business district, then right toward Port Office and RV Park.

33.8 Turn left on **Hendrickson Drive** and follow thoroughfare to starting point.

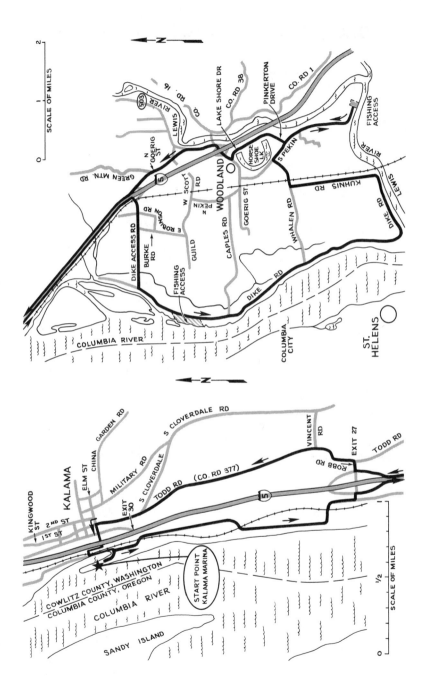

136 CASTLE ROCK–TOUTLE (Toutle River)

STARTING POINT: Along Front Street in Castle Rock. Take exit 49 from I-5 and proceed into Castle Rock on Huntington Avenue. Bear right on Front Street at city welcome sign. Park along Front Street, taking care to leave space for church parking on Sunday, and to avoid two-hour parking-limit area on other days of the week.

DISTANCE: 37 miles.
TERRAIN: Strenuous hills.
TOTAL CUMULATIVE ELEVATION GAIN: 1900 feet.
RECOMMENDED TIME OF YEAR: March through November.
RECOMMENDED STARTING TIME: 9 to 10 A.M.
ALLOW: 5 hours.
POINTS OF INTEREST
Tower Cemetery
Toutle River devastation
Volcano Interpretive Center

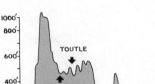

ELEVATION PROFILE

This relatively short but strenuous tour takes the bicyclist into a sparsely settled territory of Cowlitz County along the Toutle River northeast of Castle Rock. A traverse of an equally uninhabited hillside area southeast of town precedes the journey along Silver Lake and on to the Toutle.

Castle Rock is almost surrounded by the Cowlitz River as it swings around and heads south toward the Columbia, eight miles away. Farmland, Burlington Northern main-line tracks, and six lanes of I-5 share the narrow corridor of land between the Cowlitz River and the steep, forested hillsides to the east. Our tour views this part of the Cowlitz Valley before climbing into the hills on Headquarters Road. Large second-growth alder and bigleaf maple are the principal trees, though a few Douglas fir grow among the deciduous varieties.

Surprised, startled, and screaming all the way, guinea hens scatter down a side road to an isolated dwelling. Solitude returns as the route continues uphill to an intersection with Silver Lake Road, where the plunge to the Silver Lake plateau begins. Several small stump ranches enjoy a magnificent view of Mt. St. Helens and Mt. Rainier from their location high above Silver Lake. Seaquest State Park occupies a half mile of the lake's marshy shoreline, where bird watchers may have an opportunity for close encounters with nesting ducks as State Route 504 crosses a corner of the lake on a narrow causeway.

The North Fork Toutle River snuggles up to the highway as the route continues east through tall evergreen forest. Soon the route heads uphill again on Tower Road, where young tree plantings in logged-off areas speak of good forest management. As the road proceeds up and down the hills beside the Toutle River, aspen and oak trees, all hung with lichen, intersperse the fir and alder. Breaks in the trees reveal a cliff overlooking the muddy

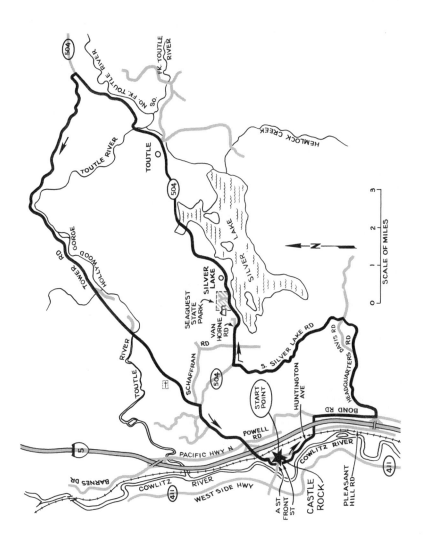

Toutle, while on the other side of the road, cattle ranches straddle the upland pastures. A section of the original road, undermined by the 1980 Mt. St. Helens mudflow, has been bypassed by a new road farther from the river. Eventually the road dives down to a crossing of the Toutle on a new concrete bridge. Cowlitz County maintains a cemetery on one of the many rolling hills that remain to be negotiated before the route again reaches State Route 504 and the final two-mile-long plunge to Castle Rock.

MILEAGE LOG

0.0 Proceed south on **Front Street** from parking area near church in Castle Rock.

0.6 Continue on **Huntington Avenue** as it joins from the left.

1.6 Continue under I-5 as Pleasant Hill Road goes right, then turn right on **Bond Road**. Rolling hills.

3.6 Turn left on **Headquarters Road** and start up a long, moderately steep hill.

7.7 Turn sharp left on **South Silver Lake Road** as Headquarters Road is marked Dead End. Start a rolling descent toward Silver Lake.

11.7 Right turn on **Spirit Lake Highway (State Route 504)**. Prepare for 10 miles of moderate highway traffic. Mt. St. Helens appears occasionally on the horizon, topping the green hillsides. Go by Seaquest State Park and the Volcano Interpretive Center at mile 13.7, and through Toutle at mile 18.3 (cafes). Cross Toutle River at 19.6.

21.9 Turn left on **Tower Road** and start up rolling hills through well-managed tree farm area. Cross Toutle River on high bridge at 31.3. Tower Cemetery on right at 32.6. Rolling hills, steep in places.

34.4 Turn right on **State Route 504** by corner grocery, and speed down long hill. Cross I-5 on overpass and continue into Castle Rock on **Huntington Avenue**.

36.8 Bear right on **Front Street** by small corner park.

37.0 Back at starting point; end of ride.

137 CASTLE ROCK–LONGVIEW

STARTING POINT: Take exit 49 (State Route 504, Castle Rock) from I-5 and follow Huntington Avenue into Castle Rock. Bear left at road fork on Front Street. Park along Front Street or side streets, but watch for parking-limit signs and keep clear of church area on Sundays.

ALTERNATIVE STARTING POINT: Intersection of Hemlock Street and Kessler Boulevard by restrooms of Sacajawea Park in Longview. Take exit 36 (State Route 432) from I-5 toward Longview. Turn right on Oregon Avenue at traffic light where S.R. 432 ends, and immediately turn left on Kessler Boulevard. Follow Kessler to Hemlock Street by restrooms. Park along Kessler by Sacajawea Park.

DISTANCE: 33 miles.
TERRAIN: Combination of hilly, moderate, and flat.
TOTAL CUMULATIVE ELEVATION GAIN: 1300 feet.
RECOMMENDED TIME OF YEAR: Any season.
RECOMMENDED STARTING TIME: 10 A.M.
ALLOW: 4 hours.
POINTS OF INTEREST
Sacajawea Park in Longview
Views of Columbia River

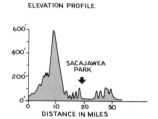

ELEVATION PROFILE

Hugging the edge of the pavement, several cyclists pedal along a crowded, shoulderless highway. Traffic piles up behind, and auto drivers become impatient and irritated. A head leans out the passenger side of a vehicle, shouting derogatory comments. Contents of a soft drink container splash out of a window as a car careens past. Sound familiar? This experience took place on the highway north out of Longview, the only obvious route for most long-distance cycle tourists. The sad part is that it is entirely unnecessary, as this tour demonstrates two alternative routes, with minimal traffic and enjoyable scenery.

Leaving Castle Rock, one route crosses the Cowlitz River and winds up the Delameter Creek Valley past homes, farms, and forest. Delameter Creek meanders by, crossing under the roadway several times. Wildflowers and gardens produce a blaze of color. Swallows swoop and dart along the road, snapping up insects on the wing. Roadway cuts reveal a bright reddish brown soil. The hard work put into the long climb is finally rewarded as the road suddenly curves over a summit and plunges down into the Coal Creek Valley. To avoid another highway at the terminus on Coal Creek Road, the route swerves onto Pacific Way and traverses the hillside along a system of sloughs leading into Longview and Sacajawea Park. Lake Sacajawea, the major feature of the park, is an oxbow lake formed from past meanderings of the Cowlitz and dredged out and kept from flooding by interconnection with Longview's system of canals, pumps, dikes, and levees. The park is attractively landscaped, with graveled jogging and cycling trails on the perimeter.

The return route to Castle Rock threads its way through Longview and Kelso on low-traffic side streets, plays leapfrog with I-5, and follows Pleasant Hill Road, a name appropriate for a road with pleasant scenery, very little traffic, and almost no hills. Side roads lead left and right, some with signs inviting passersby to fish for smelt, purchase nursery plants, or browse among the headstones of an old cemetery. Eventually Pleasant Hill Road ends, and Huntington Avenue, an almost-deserted stretch of Old Highway 99, leads into Castle Rock.

MILEAGE LOG

0.0 Starting from corner of Front Street and A Street in Castle Rock, proceed west on **A Street** and cross Cowlitz River.

0.7 Turn left on **State Route 411 (West Side Highway)**.

1.2 Bear right and uphill on **Delameter Road**.

1.4 Turn right with Delameter Road as Wren Loop Road continues across Delameter Creek. Proceed up Delameter Valley past farms and homes. Road crosses creek several times, climbing all the way.

7.2 Left turn on **Woodside Drive** as Delameter Spur continues on to dead end. Grade becomes steeper, culminating in a summit at mile 8.5, then plunges down other side.

10.1 Bear left on **Coal Creek Road**. Coal Creek General Store on right at mile 11.5.

13.1 Left turn on **Pacific Way** at bottom of hill.

18.2 Cross railroad tracks, turn left on **State Route 4 (Ocean Beach Highway)**, then turn right on **Nichols Boulevard N.E.** along edge of Sacajawea Park.

19.0 Turn left on **Hemlock Street** and cross Lake Sacajawea on pedestrian footbridge. Picnic area with tables, water, restrooms, shade trees, and lawn area at other edge of park; picnic lunch stop. After lunch, turn left on **Kessler Boulevard**.

19.1 Bear right on **25 Avenue**, then turn right on **Hudson Street**. Follow Hudson through edge of downtown Longview.

20.7 Left turn on **3 Avenue** as Hudson ends.

21.6 Turn right on **West Main Street** and cross Cowlitz River on pedestrian walkway on side of bridge.

21.8 Turn left and walk bikes across **First Avenue** immediately after crossing bridge. (No left turn for vehicles.)

22.4 Bear left on **Pacific Highway North;** a narrow, concrete two-lane roadway. *Note: Optional left turn on Cowlitz Gardens Road at mile 23.5, which rejoins 0.5 mile beyond.* Road climbs hill alongside masonry-lined cut on hillside. Main-line tracks tunnel underneath; logging railroad crosses river and goes overhead on trestle. Go under I-5 at mile 24.4 and continue alongside highway.

25.7 Turn left on **Pleasant Hill Road** and cross I-5 on 1975 overpass.

30.9 Turn left on **Huntington Avenue** and cross railroad tracks on high bridge. Enter Castle Rock.

32.4 Left turn on **A Street** in Castle Rock.

32.5 Junction of Front Street with A Street in Castle Rock; end of tour.

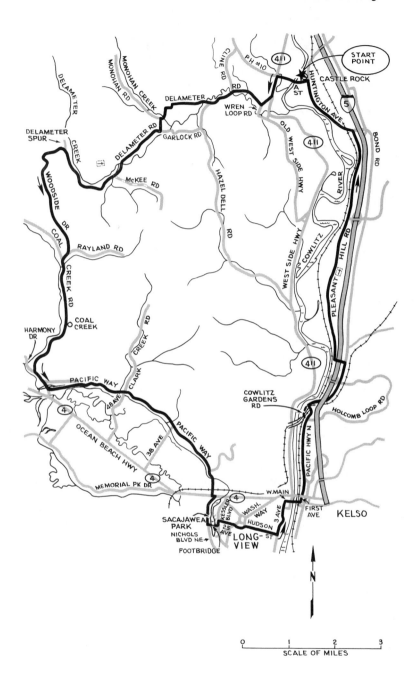

138 LONGVIEW–SKAMOKAWA

STARTING POINT: Intersection of Hemlock Street and Kessler Boulevard by restrooms of Sacajawea Park in Longview. Take exit 36 (State Route 432) from I-5 toward Longview. Turn right on Oregon Avenue at traffic light where S.R. 432 ends, and then immediately turn left on Kessler Boulevard. Follow Kessler to Hemlock Street by restrooms. Park along Kessler by Sacajawea Park.

DISTANCE: Total 69 to 93 miles: first day, 37 to 50 miles; second day, 32 to 49 miles.

TERRAIN: Flat to strenuous hills; 1.1 miles of unpaved road.

TOTAL CUMULATIVE ELEVATION GAIN: 3300 feet: first day, 2200 feet; second day, 1100 feet.

RECOMMENDED TIME OF YEAR: Any season.

RECOMMENDED STARTING TIME: 9 A.M.

ALLOW: 2 days. Camping or bed-and-breakfast.

POINTS OF INTEREST
Beaver Falls
Westport – Puget Island Ferry
Columbian White-tailed Deer Wildlife
  Refuge

ELEVATION PROFILE - FIRST DAY

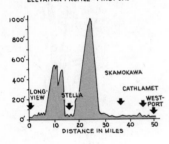

ELEVATION PROFILE - SECOND DAY

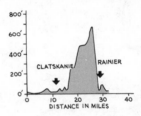

When Lewis and Clark explored the Northwest Territory of the United States of America at the beginning of the nineteenth century, the only highways available were the nation's great waterways. The Columbia River was the final such waterway leading them to the Pacific Ocean. Today the lower Columbia is still a great river. Huge ocean-going ships ply the deep, free-flowing waters where canoes and longboats transported the early American explorers in 1805. Many ships tie up at Longview to receive cargoes of aluminum and paper products and Orient-bound logs, while other ships continue up the river to Portland. This tour explores the Washington and Oregon shores of this great river and crosses it twice, once via the small Wahkiakum County ferryboat *M. V. Wahkiakum* (what else!), and again on the return via the high, arching Longview Bridge.

The tour begins well away from the water's edge, taking to the hills on the Washington side in order to escape the narrow, nondescript shoulders and heavy traffic of Washington's State Route 4. Eventually the backroads run out, and the route follows the highway along one of the few stretches with waterscape views, diverting again for the seclusion of Spruce Creek Valley.

All valleys end in a summit somewhere, however, and this valley is no exception. The high divide gives way to the Beaver Creek drainage, where young Douglas fir plantations host deer, elk, and the ethereal hoot of the blue grouse. An exhilarating downhill run levels out by the Beaver Creek Trout Hatchery, followed by a delightfully relaxing ride along the Elochoman River.

The Columbian White-tailed Deer Wildlife Refuge, encompassing several thousand acres and three islands in the Columbia River, is a treat for animal and bird watchers. Waterfowl inhabit the sluggish sloughs, while goldfinches, game birds, and deer cavort about the grassy meadows. Navigation aids for river traffic decorate the roadside as the islands part for a brief riverscape. A late evening or early morning return through the wildlife refuge almost always reaps rewards for the alert watcher.

Once past sleepy little Skamokawa, the scenery settles down to bucolic cattle farms and forest with only a brief interruption by an auto-wrecking yard. At the Wilson Creek Recreation Area, all is quiet and uncrowded, as motorized overnight tenants are excluded; only bicyclists are allowed. Picnic tables, fireplaces, and toilets make this a fine camp, although Wilson Creek is the only water supply.

The ride out of Cathlamet across the mid-river islands is flat, and roads along the levees beckon for scenic detours. With nothing to block it, however, the wind comes whistling up the river across the flat islands, increasing the motive effort.

The ride across the river on the *M. V. Wahkiakum* is yet another adventure. The meandering sloughs are reminiscent of the bayous of the Mississippi Delta. Great ships go rumbling by in the main channel. Traffic- and wind-generated swells mandate the stabilization of bicycles by hooking handlebars over railings.

Bed-and-breakfasts on Puget Island on the Washington side and near Westport, Oregon, offer accommodations. Reservations are advised.

As the tour leaves Westport, short stretches of highway shoulder are interspersed with offshoots of almost-forgotten Old U.S. 30. In Clatskanie, cafes offer early lunch fare, fuel for ascending the Beaver Creek Valley. Exposed volcanic rock along the roadsides tells of the area's fiery geologic history. The waterfall on Beaver Creek is not grandiose, as falls go, but the vertical fall from an overhanging ledge is impressive. The Columbian white-tailed deer, a staple of the early explorer's diet, still roams the forest, occasionally bounding across the road in front of startled bicyclists. Wildflowers bloom along the roadside to round out an idyllic scene.

Near the summit, bicyclists have the choice of a rapid descent along the highway with scenic turnouts, or a more leisurely set of switchbacks through the forest on the old highway. Either way leads to the approach to the Longview bridge over the Columbia River. The high, arching bridge, too narrow walkway, and lack of shoulder all contribute to keeping the adrenalin flowing. The view from the bridge summit is breathtaking, affording far-ranging inspection of port activities and river traffic below.

Once off the bridge on the Washington side, the route leaves the highway, returning quickly to the starting point in Longview's Sacajawea Park.

MILEAGE LOG

FIRST DAY

0.0 Starting from Kessler Boulevard and Hemlock Street by Sacajawea Park restrooms, head north on **Kessler Boulevard**.

0.7 Turn hard left on **Ocean Beach Highway (State Route 4)** as Kessler ends.

0.9 Right turn on **Pacific Way**. Grocery on right at 2.4.

6.1 Turn right and uphill on **Coal Creek Road** as Pacific Way ends.

6.3 Left turn downhill on **Harmony Drive** toward Eufala Heights. Cross Coal Creek and begin long climb.

7.8 Continue left and uphill on **Old Stella Road** past Eufala Store (gas-grocery). Unless a lunch has been packed, advise purchasing lunch materials here. Top a summit at 8.6 and begin undulating descent.

11.8 Right turn on **Fall Creek Road** as Old Stella Road ends. Ascend to a summit and descend steeply.

13.3 Turn hard left on **Germany Creek Road** as Fall Creek Road ends.

15.2 Right turn on **State Route 4** as Germany Creek Road ends. Viewpoints along Columbia River.

18.0 Turn right on **Mill Creek Road** and begin gradual climb along scenic Mill Creek.

19.0 Bear left across creek on **Spruce Creek Road**.

19.6 Right turn on **Cathlamet Road** toward Cathlamet as Spruce Creek Road is marked Dead End. Pavement ends at 19.8 for 1.1 miles. Enter Wahkiakum County along the way. Go over summit and begin long, winding descent as road name changes to **Beaver Creek Road**.

28.4 Cross Elochoman River and turn left on **State Route 407** as Beaver Creek Road ends by Beaver Creek Trout Hatchery. Public fishing access on left along Elochoman River.

32.0 Right turn on **State Route 4** as S.R. 407 ends. *Note: Tour may be shortened 13 miles by turning left on S.R. 4 to Cathlamet.* Pass Crown Zellerbach headquarters.

33.4 Cross Elochoman River and turn left on **Steamboat Slough Road** into Columbian White-tailed Deer National Wildlife Refuge. Proceed on a narrow, paved road through refuge, along sloughs and main channel of Columbia River. *Note: May encounter strong winds along exposed stretches.*

38.4 Cross Brooks Slough and stop at State Route 4 in Skamokawa; cafe and grocery. *Note: For bicycle camping facilities, turn left on S.R. 4, then immediately right on Skamokawa Road, continuing on East Valley Road at 39.8 to Wilson Creek Park at 44.2. Return to Skamokawa in morning.* Return along Steamboat Slough Road through refuge.

43.7 Turn right on **State Route 4** as Steamboat Slough Road ends. Cross Elochoman River.

45.7 Right turn on **State Route 409** through Cathlamet (cafe, grocery) toward ferry. Continue across bridge to Little Island at 46.2, and across Birnie Slough to Puget Island at 47.9. *Note: Bed-and-break-*

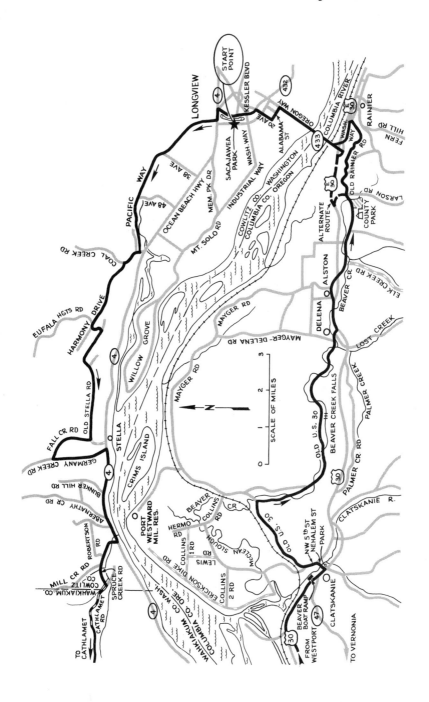

fast on Washington side is 1.9 miles right at mile 48.4 on Welcome Slough Road and N. Welcome Slough Road. Board ferry at 49.4; ferry departs hourly from 7:15 A.M. to 5:15 P.M. and then not again until 11:30 P.M. Disembark ferry in Westport, Oregon.

SECOND DAY

0.0   Continue through Westport on **Ferry Road** past Oregon-side bed-and-breakfast.

0.1   Left turn on **U.S. 30**; motel and grocery. Enter Columbia County at 0.9.

1.8   Turn right on unmarked side road, which bends left and becomes **Old U.S. 30**. Pass Woodson Store at 2.9.

3.0   Right turn on **U.S. 30** toward Clatskanie. Skirt high bluffs and rock quarry.

3.9   Turn right on unmarked side road, then left at T junction on **Old U.S. 30**.

7.7   Right turn on **U.S. 30** as old highway ends. Beaver Boat Ramp (public toilets) on left at 9.8; Flippin House National Historic Museum up hill to right at 9.9.

10.0   Turn left at traffic light on **Nehalem Street** in Clatskanie; cafes, grocery.

10.3   Left turn on **N.W. 5th Street** toward Port Westward as Nehalem Street ends. Road is promptly renamed **Old U.S. 30**.

13.3   Turn right at T junction with **Old U.S. 30**. Pass overlook to Beaver Creek Falls (listen for it) at 17.0; dirt track leads right to ford at top of falls at 17.1.

20.5   Turn left on **U.S. 30**. *Note: To avoid recrossing highway, may prefer to use left shoulder.*

21.0   Bear left toward Alston on old highway; Alston Country Store at 21.5.

21.8   Cross U.S. 30 and continue toward Vernonia on **Old Rainier Road**. Hudson-Parcher Park (Columbia County) on the right on Larson Road at 24.4. *Note: To descend hill on highway, turn left on Larson, then right on U.S. 30. Bear right toward Longview at bottom of hill.* Continue over summit and down long, winding grade. Viewpoint for Columbia River and Longview Bridge at 25.8.

27.2   Turn left on **Washington Way** toward Longview and Seattle.

27.8   Right turn past gas station and grocery, then left on **U.S. 30**.

28.0   Bear right at interchange toward Longview and Seattle; cross Columbia River and enter Longview, Washington.

30.1   Get into left turn lane at traffic light and turn left on **Alabama Street**.

30.4   Right turn on **20th Avenue**. Cross Nichols Boulevard and Lake Sacajawea.

30.8   Turn left on **Kessler Boulevard** on far side of bridge.

31.5   End of tour by restrooms in Sacajawea Park.

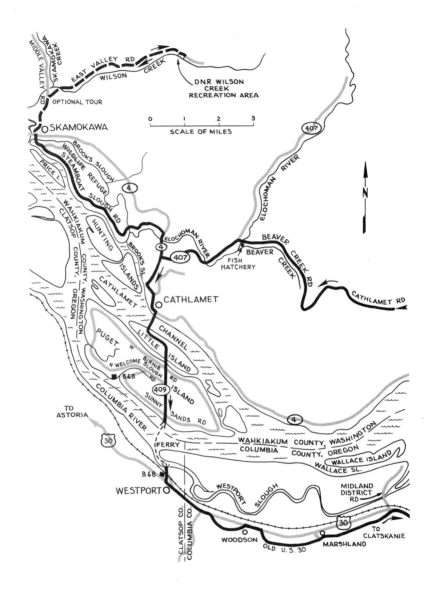

139 COLUMBIA GORGE

STARTING POINT: Vancouver, Washington, Amtrak depot. By automobile, take Exit 1C from I-5 and head west on 14th Street. Turn left on Washington Street, right on Evergreen Boulevard, right on Jefferson Street to 11th Street, then left on 11th Street to Amtrak depot parking area. Notify station agent of long-term parking intentions.

ALTERNATIVE STARTING POINT: Portland Airport parking area. By automobile, take Airport Way Exit from I-205 just south of Columbia River Bridge. Proceed toward airport and park in Economy Parking Area. By bicycle, head east on Airport Way 2.6 miles to its end at N.E. 138th Avenue, then left on 138th 0.2 mile to Marine Drive to join main route.

DISTANCE: Full tour, 338 miles; minimum daily mileages from 12 to 45. Shorter loops from 60 to 90 miles.

TERRAIN: Flat, moderate, hilly, and mountainous. Five miles of gravel road.

TOTAL CUMULATIVE ELEVATION GAIN: Full tour, 12,000 feet; daily elevations from 50 to 2600 feet.

RECOMMENDED TIME OF YEAR: June through October.

ALLOW: 7 to 10 days for full tour; shorter loops, 1 to 3 days.

RECOMMENDED ADDITIONAL GUIDEBOOKS:

1) Plumb, Gregory. *Waterfalls of the Pacific Northwest*, Seattle: Writing Works, 1983.

2) Jones, Philip. *Bicycling the Backroads of Northwest Oregon*, Seattle: The Mountaineers, 1984.

3) Allen, John E., *The Magnificent Gateway, A Layman's Guide to the Geology of the Columbia River Gorge*, Forest Grove, Oregon: Timber Press, 1984.

POINTS OF INTEREST

OREGON

Portland Women's Forum State Park

Vista House at Crown Point

Waterfalls: 5 visible from road, 15 or more accessible by short hikes

Bonneville Dam Locks, Bradford Island Visitors Center and Fish Hatchery

Rowena Overlook

Historic buildings in The Dalles

The Dalles Dam guided tours

Celilo Indian village

WASHINGTON

Maryhill Museum

Stonehenge reproduction

Goldendale observatory and museum

Ice House Park near Klickitat

Klickitat River scenery

Bonneville Dam Vistors Center

River rafting on Klickitat and White Salmon rivers

Ice caves

Mountain views

Mountain wildflowers

Government Mineral Springs

Carson Hot Springs

Beacon Rock

Pendleton Woolen Mills

Barring adverse winds, and using the primary highways on both sides of the Columbia Gorge, it is possible to travel round trip by bicycle from Camas to Maryhill in two days. If that is your objective, read no further; you don't need this book.

COLUMBIA GORGE

ELEVATION PROFILES

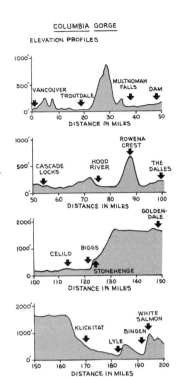

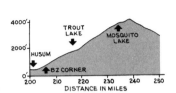

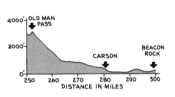

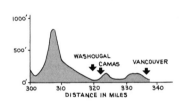

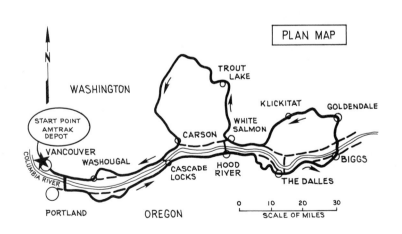

PLAN MAP

189

As implied by the Points of Interest above, this tour offers a spectacular mix of natural scenery, waterfalls, wildflowers, cultural features, diverse recreational opportunities, and history. As a bicycling vacation route, it is one of the best, offering a choice of accommodations from rudimentary campgrounds to expensive resort hotels, with several bed-and-breakfast opportunities thrown in.

Three bridges cross the Columbia River between the ends of this gorge tour, offering several options for shorter tours. The mileage log, rather than being split arbitrarily into day sections, is cumulative for the full tour, allowing the bicycle tourist to adjust the route and stopping points easily to his or her own liking.

For the botany or bird buff, the extreme variety of this tour, from sea level to high mountains and from rain forest to desert, presents a challenge to identify an unusually broad range of flora and fauna. The amateur geologist is presented with strikingly vivid layering of sedimentary and igneous formations, mountain folding, and massive earth slides. Even the amateur astronomer may have his day (or night) at the Goldendale Observatory. Cultivated fruit in season along the route includes cherries, apricots, peaches, and apples. Each major feature — waterfalls, hydroelectric dams, museums, wild rivers, ice caves, soda springs, hot springs, mountain scenery, and manufacturing plant tours — would be a reasonable objective on its own. This tour combines them all.

MILEAGE LOG

0.0 From the Vancouver Amtrak depot, head north through parking lot, cross spur track, and bear right on **West 11th Street**.

0.7 Right turn on **Washington Street** (one way), then one block farther turn left on **Evergreen Boulevard** and cross I-5 on overpass. *Note: Fort Vancouver Way goes right to Fort Vancouver Historical Museum at mile 1.2.*

4.6 Bear left as Evergreen Way is barred by a freeway exit, then right with thoroughfare on **S.E. Middle Way**.

5.4 Right turn on **S.E. Lieser Road**. Cross State Route 14 on overpass and turn left toward Camas on other side.

5.7 Bear right on **S.E. 88th Avenue**.

5.8 Left turn on **S.E. Evergreen Highway**.

6.9 Turn left on **S.E. Ellsworth**.

7.0 Right turn on **S.E. 23rd Street** for 0.2 mile, then turn left through bollards on bikeway. Cross I-205 bridge in central bike lane, fenced off from traffic by high Jersey barriers.

10.0 Left turn toward Marine Drive as Bike Route divides.

10.2 Turn right on **Marine Drive** and follow marked bikeway on shoulder. Grade-separated bikeway begins at mile 11.0. *Note: Route from Portland airport joins from right at mile 11.6.* Cross Marine Drive at 12.4 and continue along the Columbia River on a grade-separated bikeway. Rejoin **Marine Drive** at 14.1.

15.7 Turn right on bike route alongside Blue Lake Park Drive. Cross roadway and continue on grade-separated bikeway. Cottonwood roots

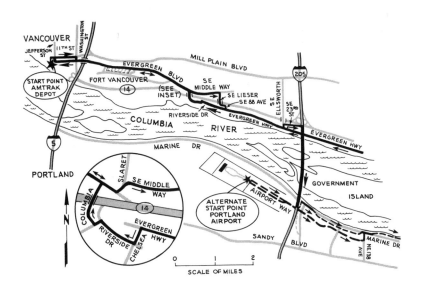

"HIGH RIDERS."

make surface bumpy. Watch for broken glass. Bikeway ends at 17.8; continue along **Marine Drive**.

18.5 Turn left with Bike Route as Marine Drive continues under I-84. *Note: Motels and cafe in Troutdale on other side of underpass.*

19.0 Right turn with Bike Route under I-84 on **Graham Street**.

19.3 Turn left on **Columbia Boulevard** toward Scenic Highway and Corbett. Continue through Troutdale business district.

20.2 Cross the Sandy River and turn right on **Crown Point Highway** toward Corbett. *Note: Bridge goes right across the Sandy River at mile 22.7 toward Gresham and Oxbow County Park; 9 miles, camping. Next campground at mile 42.1.* Dabney State Park (day use only) on right at mile 23.1. Grocery and delicatessen in Springdale at mile 24.1.

24.4 Bear right with Scenic Highway toward Multnomah Falls. Grocery in Corbett at 27.3. *Note: Memorial to pioneers by grange hall on side loop to right toward Littlepage Road at mile 27.5.* Portland Women's Forum State Park on left at mile 28.6; memorial to Sam Hill, road builder. Vista House on Crown Point at mile 29.9.

32.4 La Tourell Falls on right; walking trail to falls continues back through Talbot State Park and returns to scenic highway. Falls in Shepperd's Dell State Park on right at 33.6. Bridal Veil State Park on left at 34.5; 0.5 mile trail to falls. Wahkeena Falls on right at 37.9.

38.5 Multnomah Falls on right; trail to falls viewpoint and Upper Falls; cafe and restaurant. *Note: Oneonta Trail #424 goes right at mile 40.6 to Oneonta Falls, Triple Falls, and Upper Horsetail Falls; recommended side trip if bicycles are locked to trees 1/4 mile up trail.* Oneonta Botanical Area on right at 40.8. Ainsworth State Park (camping) on right at mile 42.1.

42.4 Bear right toward Hood River and I-84 East.

42.7 Bear right on **Frontage Road**. Trail to Elowah Falls goes right at mile 44.8.

45.0 Join **I-84** and continue on shoulder. Beacon Rock appears across Columbia River. Narrow bridge at mile 46.4.

47.5 Bear right on Exit 40 toward Bonneville Dam. Turn left at stop sign and follow arrows to Visitors Center. Be careful of rails in roadway by power house.

49.0 Bradford Island Visitors Center. Tour visitor center and follow exit arrows past fish hatchery to I-84.

50.8 Go under I-84 and take up-ramp to **I-84 East**. Go through lighted tunnel at mile 51.7.

54.0 Take Exit 44 **(U.S. 30 East)** toward Cascade Locks. *Note: Tour may be short-cut by taking grating-decked toll bridge across Columbia River here.* Continue through town on **WA-NA-PA Street** (motels and cafes). Cascade Locks Marina, museum, and Amtrak station on the left on Portage Road at mile 55.0.

55.4 Left turn on **Forest Lane Road** toward Airport and Industrial Park. KOA Campground on the left at mile 56.4.

57.3 Cross bridge over I-84 and bear left toward Herman Creek Road.

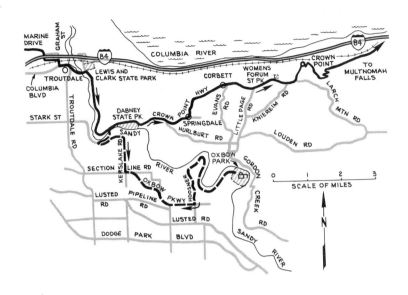

"LOOK AT THE NEAT LITTLE LIGHTS ALONG THIS ROAD."

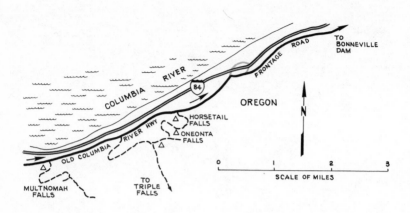

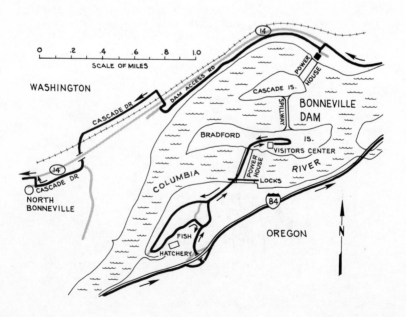

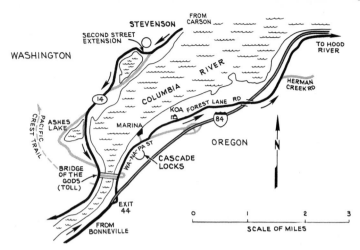

58.3 Bear left toward Hood River as Herman Creek Road goes right. Continue on shoulder of **I-84**.

66.0 Bear right into highway rest area. Memorial to construction of Columbia River Highway, begun here in 1912. Picnic area and trails to Starvation Creek Falls and Cabin Creek Falls. Return to I-84 at mile 66.2. *Note: Exit 56 goes right at mile 67.1 to Viento State Park; camping.*

73.2 Bear right on Exit 62 toward West Hood River. *Note: For a more-than-you-can-eat breakfast by reservation, turn left at stop sign, cross overpass, then left on Westcliff Drive to Columbia Gorge Hotel. Lower-priced motels nearby.* Continue on **W. Cascade Avenue** down the hill into Hood River. Road changes name to **Oak Street**.

74.5 Turn right on **Front Street** by Amtrak station as Oak Street ends, then left on **State Street**. Cross Hood River.

74.7 Left turn on **State Route 35** toward I-84.

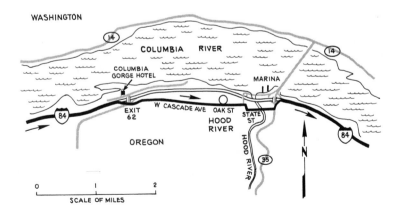

74.9 Right turn at entrance to **I-84 East** toward Celilo, and continue on shoulder. *Note: S.R. 35 continues across Columbia River to Bingen; possible tour shortcut.*

80.2 Take Exit 69 and continue on **U.S. 30** toward Scenic Loop and Mosier. Old road returns from right. Grocery, cafe, and lodging at 80.6; cherry orchards at 82.1.

87.1 Turn right into Rowena Crest Viewpoint for overlook. Return to U.S. 30 at 87.5. Tom McCall Preserve on left at next bend; Mayer State Park at bottom of hill at 89.7.

96.5 Left turn with U.S. 30 on **Webber Street**, go under I-84, then right on **2nd Street**. Tourist Information Center in old Wasco County Courthouse in The Dalles at 98.5 (maps and lists of historic structures in The Dalles). All services in The Dalles.

98.6 Turn right, then left on **3rd Street** with one-way grid.

99.6 Rejoin **2nd Street** with U.S. 30.

100.9 Keep right with U.S. 30 toward State Route 197.

101.1 Turn left on **State Route 197** toward freeway and Yakima. Cross overpass and turn right toward The Dalles Dam.

102.4 Stop at The Dalles Dam Visitors Center for free tram ride and dam tour, then return to S.R. 197.

103.4 Turn left on **State Route 197**, cross overpass, and turn left on entrance to **I-84 East**. *Note: S.R. 197 continues north across Columbia River to Washington's Horsethief Lake State Park; camping and possible shortcut to tour.*

113.5 Bear right on **Exit 97 (State Route 206)**, then turn right with S.R. 206 as left goes under freeway to Celilo Park; restrooms, water, picnic tables, green lawns, views of Columbia River.

113.6 Left turn with S.R. 206 East as right goes to Celilo Indian Village; tourist displays, salmon bake on second weekend in April. Cross Deschutes River at 116.7 and pass Deschutes River State Park; camping, picnicking.

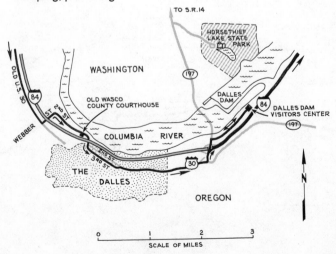

118.7 Continue on **U.S. 30** as S.R. 206 turns right.

121.6 Turn left on **U.S. 97** in Biggs; grocery, motels, cafes. Cross Columbia River into Washington State.

122.6 Right turn toward Maryhill State Park. *Note: No group camp, no reservations; campground full every night from mid-June to mid-September.* Continue past park on old roadway toward Stonehenge.

123.2 Turn left toward Stonehenge at stop sign in Maryhill by old church. Cherry and apricot orchards.

124.6 Left turn into Stonehenge entrance. Stonehenge replica at 124.7. Tour the replica, view monument to Sam Hill, and head back out to entrance.

124.8 Turn left toward State Route 14 at entrance.

125.5 Left turn on (Washington State) **State Route 14**.

126.5 Turn right (uphill) on **U.S. 97**. *Note: Maryhill Museum is 2.6 miles farther west on S.R. 14; open 9 A.M. to 5 P.M.* Mountain viewpoint at 131.5; top of grade (elevation 1700 feet).

144.6 Left turn on **Old 97** toward Goldendale and immediately bear right with main thoroughfare. Enter Goldendale on **Columbus Street**.

147.9 Turn left on **State Route 142 (West Broadway)** in Goldendale. Groceries, cafes, motels, coin laundry, museum; Washington State Goldendale Park Observatory open to public Wednesday through Sunday evenings. *Note: Glenwood Road goes right at mile 159.4 to Glenwood, 24 miles; Trout Lake, 42 miles; 1200-foot climb out of Klickitat Gorge to Glenwood.* Start down long, steep hill with switchbacks at 160.0. Department of Wildlife Conservation Park on left at 167.4; soda spring, pit toilets, Klickitat River. Town of Klickitat at 169.6; cafe, grocery. Continue down Klickitat Canyon.

183.1 Right turn on **State Route 14** as S.R. 142 ends. Chamberlin Lake Rest Area at 185.0.

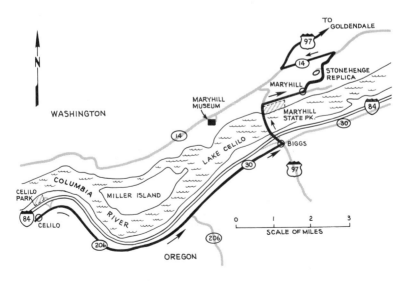

192.8 Turn right toward White Salmon on **State Route 141** in Bingen; grocery, cafes, campground/dormitory, motel, B & B, winery, Amtrak station. Town of White Salmon at 194.5; cafe, grocery, B & B. *Note: Side road goes left 0.5 mile to Northwestern Lake at mile 199.6; camping, food concession, raft trips.* Husum Cafe at 201.6, BZ Corners grocery at 205.4. Go through Trout Lake at 217.4; cafe, grocery, sleeping rooms in back of general store, camping in county park. Ranger station at 218.1.

219.0 Right turn on **Forest Road 88** (U.S. Forest Service). *Note: Ice caves picnic area and campground 5.1 miles farther on S.R. 141 and Forest Road 24.*

231.8 Continue on **Forest Road 8851** as Road 88 turns right at Tire Corner. *Note: Langfield Falls trail head is 0.1 mile right on Road 88.* Cross Pacific Crest Trail at mile 234.5, 3900 ft. elevation; go by Mosquito Lake at 234.6.

235.2 Bear left on **Forest Road 24** as Road 8851 forks right.

238.6 Bear right on **Forest Road 30** as Road 24 turns left up a steep hill and turns to gravel. *Note: Road 580 goes left at mile 240.1 up steep hill to Mt. St. Helens viewpoint with pit toilets, but just as good a viewpoint is 0.5 mile farther along Forest Road 30.* Pavement ends at mile 241.4 for 5.3 miles of gravel surface.

246.7 Turn left on **Wind River Road** (paved!) as Road 30 (Lone Butte Road) ends. Watch for logging trucks. Crest of Old Man Pass (3000 ft.) at mile 251.1; sno-park restrooms. Paradise Creek Campground on left at mile 256.6 (campsites and pit toilets but no potable water).

263.5 Right turn on **Mineral Springs Road**.

263.9 Cross Wind River and turn left on **Little Soda Springs Road**; unpaved, but hard-packed. *Note: Government Mineral Springs picnic area 1.0 mile farther on Mineral Springs Road; soda springs, historical signboards, pit toilets.*

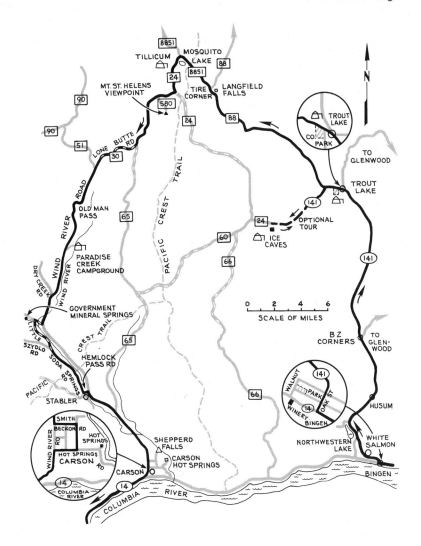

266.7 Continue on Little Soda Springs Road (now paved) as Szydlo Road joins from the right.

270.3 Left turn on **Hemlock Pass Road** as Trout Creek Road continues.

270.6 Turn right on **Wind River Road** at stop sign in Stabler.

273.5 Bear left on **Old State Road**.

275.3 Left turn on **Wind River Road** as Old State Road ends.

276.3 Cross Wind River and turn left on **High Bridge Road**. Cross Wind River Road at 276.7.

277.2 Turn right on **Metzger Road**. Cross Wind River Road by grocery at mile 277.9.

278.4 Left turn on **Smith Beckon Road**. *Note: Shepperd Falls Road goes left at 278.8 to falls on Wind River.*

279.2 Right turn on **Hot Springs Road**. *Note: St. Martin Hot Springs hotel, cafe, and spa is left 0.4 mile on St. Martin Hot Springs Road.*

280.1 Left turn on **Wind River Road** at four-way stop sign in Carson.

281.1 Turn right on **State Route 14** as Wind River Road ends. Enter Stevenson at 284.0; cafes, grocery.

284.5 Bear right on **Second Street Ext** in Stevenson and ride past Skamania County Fairgrounds and Rock Creek Park.

285.8 Turn right on **State Route 14** as Second Street ends. Historical markers at 286.8, 287.3, and 288.6. Bridge of the Gods (toll, grating-decked) goes left to Cascade Locks at 287.5. Cross Pacific Crest Trail at 287.7.

289.6 Left turn into Bonneville Dam North Shore Visitors Center. After dam visit, bear left (west) on **Dam Access Road**.

291.0 Turn right toward highway as road is marked No Outlet. Cross State Route 14, go under railroad trestle, and turn left on **Cascade Drive**.

292.3 Turn right in North Bonneville on side road to highway and turn left on **State Route 14** toward Vancouver. Beacon Rock State Park rest area, Beacon Rock trail, and campground at 297.0. Cafe in Skamania at 299.0.

304.9 Right turn on **Krogstad Road** as passing lane ends on uphill grade.

305.7 Turn right on **State Route 140** as Krogstad Road ends. Continue uphill. Cross Salmon Falls Road at 306.6, just short of summit. Skamania County Prindle Park (day use only) at 308.9.

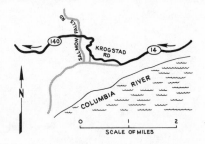

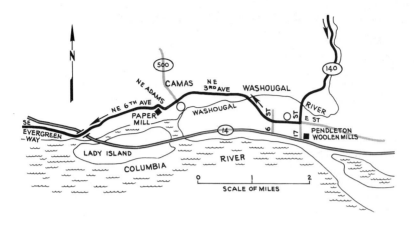

309.9 Cross Washougal River and turn left with S.R. 140; grocery.

319.9 Right turn on **E Street** at traffic light in Washougal. *Note: Pendleton Woolen Mills at 17th and A streets; only motel is left from E Street on 6th Street.* Enter Camas at 320.5 where road is renamed **N.E. 3rd Avenue**.

322.7 Turn right with thoroughfare on **N.E. Adams Street** and pass Crown Zellerbach paper mill.

322.8 Turn left with thoroughfare on **N.E. 6th Avenue**.

323.9 Turn hard left with **N.W. 6th Avenue** toward Washougal at highway interchange. Cross overpass and continue on old highway.

327.9 Bear left on **S.E. Evergreen Highway** toward State Fish Hatchery as road forks. Fish hatchery and historical monument at 330.1. *Note: Bike route goes right at 330.9 on S.E. Ellsworth and S.E. 23rd Street across I-205 bridge to Marine Drive, Portland Airport, and alternative start point.*

333.0 Left turn with bike route on **S.E. Chelsea**, then right on **Riverside Drive**.

333.6 Bear left at stop sign, then right across overpass on **Columbia Way**.

333.9 Left turn on **E. Evergreen Boulevard**. Cross I-5 on overpass in Vancouver at 336.7.

337.4 Turn right on **Jefferson Street** as Evergreen is blocked by Exit Only signs, then left on **11th Street** to Amtrak terminal; end of tour.

ALPHABETICAL INDEX

MILEAGE INDEX – DAY TOURS

MILEAGE INDEX – OVERNIGHT AND MULTI-DAY TOURS

WASHINGTON STATE PARKS

PARK	TOUR NUMBERS
Belfair	109
Battle Ground Lake	134
Federation Forest	106
Flaming Geyser	7, 97
Fort Canby	133
Jarrell Cove	110
Kopachuck	94, 95
Lake Sylvia	117
Leadbetter Point	133
Lewis and Clark	128, 129, 130
Loomis Lake	133
Manchester	44, 95
Millersylvania	47, 48, 49, 50, 51, 120, 121

PARK	TOUR NUMBERS
Nolte	8, 97
Ocean City	111, 112
Pacific Beach	112
Pacific Pines	133
Palmer-Kanaskat	97
Paradise Point	134
Penrose Point	95
Rainbow Falls	132
Schafer	46, 115
Seaquest	131, 132, 136
Tolmie	119
Twanoh	107

TOURS WITH BED-AND-BREAKFAST ACCOMMODATIONS

TOUR NO.	NAME	B&B LOCATION	PHONE NO.
94	Southworth–Gig Harbor	Gig Harbor	(206) 851-8654
106	Mt. Rainier	Ashford	(206) 569-2739
		Eatonville	(206) 832-6506
108	Mason Lake–Grapeview	Allyn	(206) 275-5378
113	Aberdeen–Hoquiam–Wishkah	Hoquiam	(206) 533-2320
117	Oakville–Brooklyn–Montesano	Montesano	(206) 249-3453
119	Priest Point–Tolmie State Park	Olympia	(206) 754-0389
		by Tolmie Park	(206) 459-1676
120	Millersylvania–Delphi–Olympia	Olympia	(206) 754-0389
133	Long Beach Peninsula	Seaview	(206) 642-4177
134	Lewis River	Battle Ground	(206) 687-5525
		Battle Ground	(206) 686-3029
138	Longview–Skamokawa	Westport, OR	(503) 455-2400
		Puget Island	(206) 849-4328
139	Columbia Gorge	Bingen	(509) 493-2838
		Hood River, OR	(503) 386-5566
		Husum	(509) 493-3024
		The Dalles, OR	(503) 296-2793
		Trout Lake	(509) 395-2264
		White Salmon	(509) 493-2335

TOUR JUNCTIONS

Note: Rides 1 through 54 are found in *Bicycling the Backroads Around Puget Sound,* and rides 55 through 93 are found in *Bicycling the Backroads of Northwest Washington* (The Mountaineers, Seattle, Washington).

TOUR JUNCTION	TOUR NUMBERS	TOUR JUNCTION	TOUR NUMBERS
Aberdeen	113, 114	Graham	103, 104
Adna	125, 130, 132	Grand Mound	51, 124
Algona	96	Grapeview	108
Allyn	108	Greenwood	113, 114
Amboy	134	Hood River, OR	139
Auburn	6, 7, 96, 98	Hoquiam	113
Battle Ground	134	Ilwaco	133
Belfair	109	Independence	125
Biggs, OR	139	Kalama	135
Black Diamond	7, 8, 97	Kanaskat	8, 97
Boistfort	132	Kapowsin	52, 103, 104, 105, 106
Bonney Lake	99	Kelso	137
Boston Harbor	119	Kent	3, 6, 96
Brooklyn	117	La Center	134
Buckley	53, 98, 101, 106	Lacey	119
Bucoda	50, 126	Little Rock	5, 120, 121
Camas	139	Long Beach	133
Carson	139	Longbranch	95
Cascade Locks, OR	139	Longview	137, 138
Castle Rock	131, 132, 136, 137	Maple Valley	5, 97
Cathlamet	138	McCleary	46, 116
Cayuse Pass	106	McKenna	50, 102, 123
Centralia	50, 51, 124, 125, 126, 127	Moclips	112
Chehalis	127, 128	Montesano	114, 117
Claquato	127	Napavine	128
Clatskanie, OR	138	Nisqually	102
Cloquallum	46, 115	Oakville	116, 117, 124
Copalis Crossing	112	Ocean City	112
Cumberland	8, 97	Ocean Shores	111
Curtis	130	Ohanapecosh	106
Doty	102	Olympia	47, 119, 120
Du Pont	102	Onalaska	129
East Olympia	120	Orting	52, 101
Eatonville	50, 52, 105, 106	Oyster Bay	118
Elbe	50, 106	Oysterville	133
Elma	46, 115, 116, 117	Pacific	96, 99
Enumclaw	8, 98, 106	Pacific Beach	112
Galvin	51, 124, 126, 127	Pe Ell	132
Gig Harbor	94, 95	Portland, OR	139
Goldendale	139	Port Orchard	44, 95
		Porter	116

Authors Erin and Bill Woods have put more than 20,000 miles on their bicycles researching and updating the three books in their cycle tour guide series that also includes: *Bicycling the Backroads of Northwest Washington* and *Bicycling the Backroads Around Puget Sound*. Residents of Redmond, WA, they are active members of the Boeing Employees Bicycle Club and The Mountaineers bicycle group.